Hemingway and Film

TEACHING HEMINGWAY
Mark P. Ott, Editor
Susan F. Beegel, Founding Editor

Teaching Hemingway's *The Sun Also Rises*
EDITED BY PETER L. HAYS

Teaching Hemingway's *A Farewell to Arms*
EDITED BY LISA TYLER

Teaching Hemingway and Modernism
EDITED BY JOSEPH FRUSCIONE

Teaching Hemingway and War
EDITED BY ALEX VERNON

Teaching Hemingway and Gender
EDITED BY VERNA KALE

Teaching Hemingway and the Natural World
EDITED BY KEVIN MAIER

Teaching Hemingway and Race
EDITED BY GARY EDWARD HOLCOMB

Hemingway in the Digital Age: Reflections on Teaching, Reading, and Understanding
EDITED BY LAURA GODFREY

Hemingway's Short Stories: Reflections on Teaching, Reading, and Understanding
EDITED BY FREDERIC J. SVOBODA

Hemingway and Film: Reflections on Teaching, Reading, and Understanding
EDITED BY CAM COBB AND MARC K. DUDLEY

Hemingway and Film

Reflections on Teaching, Reading, and Understanding

Edited by Cam Cobb and Marc K. Dudley

The Kent State University Press   Kent, Ohio

© 2024 by The Kent State University Press, Kent, Ohio 44242
All rights reserved

No part of this book may be used or reproduced, in any manner whatsoever, without written permission from the Publisher, except in the case of short quotations in critical reviews or articles.

ISBN 978-1-60635-482-7
Manufactured in the United States of America

Cataloging information for this title is available at the Library of Congress.

28 27 26 25 24   5 4 3 2 1

Contents

Foreword
    MARK P. OTT   vii
Introduction
    CAM COBB AND MARC K. DUDLEY   ix

Part I. Early Stories

Hemingway and the Language of Film Noir: Robert Siodmak's Deceptive Flashback
    ALICE MIKAL CRAVEN   3
Seeing and Nothingness: Doing Film/Theory with Hemingway's "The Killers"
    CHRISTINA PARKER-FLYNN   17
Rhythmic Cycles in *The Sun Also Rises, For Whom the Bell Tolls,* and *The Fifth Column* and Their Film/Theater Adaptations
    JEAN JESPERSEN BARTHOLOMEW   35
Teaching Hemingway's *The Sun Also Rises* as Novel and Film
    DONALD A. DAIKER   59
Visual Values: The Success and Failure of Hemingway's Ethics in Film
    SEAN C. HADLEY   73

Part II. The Middle Years

A Thrice-Told Tale: *To Have and Have Not* and Adaptation Studies
    KIRK CURNUTT   85
To Have and Have Noir: A Tale of Two Hemingway Films
    JAMES PLATH   110
From the Harbor to the Hotel: Visual Equivalents in Howard Hawks's *To Have and Have Not*
    TIMOTHY PENNER   131

Hemingway's *Fifth Column,* Howard Hawks, and the Movies
PETER L. HAYS   142

Part III. Later Works and Myths

Teaching *The Garden of Eden*
SUZANNE DEL GIZZO   153

Teaching Hemingway through Fiction Film: *Midnight in Paris* and *Hemingway & Gellhorn*
TATIANA KONRAD   165

Films Like White Elephants: Hemingway in Woody Allen's *Manhattan* and *Midnight in Paris*
STEPHEN WHITTAKER   173

Appropriations of Hemingway in *The Long Goodbye* and *A History of Violence*
SCOTT D. YARBROUGH   191

Contributors   205
Index   208

Foreword
Mark P. Ott

Ernest Hemingway—his writing, his life, and his enduring presence in our cultural life—continues to unite, divide, and fascinate us as each generation, each historical moment, conjures up its own Hemingway, rife with fresh, contested significance. How should the work of Ernest Hemingway be taught in the year 2024, sixty-three years after his death in 1961 and a hundred years since the publication of his pathbreaking and enduring collection of short stories, *In Our Time* (1924)? Now more than ever, Hemingway's place in the curriculum continues to inspire discussion among writers and scholars about the lasting value of his work. Yet readers of this volume will once more find affirmation that his life and writing remain vital, meaningful, and still culturally resonant for today's students.

Books in the Teaching Hemingway series have built on the excellent work of founding series editor Susan F. Beegel, who guided into publication the first two volumes of this series: *Teaching Hemingway's* The Sun Also Rises, edited by Peter L. Hays (2008), and *Teaching Hemingway's* A Farewell to Arms, edited by Lisa Tyler (2008). In an effort to continue to be useful to instructors and professors—from high schools, community colleges, and universities—the newest volumes in this series are organized thematically, rather than around a single text. This shift attempts to open up Hemingway's work to more interdisciplinary strategies of instruction through divergent theories, fresh juxtapositions, and ethical inquiries, often employing emergent technology to explore media beyond the text.

As the final volume of the Teaching Hemingway series, Cam Cobb and Marc K. Dudley's *Hemingway and Film: Reflections on Teaching, Reading, and Understanding* is an exciting, intriguing conclusion to the ongoing conversation about how to introduce students to Hemingway's texts. This collection of essays speaks to the most important issue of intense interest today: how do films of Hemingway texts inform our interpretations of his work? Students today are saturated in a visual culture that demands their attention and carry around smartphones that are designed to addict them to relentless streams of stimulation; images of Hemingway with distorted or misattributed quotations from his work pop up on TikTok, on Instagram, and in relentless unfiltered reels on YouTube.

Thus, the time is right for this important collection of essays. An unexpected yet welcome dimension to this collection is the thread of joy that unites them; these scholars are enjoying the exploration of how Hemingway's texts have been depicted in films. The examination of casting decisions, script variations, setting, and directing are captivating to investigate, and these scholars want to share their enthusiasm with their students and other scholars of Hemingway and film. These diverse essays exploring representations of Hemingway's persona and the adaptations of his works are useful to those new to the classroom as well as seasoned veterans. Written by well-known Hemingway scholars with a broad range of experience from public high schools, community colleges, and large and small universities, these essays refresh our understanding of how to introduce Hemingway's work.

In sum, these essays revise our understanding not only of Hemingway but of how to refresh his work for students and in 2024.

Indeed, this volume demonstrates that not only is Hemingway's work being taught in more thoughtful, creative, and innovative ways in today's classrooms and lecture halls than ever before, but scholars are extending the classroom and taking the Hemingway text into new, exciting places that show us now, more than ever, his enduring relevance.

Introduction
Cam Cobb and Marc K. Dudley

The sun reflected off the water of the canal. At times it was almost blinding. As the boat cut forward, the pier and its piazza backdrop loomed larger and larger. While the water taxi was half empty, the pier was bustling with people, as shoppers and sellers hurried here and there, sometimes intermingling, but mostly ignoring one another on a very warm early summer afternoon. Getting off the boat, my wife and I noticed a man trying to get his bearings in the crowd. He had a map in hand. We'd seen him give a presentation on the island of San Servolo earlier that day, and years before, I'd read his book on Hemingway and race. We approached the man and offered to help. As it turned out, we were all staying at the Hotel Bisanzio, which was only a few hundred meters, but perhaps a dozen corridor-turns, away. Over the next several days, we broke bread and trekked the city of Venice together, and we chatted about books and music and all manner of things, like old friends. In truth, it was just the beginning of our friendship. That chance meeting on that busy pier in Venice on Tuesday, June 24, 2014, was also the origin of this book—Teaching Hemingway and Film.

Hemingway had a contentious relationship with film. He was skeptical of the industry, but he also loved the art. In 1947, when an interviewer for *Time* suggested he could make "big money" writing for Hollywood, the writer curtly replied, "Most whores usually find their vocations" (51). He had, just years earlier witnessed friend F. Scott Fitzgerald follow that siren song west and fall victim to her wiles, hating himself for it all the while. In that same interview, when pressed, Hemingway conceded, "But Hollywood has proven [it] can make good pictures from good stories honestly written" (51). Indeed, he also knew just how lucrative that Hollywood connection could be.

Years later, when A. E. Hotchner asked the writer if he frequented the movies, Hemingway responded, "Yes, I see quite a lot of them. This past year, the best ones were *The Bridge on the River Kwai* and *Around the World in Eighty*

Days." Elaborating, the Nobel laurate offered a rare glimpse into his feelings as a filmgoer, "*Around the World* starts dull and slow but it develops a wonderful quality like a dream—that dream quality is a unique thing that a good movie can generate" (147–48). Hemingway saw the magical potential in cinema. Moreover, while he was weary of the industry, he could at times be swept away by that narrative magic. As with many things, his views were complicated and sometimes conflicting.

Throughout Hemingway's career, his avocation repeatedly intersected with Hollywood. Sometimes it was a head-on collision. Like F. Scott Fitzgerald, William Faulkner, and John Steinbeck, Hemingway had interactions with producers, screenwriters, and directors that stretched across decades and eras as stories were adapted, expanded, condensed, and then revisited, and changed all over again, sometimes multiple times.

When *Esquire* asked about film adaptations, he erupted: "Jesus! . . . Usually I couldn't have anything to do with the pictures, or didn't want to. The properties had usually been sold or resold. . . . I have lent a hand with *The Old Man and the Sea*, though, mostly trying to get the big marlin, but even there didn't make out so well. I don't know" (160). In fact, in July 1955 Hemingway shelved a manuscript that had dogged him and would continue to dog him for years—his unfinished "Africa book," posthumously published as *True at First Light* (1999) and then *Under Kilimanjaro* (2005)—to work on *The Old Man and the Sea* (1958), starring Spencer Tracy. After laboring on the production for months, he walked away and made a beeline for his manuscript. Unthinkable as it may be, for that handful of months, "movie work" took priority over "book work."

Interviewing Hemingway for the *New York Herald Tribune* in 1959, Hotchner asked, "Do you enjoy pictures based on your books?" Hemingway coldly responded, "I usually can't stand them. The only one of those movies made by Hollywood I liked was *The Killers*. I had to walk out on all the others except *The Old Man and the Sea*." With a tinge of regret, he added, "I was responsible for that one" (147). Perhaps Hemingway's reticence to *fully* participate in a film from start to finish was not solely caused by his bad encounters or his disappointment with various adaptations. Perhaps it stemmed from his experiences with the theater.

Recalling his time developing *The Fifth Column* (1940), his one and only play, the writer philosophized, "If you write a play, you have to stick around and fix it up. . . . They always want to fool around with them to make them commercially successful, and you don't like to stick around that long. After I've written, I want to go home and take a shower" (182).

Yet the writer *did* get his hands dirty with filmmaking, and on more than one occasion. In 1940, the *Kansas City Times* reported, "Hemingway said he was pleased that the studio which purchased *For Whom the Bell Tolls* had selected Gary Cooper to play leading role. . . . He pointed out that Cooper rather fitted the character of Robert Jordan" (23–24). The following year, Hemingway repeated this sentiment when speaking with the *San Francisco Chronicle* (28). As these early press snippets indicate, Hemingway had very definite ideas as to how his stories could and perhaps should be cast. Yet, as the film went into production, his interest in it dwindled; and when it was released to much fanfare in 1943, the writer seemed unimpressed. Although the popular film later garnered eight Oscar nominations, and even an award, Hemingway remained resolute in his indifference. Of course, he stayed friendly with the film's leading stars, Cooper and Ingrid Bergman. When the *New Yorker* asked about Bergman a few years later, he confided, "She's an old friend of mine. She was in the movie of *For Whom the Bell Tolls,* but I'd better not tell you what I thought of that" (49). His enduring friendship with Cooper has been well-documented.

In the late 1940s, a *Time* reporter asked Hemingway about "his own attitude toward writing for Hollywood," and the writer snapped back, "Never done it" (51). Of course, that wasn't entirely true. Speaking with *Esquire* eleven years later, he casually recalled, "I made a documentary film once, myself—*The Spanish Earth,* 1937. I wrote it, but Archie MacLeish and John Dos Passos were supposed to have done it. I think I was a grip too" (160). Perhaps not uncoincidentally, Hemingway's close involvement with this documentary unfolded shortly after he'd written two experimental nonfiction books, *Death in the Afternoon* (1932) and *Green Hills of Africa* (1935). Both releases were written documentaries of a sort, and together this multimedia suite formed a nonfiction triptych. *The Spanish Earth* also marked a transition for Hemingway, as it directly preceded (and proved to be a preamble for) two of the writer's most political works—*To Have and Have Not* (1937) and *For Whom the Bell Tolls* (1940). In a way, Hemingway's film documentary (developed with director Joris Ivens) can be linked to these two novels as a very different sort of triptych, a sociopolitical one.

Yet this isn't a book about Hemingway's dabbling with the filmmaking process. It isn't a book about Hemingway novels being adapted to film in different decades and in different centuries. It isn't a book about the author's dealings with moviemakers, either. Moreover, while it isn't any *one* of these things, it's a bit of each of them. And it's something different, as well. *Hemingway and Film: Reflections on Teaching, Reading, and Understanding* is about exploring his work through the cinematic lens. It's about the publishing trade, the film business, and the mythmaking industry. It's about teaching and learning Hemingway's work alongside and through film. Indeed, it is very much a book about literature and cinema, two media coexisting in tension, one sometimes complementing the other, at other times clashing with it. This tension is, quite honestly, often a function of alchemy. Hollywood has proven through the years that a novel's translation is not a perfect art; in fact, it is often a woefully flawed one, often dependent on that right combination of writing (screen adaptation), editing, directing, casting, timing. One truism persists as a through line, though, when examining Hemingway's relationship with film, when considering the successes and/or failures in translation: the author's stories continue to speak to us and persist in being recast and retold and retranslated, simply because they're complex and because they're timeless.

While the possibilities are several, we organized this book into three parts that coincide with distinct phases of Hemingway's career: "Early Stories," "The Middle Years," and "Later Works and Myths."

"Early Stories" includes five chapters. In "Teaching Hemingway and the Language of Film Noir: The Case of 'The Killers,'" Alice Mikal Craven kicks off the set with an insightful look at Hemingway's preemptive intersection with a popular film genre. Next, Christina Parker-Flynn offers sharp insights into the same 1946 classic film in "Seeing and Nothingness: Doing Film Theory with Hemingway's 'The Killers.'" Jean Jespersen Bartholomew shares noteworthy ways that *The Sun Also Rises* (1957) and *For Whom the Bell Tolls* (1943) as well as the writer's solitary play—"The Fifth Column" (1940)—act as three gateways through which we may step into Hemingway's Spain in "Weaving Film, Stage, and Text." Donald A. Daiker, a stalwart of the Teaching Hemingway series, follows with a perceptive discussion of Hemingway's breakout, classic novel and how it may be examined in a self-contained minicourse, in "Teaching Hemingway's *The Sun Also Rises* as Novel and Film." Closing out the first segment of the book, Sean C. Hadley considers morality and ethics in three films—*The Sun Also Rises* (1957), *The Macomber Affair* (1947), and *The Old Man and the Sea* (1958)—in his fascinating entry, "Visual Values: The Success and Failure of Hemingway's Ethics in Film."

The second portion of this book, "The Middle Years," includes four chapters. Kirk Curnutt—who published *Reading Hemingway's* To Have and Have Not just a few years ago—opens with "Teaching *To Have and Have Not* and Adaptation Studies." James Plath returns to the 1937 novel, offering further teaching insights in "To Have and Have Noir: A Tale of Two Films." Timothy

Penner extends the examination and adds a third perspective on using film to teach this cinematic (and yet quite problematic) novel in "From the Harbor to the Hotel." Finally, concluding this segment, Peter L. Hays discusses some intriguing connections between Hemingway and a classic Hollywood director in "Hemingway's *Fifth Column,* Howard Hawks, and the Movies."

"Later Works and Myths" begins with Suzanne del Gizzo's discerning look at how a failed 2008 adaptation of one of Hemingway's most startling (and most truncated) posthumous works may be scrutinized in "Teaching *The Garden of Eden.*" Tatiana Konrad next transports us into the realm of celluloid myth-making in "Teaching Hemingway through Fiction Film: *Midnight in Paris* and *Hemingway & Gelhorn.*" Continuing along this path, Stephen Whittaker presents another shrewd examination of Woody Allen's *Midnight in Paris* (2011) in "Films Like White Elephants." Closing out the volume is Scott D. Yarbrough's astute aerial-view reflection on delving into text with and through film in "Appropriations of Hemingway in *The Long Goodbye* and *A History of Violence.*"

Examining Hemingway's writing *and* film, *through* film, and *alongside* film allows for rich crossovers between literary criticism, film studies, and, yes, pedagogy. Hemingway's writing is very cinematic, his stories are objects of cinema, and the man himself has been mythologized on film. At heart, this collection is about learning. It's a book about making connections among people, between teachers and students, and through readers and texts. With a baker's dozen of chapters, this volume shares a variety of teaching strategies that spark critical engagement. *Hemingway and Film: Reflections on Teaching, Reading, and Understanding* is a useful volume for scholars, teachers, and lay learners alike.

While Hemingway's influence on twentieth-century fiction has been extensively mined, his impact on and through film has received far less attention. Even this volume, in all its spirited ambition, presents the reader with merely a beginning point and is notable for both what is present as well as what is absent. For example, while *To Have and Have Not* and "The Killers" are amply represented, the several film adaptations of *A Farewell to Arms* and stories like "Soldier's Home," "The Short Happy Life of Francis Macomber," and "The Battler" are not. And what of Hemingway's later, problematic works, besides *The Garden of Eden,* like *Islands in the Stream?* Or the recently adapted *Across the River and into the Trees?* The future of Hemingway film studies is, in a word, promising.

With a focus on the relationship between written and cinematic text, traversed through the lens of pedagogy, this collection draws something new from the master's well.[1] Pulling from a range of leading thinkers in the fields of literature and film studies, *Hemingway and Film: Reflections on Teaching, Reading, and Understanding* points to new possibilities and directions in the robust field of American literature. We close this introduction with another snapshot, from another time.

Climbing the flight of stairs, Marc and I stepped into the opening foyer. The building stood about a kilometer east of the Eiffel Tower, on rue du Colonel Combes. It was just a few steps south of the Seine. Turning left, we entered the lounge and stepped past the bar, which featured a large coffee urn, along with an arsenal of cups and packets of sugar, cream, and milk. Running along the south wall was a row of arched windows, which looked out to the street below. We walked to the opposite side of the room, where a dozen or so chairs and sofas were arranged in front of a large wooden bookcase, and sat down. After reviewing our notes, we exited the lounge and climbed the stairs to the second floor of the Combes Building. At 3:20 P.M., a small group of panellists presented papers on Hemingway and the movies. While Alice Craven reflected on film noir and Christina Parker-Flynn discussed overlaps between film and literary analysis, Peter Hays cast his eye back to the Golden Age of Hollywood. At the end of the session, we chatted with Alice and Christina about our vision for this book, and they each agreed to contribute. Peter Hays was a generation older than we were, and we were a bit apprehensive about approaching him. As fortune would have it, though, he sent us an email a few weeks after that Friday afternoon in the summer of 2018, and over the next year and half, we corresponded with him (along with twelve other contributors) as this collection took form. But things slowed with the onset of the pandemic, as we tried to navigate all the uncertainty and change. We were saddened to hear of Peter's passing in the spring of 2022, and that news moved us to complete the work we set out to do all those moons ago in Venice. Peter Hays was a thoughtful and reflective man and a wonderful storyteller, and we dedicate this book to his memory.

Note

1. We would be remiss not to mention three books at this juncture, and we encourage you to seek them out. In 1980, film and literature scholar Gene D. Phillips published *Hemingway and Film*. It was the first book-length venture into Hemingway's work on the silver screen. The following year, Frank M. Lawrence added his own perspective with *Hemingway and the Movies*. More recently, Candace Ursula Grissom updated the conversation, with *Fitzgerald and Hemingway on Film* (2014). Rather than competing with these titles, *Hemingway and Film: Reflections on Teaching, Reading, and Under-*

standing is meant to complement them and to extend this trajectory of Hemingway studies—with the added dimension of pedagogy.

Works Cited

Around the World in 80 Days. Dir. Michael Anderson. Perf. David Niven, Cantinflas. Michael Todd Company, 1956. Film.

The Bridge on the River Kwai. Dir. David Lean. Perf. William Holden, Alec Guinness. Horizon Pictures, 1957. Film.

Delaplane, Stanton. "He Was a Right Guy and the Woman with Him Was Good [reprinted from *San Francisco Chronicle* (31 Jan. 1941)]." *Conversations with Ernest Hemingway,* edited by Matthew J. Bruccoli, UP of Mississippi, 1986, pp. 27–28.

For Whom the Bell Tolls. Dir. Sam Wood. Perf. Gary Cooper, Ingrid Bergman. Paramount Pictures, 1943. Film.

Ginna, Robert Emmett. "Life in the Afternoon [reprinted from *Esquire* (Feb. 1962)]." *Conversations with Ernest Hemingway,* edited by Matthew J. Bruccoli, UP of Mississippi, 1986, pp. 154–64.

Grissom, Candace Ursula. *Fitzgerald and Hemingway on Film: A Critical Study of the Adaptations, 1924–2013.* McFarland, 2014.

Hemingway, Ernest. "Hemingway in the Afternoon [reprinted from *Time* (4 Aug. 1947)]." *Conversations with Ernest Hemingway,* edited by Matthew J. Bruccoli, UP of Mississippi, 1986, pp. 50–51.

Hotchner, A. E. "Hemingway Talks to American Youth [reprinted from *New York Herald Tribune* (18 Oct. 1959)]." *Conversations with Ernest Hemingway,* edited by Matthew J. Bruccoli, UP of Mississippi, 1986, pp. 143–49.

"Indestructible [reprinted from the *New Yorker* (4 Jan. 1947)]." *Conversations with Ernest Hemingway,* edited by Matthew J. Bruccoli, UP of Mississippi, 1986, pp. 48–49.

Kansas City Times. "Back to His First Field [reprinted from *Kansas City Times* (26 Nov. 1940)]." *Conversations with Ernest Hemingway,* edited by Matthew J. Bruccoli, UP of Mississippi, 1986, pp. 21–24.

Lawrence, Frank M. *Hemingway and the Movies.* Da Capo, 1982.

Manning, Robert. "Hemingway in Cuba [reprinted from the *Atlantic Monthly* (Aug. 1965)]." *Conversations with Ernest Hemingway,* edited by Matthew J. Bruccoli, UP of Mississippi, 1986, pp. 172–89.

Phillips, Gene D. *Hemingway and Film.* Frederick Ungar, 1980.

The Old Man and the Sea. Dir. John Sturges. Perf. Spencer Tracy. Warner Bros., 1958. Film.

Part I

Early Stories

Hemingway and the Language of Film Noir
Robert Siodmak's Deceptive Flashback

Alice Mikal Craven

At its inception, the cinematic language of film noir distinguished itself through its use of the voiceover flashbacks. Innovations in sound technology in the 1940s, following the appearance of Orson Welles's *Citizen Kane* (1941), allowed cinema to move beyond the simplistic practice of matching sound to the human voice as was the standard practice in the age of the talkies. Indeed, in his "Statement on Sound," written shortly after the advent of sound, Soviet filmmaker and theorist Sergei Eisenstein recommended experimentation in asynchronous sound. He argued that sound innovation in the cinema should not be sacrificed to the mundane use of sound as a vehicle for simple dialogue (Eisenstein, Pudovkin, Alexandrov).

Fifteen years later, with the voiceover flashback, noir filmmakers sought to deepen relations between sound and screen even more. The voiceover flashback provided for greater control over temporal dimensions within the screen space of a given film. As Mary Ann Doane argues, flashbacks allowed for sophistication in sound use and bodily representation in the screen space of the film noir. Though most film noir directors experimented with these new possibilities, Robert Siodmak, in his 1946 film *The Killers,* based on Ernest Hemingway's 1927 short story of the same name, took these innovations to new heights. In essence, he linked his experimentation with an in-depth exploration of Hemingway's style. He linked the early twentieth-century literary practices forged by Hemingway with the cinema's own capacity for a modernist aesthetic.[1] Siodmak's introduction of a *deceptive flashback* allows the viewer and indeed the student to understand how cinema evolved to adapt and add nuance to its language in ways that rivaled modernist literary styles, in this case Hemingway's elliptical style.[2]

Hemingway anticipated and in many ways helped to create the language of noir. Noir's techniques for defining narrative and screen spaces were prefigured in Hemingway's prose (see Naremore). An analysis of *The Killers* suggests that Siodmak was a close reader of Hemingway and used Hemingway's ellipses as a way to explore the potentials of noir filmmaking. In keeping with the critical practice initiated by James Naremore, I refer to *film noir* as a phenomenon rather than a genre, since its impact goes far beyond the rules of a specific genre. In his introduction to his critical work on noir, Naremore indeed begins by suggesting that studying noir is studying the history of an idea or phenomenon rather than trying to define a genre. There is a plethora of directors and a massive variety of generic styles within the noir phenomenon.

Broadening the critical term *noir* is essential to understanding Hemingway's contribution to its evolution. The striking parallels, in terms of anticipation and innovation, between Hemingway's short story and Siodmak's film show the crucial ways that the literature eventually influenced cinematic language. Hemingway's story leaves many questions unanswered, since it gives us only the barest glimpse of an *impending* violent encounter. The hitmen of the story, Max and Al, show up in a small town and invade George's lunch counter. When asked why they are there, they claim that they are going to kill the Swede, Ole Anderson. They are obviously working on the clock, since references to the precise time and the fact that George's clock is running late reverberate throughout the story. George; his cook, Sam; and the primary client, Nick Adams, are all both terrorized and mesmerized by these out-of-place café patrons. Though Nick goes to warn Ole of the hitmen's plan, Ole remains immobile, powerless to escape his certain fate.

The treatment of violence is elliptical in Hemingway's story, as it is primarily restricted to mere references to pending violence through dialogue. Siodmak used the then current evolution of sound in film as well as Hemingway's narrative ellipses to find a visualization of violence that could approximate the power of Hemingway's prose. For example, in the film, the Swede's killing, which is only alluded to in the short story, is shown at the beginning but kept off camera. The only direct screening of the death is done through a close-up of the Swede's hand as it slides down the edge of the bed after he has been killed. Not content to be simply a disciple of noir tendencies, Siodmak used *The Killers* to question the "why" of film noir.³ This meant that his screen techniques had to be attentive to both direct and indirect aspects of his adapted narrative.

Siodmak relied on noir to fill in the ellipses of Hemingway's short story. That his characters acted how they did is directly linked to what Paul Schrader and others argue was one of the pivotal ideas of noir, namely, postwar disillusionment. Schrader specifically names Siodmak's *The Killers* as an example of the movement toward postwar realism and the need for American audiences to take stock of the war's effects on their own realities. The visualization of violence was a key to making that link. Siodmak uses the common trope of the domesticated protagonist, insurance agent Reardon, who represents the American man paradoxically relieved to be free from the war's traumas but still desirous of the battlefield's exhilaration. Whereas Hemingway's short story never directly refers to wartime trauma, its evocation of violence is precisely the source for crime films such as Siodmak's, as Schrader notes (583). As in the short story, direct encounter and representation of onscreen violence do not occur until later in the film, when Reardon is indeed exposed to violent encounters that are visible to the viewer.

Structurally, the film explores the story's ambiguities by linking a series of narrative flashbacks, which provide a story beneath the surface of Hemingway's elusive text. Siodmak's story is his alone, though it is crafted to interpret what was implied in Hemingway's story. The film creates a history behind the dramatic encounter between the hitmen of Hemingway's story and the Swede, who is trying desperately to escape his past. As the film and the short story suggest, Ole cannot easily turn to the present or even the future. Schrader notes that "noir heroes dread to look ahead, but instead try to survive by the day, and if unsuccessful at that, they retreat to the past." Schrader goes on to say that this retreat to the past is nostalgic; the past is ultimately more a haunting presence than a cure to their present-day struggles (587).

Film noir can thus be seen as cinema's way of coping with postwar trauma and nostalgic desire, with the return of the American soldiers, who came back to the United States scarred but were nonetheless treated as heroes. Settling back into everyday routines eventually diminished their heroic status, and the films of the late 1940s and early 1950s provide entertainment and solace in the form of new and dark confrontations with violence and crime. From Charles Vidor's *Gilda* to Billy Wilder's *Double Indemnity*, films of this period evince what Barbara Hales refers to as the "crisis of male identity" resulting from their reactions to the postwar environment. She contends that this crisis is projected onto the figure of the femme fatale, as both a challenge to the male protagonists and a symbol of dangerous desire (225).

Though more subtle, Hemingway's story is rooted in a similar revisitation of the traumatic lived experiences of World War I soldiers, displaced into an everyday gangster context that Nick Adams and George can only imagine.[4] In her article "The Aesthetics of Revealing/Concealing in 'The Killers' by Ernest Hemingway and Its Adaptation by Robert Siodmak," Linda Collinge-Germain sums up the critical common places of the comparison between the film and the short story. Despite that her primary sources are French and scholarly, she considers many of the international critical findings on this film-text comparison. She argues that Siodmak ultimately succeeded in providing a "filling in of [the] gaps" of Hemingway's elliptical style (69).

Outlining his ellipses as well as his dependence on implicit references, Collinge-Germain primarily appeals to Hemingway's 1923 work "Out of Season" and his 1932 *Death in the Afternoon* as sources for understanding his aesthetic. She also rightly evokes his "iceberg theory." She quotes Hemingway's explanation that a writer is able to omit many things if he is writing about what he knows. Hemingway claims that the reader will feel those things "as strongly as though the writer had stated them. The dignity of the movement of an iceberg is due to only one-eighth of it being above water." Other modernist writers—like Henry James who focuses on the idea of *explicit* ambiguity in his preface to *The Turn of the Screw*—also explore this aesthetic move. James evokes the concept of adumbration and suggests that the reader's "own imagination, his or her own sympathy (with the children) and horror (of their false friends) will supply him quite sufficiently with all the particulars" (128).[5]

Collinge-Germain argues that as in many modernist works, Hemingway places his readers in the position of detectives needing to find solutions to enigmas confronting them. She relies on Gerard Genette's concept of the *external focalizer* to stress the absence of an authoritative narrative voice in Hemingway's short story. This concept upon is in many ways like the camera's perspective in the cinematic language of film in general and film noir in particular. The flashback voiceover must be viewed as a quasi-contender to the power of the camera's storytelling. The camera renders all flashback narratives as subjective and to a certain extent suspect until the film's narrative as implicitly certified by the objectivity of the camera's gaze has unfolded and been confirmed by the external narrative source.

Though Collinge-Germain credits the idea of the first and second narrative of detective fiction to Dominique Sipière (1999), Sipière's arguments are derived either directly or indirectly from Tzvetan Todorov's "Typology of Detective Fiction" (1977). For both Sipière and Todorov, the two parts of the narrative of detective fiction, which may also be applied to film noir, are the narrative of the *event* and the narrative of the *investigation* of the event. The seminal definition of *film noir* in Collinge-Germain's article is derived from Anthony Slide and focuses on the use of low-key lighting as well as the redemptive nature of pre-noir gangster films. From 1930 to 1968, redemption in gangster films was necessarily determined by the moral impositions of the Hays Code.

The extensive use of flashback narrative in film noir, and in particular in Siodmak's *The Killers,* is elaborately mapped in Gilles Menegaldo's essay "Flashbacks in Film Noir." Critics generally agree that Siodmak made great innovations in the complications of flashback structure in *The Killers*.[6] Though much critical attention has been given to this technique in the film, almost none has been given to the collapse of the flashback sequencing in its middle.

Though Collinge-Germain also analyzes the prominence of dialogue rather than narrative in Hemingway's "The Killers," in terms of narrative theory, Hemingway's short story completely elides all elements of *séries noire* fiction and film noir films. Siodmak's excellent anticipation of what becomes important in film noir style in terms of sound innovation derives from his efforts to render the implicit explicit. The real key to seeing the innovation effected by Siodmak and the genius of Hemingway's story has been compacted into the deceptive flashback of the film to which I now turn.

Flashback sequencing is one of the first attempts after the advent of sound films to move away from a privileging of sound originating from the human body. The approximation of a voiceover flashback was nonetheless created in the silent period through the collective efforts of Fritz Lang and Robert Wiene in *The Cabinet of Dr. Caligari*. Lang would go on to become one of the seminal directors of film noir in 1940s Hollywood.[7] In addition, three years prior to the birth of film noir, one of the first questions Welles asked and one that Siodmak also entertained, is the question of how sound should affect both the diegetic, or narrative, space of the film as well as the extra-diegetic space.

In her reading of Siodmak's *The Killers,* Doane suggests (though she does not evoke Hemingway per se), that the dialogic nature of Siodmak's source material made it possible for him to subvert the dominance of narrative in the classical Hollywood cinema, as Bordwell theorizes. The film does not work against the idea of a seamless narrative, which is characteristic of classic Hollywood cinema, but it does complicate and disrupt the temporal sequencing in the film's narrative. Though Doane does not expressly make the comparison between Hemingway and Siodmak, her analysis enables us to concentrate more on the dialogic intonation one finds in Hemingway's short story and how it is captured in the film (321). Doane's main observations concern the ability to create multiple spaces within one narrative simply by allowing flashback to dominate. Ole Anderson, "the Swede," of Hemingway's story thus becomes a phantasmatic body in the film, which is to say a body constructed by the fragmented flashback narrative (322). Since Anderson is killed by the hitmen at the opening of the film, the spectator's only access to him is through the multiple recollections of his past offered by numerous characters.

We can use Doane's findings to argue that the femme fatale, Kitty, functions as a camera code, allowing for the films disparate spaces to come together. Since Kitty ultimately represents the paradox of post–World War II trauma and desire, she is not a protagonist; rather she allows for the protagonists to shift their goals with respect to the driving narrative. By matching trauma and desire as effects of the war, the suggestion is that there is a paradoxical need to revisit the vital experiences of war as an authentic encounter with death. Siodmak creates his film to try and make sense of what is left out in Hemingway's story. Kitty is a central mechanism controlling what is revealed and concealed in the film and one that helps the viewer to explore how those revelations and concealments are anticipated in Hemingway. She is there to incite the protagonist, Reardon, to look again beneath the surface of a violent encounter.

Hemingway's ellipses nonetheless make space for three temporally distinct sets of protagonists: the hitmen of the short story (Max and Al); the insurance agent Reardon, who functions as an investigator but is not the tough investigator cited by Collinge-Germain; and the Swede. In terms of the narrative, the Swede must be considered the central figure in the group of Prohibition Chicago–type gangster cohorts he frequents in the flashbacks describing his rise and fall. Each set of protagonists is defined by goals characteristic of specific genres within film noir. The hitmen's goals of are unexamined and stereotypical. These men just want to kill, since that is what they do. Later articulations of narratives about hitmen attempt to make their treatment of such characters nuanced by exploring more deeply the how and the why of hitman characters. Martin Mcdonagh's 2007 neo-noir film *In Bruges* is a prime example of this evolution.

The gangsters of the Swede's entourage want money from the Prentiss Hat Factory heist. Once the Swede has been killed, Reardon wants to recover the money for his insurance company. With the Swede's murder, the remaining gangsters of his entourage set out after the money, which he supposedly took when he double-crossed them. These characters—Kitty, Big Jim, Blinky Franklin, and Dum Dum—are out for that money, but they are also out for revenge against the Swede for his apparent betrayal.

These goals all fit postwar cinema and the aspirations of post–World War II America's attempt to restore a sense of order and safety at home. The goals are also a common trope of some noir films such as *Gilda,* which resolves itself in a depletion of the American man's ability to solve the problems fomented by the end of the war. At the film's ending, Gilda and Johnny, who have been battling each other throughout, recognize that they are indeed in love and resolve to leave Europe. They want to go home and to leave behind the traumas of the war and the postwar environment that defined them throughout the film. We can see that, in keeping with their goal of returning to a peaceful existence, violence can be contained if it is kept in the urban settings. Men can provide for themselves and their families if they take safe jobs as insurance agents, even though they may yearn for the dangers of the war they won and left behind. By extension, American women can return to their appropriate places as those the men went to war to protect.

What is interesting about Siodmak's *The Killers* is how the insurance agent's goals shift once the disparate spaces of the film get filled in by the flashback structure and collapse the validity or believability of those goals. A little over halfway into the film, the definitive collapse is provided by the *deceptive flashback.* Up to this point, the screen and narrative's temporal space is divided into the world of Reardon, who is in the present seeking to solve the mystery of the disappearance of the Prentiss Hat Factory money stolen by the gangsters in the past.

The hitmen's world is defined by the opening café sequence, after which they disappear until the end when the disparate spaces of the film come together. The Swede's life and the Prentiss Hat robbery are definitively part of a past that the film seems destined not to be recovered, due to the fact that the Swede has been killed.

To understand how Reardon's desire to step into the Swede's place is realized, we must study the rules of flashback structure Siodmak proposes throughout the film. The opening half is controlled by slowly dissolved flashbacks where characters who were part of the world in which the original crimes of the hat factory heist took place recount their involvement in that world. Each flashback begins with a voiceover as the transition from present to past is made, and then the past takes over and the voiceover narration disappears. Having been killed in the film's opening moments, the Swede functions throughout these screen spaces as a phantasmatic body. Having "gone straight" or in other ways "gotten out of the game," none of these early characters have any further access to that criminal world belonging to the Prentiss Hat robbery.

Reardon is initially searching for a way to recover the money lost in the factory raid, but he becomes increasingly absorbed by the past world of gangsters he is trying to penetrate. He finally encounters one of the characters who was *and still is* part of that world, and the narrative spaces of the film begin to collide. Reardon encounters Blinky Franklin, close to death and ranting deliriously on his deathbed. There is no way of determining, therefore, whether his flashback narrative is reliable or consistent with what happened during the days of the heist. His flashback narrative nonetheless echoes the fantasies and speculations of Hemingway's George and Nick Adams about what gangsters can be expected to do or indeed why they might be killed. As George says when Nick speculates on why they might want to kill the Swede: "Double-crossed somebody. That's what they kill them for" (222). As a result, it feeds Reardon's desire to get closer not only to the narrative itself but to the narrative's actual screen space. In other words, one basic rule of film theory is that there is always a discrepancy between what happens in the diegetic or narrative space of the film and in the screen space. Reardon is only ever exposed to direct violence and adventure once he is *onscreen* with the criminals he pursues, namely the hitmen, Blinky Friedman, Dum-Dum, Big Jim, and eventually Kitty. This discrepancy between what the narrative relates and how it is visualized onscreen is a fundamental rule of cinematic language's grammar.

Reardon is indeed closer to the crime space itself but is still pushed away in that he cannot guarantee the veracity of Franklin's story, and Franklin gets himself "out of the game" when he dies at the close of the flashback. By now, the viewer has been lulled into watching a film controlled by flashbacks. The police, also after the killers, have been convinced that Reardon is close enough to danger that he needs to carry a gun. This will be Reardon's first step into the separate narrative space of the criminal world. The next flashback, the deceptive one, is when Reardon catches another of the criminals, Dum Dum, holding a gun on him and essentially asks him to tell his side of the story. Reardon is in direct contact with a violent encounter. He is in a position to live or relive a traumatic episode.

At this juncture, Reardon is left with a desire to relive the true story of the original traumatic event experienced by the Swede. Similarly, in Hemingway's story George and Nick Adams question what precisely is beneath the surface of the plan to kill Ole Anderson, to which they are occasional witnesses. Their desire for a repetition of the trauma underlying this event echoes the desire one can sense in Reardon's actions from this point forward.

In Reardon's crucial encounter with Dum Dum, Siodmak uses the slowly dissolving pre-shot to the flashback sequence, which has become the main structure of the film's language. However, rather than lapse into a flashback, Dum Dum disrupts the spectator's expectations by grabbing Reardon's gun, thus breaking the rules of the flashback sequencing. From this point forward, all three worlds—of Kitty and the other gangsters, of the hitmen, and of Reardon—all become one space within the film, and the flashback sequencing all but disappears.

Most important about this shift is that Siodmak illustrates in some ways just how spatially disparate Hemingway's characters are from each other. Sam, the black cook, is confined in the kitchen. The Swede cannot to leave his own bedroom. George remains stuck behind the counter of his business enterprise. Nick Adams is the only character trying to pull these worlds together and to understand how to save the Swede from his past. Reardon recognizes that it is not enough just to want to recuperate the heist money for his company. He wants to know the gangsters' whole story. He does not want to be left out, and, indeed, in this final space where all characters of this world are united, he meets the femme fatale Kitty, who has become a symbol of his desire to experience the thrill and danger of the criminal world. While we cannot be certain, it is entirely possible that the author favored the casting of Ava Gardner as Kitty. After all, the bond between the two not only crops up in Hemingway's correspondence but also shines through as one peruses various entries posted on the official *Ava Gardner Blog* (see also Mulvey).

Reardon's sense of adventure and his desire to relive trauma is rewarded by his ability to get as close as possible to the real story of crime and violence lurking beneath the narrative veneer of Siodmak's film noir structure. Reardon is allowed time onscreen with the protagonists of a narrative that he has only enjoyed vicariously up until the deceptive flashback. In this small instance at least, Reardon differs from Nick, who shies away from getting directly involved, though he is the only character brave enough to go and warn the Swede. He wants to be part of the action but, paradoxically, "doesn't know if he can think about it" (222). Hemingway's articulation is indeed that of the paradox of trauma and desire outlined through Siodmak's flashback structure.

The film's flashback structure is also inexorably tied to the Swede's experience of post-traumatic stress disorder (PTSD). When the two hitmen show up in Brentwood and the ex-boxer retreats to his room, a place where they are prepared to kill him, the specter of PTSD looms large. Watching as the Swede makes no attempt to escape, the reader (or film spectator) is helpless, watching as a tragic chain of events unfolds. The audience is stuck, unable to urge the Swede to run or to help him overcome the stress of the trauma of his past. It is as though the flashbacks reach forward from the past, taking form as the weight of the Swede's PTSD, holding him down in the present.

Hemingway makes one of his most elliptical moves when he ends his story with the lunch-counter owner George suggesting to Nick that if he doesn't think he *can* think about it, then perhaps he shouldn't. Just as the Great War perhaps needed to be elided over in the 1920s, Siodmak makes use of the cinematic technique by which film noir placed WWII into a parallel ellipsis. Freud's 1914 essay, "On Disillusionment," in which he claims that WWI disillusionment consisted of humanity's desire to repress the brutality of what it had witnessed is an echo of the greater excellence of Hemingway's elliptical style and his creative vision, which German Jewish film director Siodmak sought to understand and recreate in his film. The film exemplifies why this literary generation, and, in particular, Hemingway, felt lost but nonetheless created ways for later generations to experience loss productively.

Appendix: A Guide to Student Learning

Students being initiated into the language of film noir can benefit greatly from a comparative analysis of Hemingway's short story and Siodmak's film. Here are some suggestions:
1. Siodmak's film is one of the more successful and intriguing exercises in film adaptation of an original literary source. Keeping in mind the context of Siodmak's film at the height of the film noir period, close analysis of his use of a film noir aesthetic to give voice to Hemingway's ellipses can be a profitable exercise. Adding to this exercise a parallel analysis of Don Siegel's 1964 adaptation of the film and Tarkosvsky's 1956 short student film, helps students learn how to understand adaptation theory and how

it can be applied in the varied phases and cultural areas of the evolution of cinematic language. For example, narrative voiceover flashback is absent from Siegel's adaptation, since the exploration of sound innovations is no longer of central concern in 1964.

2. Handing out a list of the series of flashbacks in the film, provided by Gilles Menegaldo, and doing a comparative analysis of how they function differently within the film can add to a student's understanding of how sound functions in film and how the flashback provides innovative techniques in the use of sound in cinematic language.

3. If one considers Hemingway's short story as a screen space, then it is abundantly clear what is left out and only implied in that space. A close analysis of the prose in Hemingway's text and how Siodmak's film supplements it can help in instructing the student in the differences between what is explicit and implicit both in literature and in film. Siodmak's version of what lay beneath the surface in Hemingway's short story is filled in primarily by the diegetic space rather than the screen space. If a creative angle were to be employed, students might be invited to invent their own versions of what was elliptically implied in the short story and how it might be developed into a film script. This would also provide an opportunity to deepen the student's understanding of the difference between the narrative of the event and the investigative narrative of the event, as introduced by Sipière and Todorov.

4. The paradox of trauma and desire that informs modern capitalism and was born of the modernist aesthetic and still shared by the filmmakers of the noir period is an area for further student research. What effects did the two world wars have on the imaginations of writers and artists and how do the Freud's psychoanalytic theories affect the structures of modernist texts and film noir? What is it precisely that Nick Adams is incapable of thinking about? A good place to begin with this project would be the article cited in this chapter, "On Disillusionment" which was written at the outbreak of World War I and formed the base for what later became his work *Civilization and Its Discontents* (1929). Another creative project would be to have students write a page of Nick Adams's diary, about the day he witnessed the appearance of the hitmen, as he speculates on what happened to put Ole Anderson into such danger.

5. The violent encounter of Hemingway's short story, the pending killing of Ole Anderson, occupies both a past and a present position. The Swede has done something linked to a past and it is intimated that that past

was violent. Midway through the film, there is a significant third-person flashback narration of a newspaper article citing the salient details of the Prentiss Hat factory robbery, and this is differentiated from the rest of the flashbacks narrations, which are always linked to specific characters. What is the purpose of this third-person voiceover narration? What does it accomplish? Siodmak, like many of his German exiled compatriots uses the concept of the narrative elaboration of a journalistic *fait-divers* to develop his narrative. This technique is of central importance to the noir period. If students are involved in a more creative course, a related study might be to find their own newspaper articles and construct fuller narrative structures for that newspaper, suitable for a noir script.

6. The exercise in constructing noir narratives from newspaper or social media sources could be expanded into a study of genres such as melodrama or even science fiction. How do our realities create our fictions on the screen?

Notes

1. Doane's primary purpose is to speak uniquely to the question of sound innovation in film with the advent of the flashback. I rely on her findings to show how Hemingway's prose anticipated those innovations.

2. The term *deceptive flashback* is my own and is intended to indicate a moment when the camera language used throughout the film suggests that a flashback will occur. In the one instance I discuss, Siodmak deliberately lulls the viewer into accepting his rules for how a flashback is introduced in the film and then thwarts them by skipping over the introduction of a flashback.

3. Alpi and Greco both provide more insight into Siodmak's attitudes toward the demands of his filmmaking work in Hollywood.

4. For a complete coverage of the questions posed by Hemingway on the negative effects on war, See *Hemingway on War*.

5. For more information on this text and its use in pedagogic practices, see Beidler.

6. Menegaldo, Doane, and Naremore are some of the essential sources for this argument. In *Narration in the Fictional Film,* David Bordwell additionally points out that *The Killers* is one of the most elaborate films when it comes to the use of flashback as a fictional device (194).

7. Tom Gunning's is the most comprehensive text on the films of Fritz Lang.

Works Cited

Alpi, Deborah Lazaroff. *Robert Siodmak: A Critical Analysis of His Film Noirs and a Filmography of All of His Works.* McFarland, 1998.

Ava Gardner Blog, Ava Garber Museum, Smithfield, NC, https://www.johnstoncountync.org/ava-gardner/blog/.

Beidler, Peter G. "Reader-Response and *The Turn of the Screw.*" Henry James, *The Turn of the Screw: Complete, Authoritative Text with Biographical and Historical Contexts, Critical History, and Essays from Five Contemporary Critical Perspectives,* edited by Peter G. Beidler, Macmillan Education, 1995, pp. 152–78.

Bordwell, David. *Narration in the Fictional Film.* Routledge, 1987.

Collinge-Germain, Linda. "The Aesthetics of Revealing/Concealing in Ernest Hemingway's 'The Killers' and its Adaptation by Robert Siodmak." *Journal of the Short Story in English,* vol. 59, special issue, *Short Story and Cinema,* Aug. 2012, https://journals.openedition.org/jsse/1323.

Doane, Mary Ann. "The Voice in the Cinema: The Articulation of Body and Space," *Film Theory and Criticism,* edited by Leo Braudy and Marshall Cohen, 7th ed. Oxford UP, 2009, pp. 318–39.

Eisenstein, Sergei, Vsevelod Pudovkin, and Grigori Alexandrov. "Statement on Sound," *Film Theory and Criticism,* edited by Leo Braudy and Marshall Cohen, 7th ed., Oxford UP, 2009, pp. 315–17.

Freud, Sigmund. *Civilization and Its Discontents,* translated by Christopher Hitchens and Peter Gay. 1929. Norton, 2010.

Greco, Joseph. *The File on Robert Siodmak in Hollywood, 1941–1951.* Universal-Publishers. 1999.

Gunning, Tom. *The Films of Fritz Lang: Allegories of Vision and Modernity.* British Film Institute, 2000.

Hales, Barbara. "Projecting Trauma: The Femme Fatale in Weimar and Hollywood Film Noir." *Women in German Yearbook,* vol. 23, 2007, 224–43.

Hemingway, Ernest, *Death in the Afternoon.* Scribner & Sons, 1932.

———. *Hemingway on War.* Scribner, 2004.

———. "The Killers." *The Complete Short Stories of Ernest Hemingway: The Finca Vigía Edition.* Scribner, 1987, pp. 215–22.

———. "Out of Season." *The Complete Short Stories of Ernest Hemingway: The Finca Vigía Edition.* Scribner, 1987, pp. 133–40.

James, Henry. *The Turn of the Screw,* edited by Deborah Esch and Jonathan Warren, Norton, 1999, pp. 123–29.

Menegaldo, Gilles. "Flashbacks in Film Noir." *Sillages Critique,* vol. 6, 2004, pp. 157–75.

Mulvey, Laura. "Visual Pleasure and Narrative Criticism." *Film Theory and Criticism,* 7th ed., edited by Leo Braudy and Cohen Marshall, Oxford UP, 2009, pp. 711–23.

Naremore, James. *More Than Night: Film Noir in Its Contexts.* U of California P, 1998.

Schrader, Paul. "Notes on Film Noir." *Film Theory and Criticism,* 7th ed., edited by Leo Braudy and Marshall Cohen, Oxford UP, 2009, pp. 581–91.

Slide, Anthony. *The New Historical Dictionary of the American Film Industry*. Fitzroy Dearborn, 1988.
Sipière, Dominique. "Avant-Propos." *Les récits policiers au cinéma*, edited by Dominique Sipière and Gilles Menegaldo, Licorne, 1999, pp. 3–6.
Todorov, Tzvetan. "The Typology of Detective Fiction." *The Poetics of Prose*, translated by Richard Howard, Cornell UP 1977, pp. 42–52.

Seeing and Nothingness

Doing Film/Theory with Hemingway's "The Killers"

Christina Parker-Flynn

Columnist Louella Parsons once praised Ernest Hemingway as not only one of the greatest novelists of the era but one of the greatest screenwriters as well. Indeed, more than thirty major films, series, and the like have been made by adapting the author's novels and short stories. In 1932, Gary Cooper starred in the first screen version of *A Farewell to Arms,* and some other, famously glossy Hollywood adaptations soon followed, including the Humphrey Bogart–helmed film version of *To Have and Have Not* (1944), for which William Faulkner cowrote the screenplay with director Howard Hawks. Yet, it was one of Hemingway's most sparing works, his short story "The Killers," that possibly commands the prize for inspiring many, as well as one of the most successful, film adaptations. Released in 1946 and directed by German émigré Robert Siodmak, *The Killers* serves an instructive imperative for understanding adaptation as a complex relationship between text and film. Siodmak's adaptation performs an erudite reading of Hemingway's brutally modernist short story, capitalizing on both its expansive potential for cinema as well as the parallelism between the story's main themes and the central concerns of film noir, including radical externalism, nihilism, and the postwar crisis of masculinity as an inverted performance.

First published by Scribner's in 1927, "The Killers" illustrates the principle of Hemingway's theory of omission in action, a theory that became, upon the author's own edict, the central evaluative basis for many of his short stories. The first, major component to teaching this lesson is to acknowledge the nullity built into Hemingway's short story, which requires a foundational understanding of his iceberg theory. In a *Paris Review* interview with George Plimpton (1958), Hemingway admits to trying "to write on the principle of the iceberg. There is seven-eighths of it underwater for every part that shows. Anything you know you can eliminate and it only strengthens your iceberg. It is the part that doesn't show" (88). Though the story was set in Chicago, Hemingway admitted that it "probably had more left out of it than anything I ever wrote. I left out all of Chicago, which is hard to do in 2951 words" (P. Smith 277). Almost entirely composed of dialogue—the speaker of which is sometimes maddeningly unclear—and lacking overall in adverbs or adjectives, Hemingway's "The Killers" has been praised for its minimalist realism. Two men enter Henry's lunchroom and initiate a threateningly banal back-and-forth about the menu with the counterman, George. They hold George, the cook, and young Nick Adams hostage while waiting for the Swede, a boxer named Ole Andreson, to arrive for dinner. They leave when he doesn't show, and Nick runs to the Swede's rooming house to warn him that these men have come to kill him, to which the Swede responds repeatedly, "There ain't anything to do" (221). Nick returns to the lunchroom where George instructs him to "better not think about it" (222).

I might acknowledge here how strange it is to discuss a story that shows so little, and then work upon the premise of how said story becomes adapted into a visual medium that seemingly shows so much. But taken in conjunction with its 1946 film adaptation, "The Killers" can be used to approach a multitude of film theories, including brief points about narrative theory, adaptation studies, montage theory, feminist film theory, film noir, and existentialism proper. Specifically, I propose that Hemingway's short story offers a surprisingly meta-cinematic imperative or at least, organically intersects with some central components of film form and theory.

As early as the seventeenth century, writers began to put various arts under a single category, thus drawing parallels among them. As far back as antiquity, Horace's *ut picture poesis* equated poetry and painting, lending to the idea that the lyrical literature might operate as speaking picture. By the Victorian period, Charles Dickens had drawn the analogy between novels and the theater in that every writer, hoping to achieve some dramatic potential in their work, "writes in effect for the stage" (Pullman 13). More accurately, many of Dickens's texts presage filmic effects and see—or allow the reader to see—cinematically. In the opening of *Bleak House,* for instance, Dickens cuts from wide landscape views to close-ups on the fingers and toes of the little prentice boy (13). Soviet montage theorist and filmmaker Sergei Eisenstein theorized on the development of film form from the soil of montage structures found in Dickens's writing, The visual mechanics of Dickens's writing directly resembled what would become the most important principle of building and construction in the cinema, montage (204). Eisenstein determined that the method of parallel action in the films of D. W. Griffith, for instance, was directly inspired by Dickens's work (something Griffith testified to as well). The "extraordinary plasticity" and optical qualities of Dickens's work proved necessary antecedent to early cinema, according to Eisenstein, who, in his essay "Dickens, Griffith, and the Film Today" offers an early testament to the importance to understanding literature to film adaptations on a theoretical, structural, and even molecular level (204–7).[1]

Modernist Henry James presupposed the novel to be a pictorial art, fulfilling man's appetite for a picture. As David Bordwell argues in *Narration in the Fiction Film,* books like James's *The Wings of the Dove* evoke stages in perspective relevant to Renaissance painting, and equally relevant to the new medium of artistic representation, modern film. Bordwell suggests that by "confining the text to the limited viewpoint of the implied subject of the perspective picture, the novelist makes language a vehicle for vision"—a "scenic" method (8). However, in many ways, Hemingway's short story specifically makes us *not* see, as if operating on both levels of form and content as an explicit refusal to see or to know. In his theoretical analysis of narrative discourse, Gérard Genette suggests that Hemingway's story takes external focalization to such an extreme as to become riddle-like. Popularized by pulp fiction writers like Dashiell Hammett, a narrative with external focalization offers its main characters from the outside or external perspective, not allowing the reader to access their internal thoughts or desires, only superficial looks and actions (Genette 190). Siodmak's film adaptation reads and re-presents the Swede (Burt Lancaster) as central riddle of circumspection, and the near absence of (internal) focalization in the story and film becomes a focalization proper, one that directly suits the nihilism that runs deep in Hemingway and the equivalent fatalism that exemplifies noir.

Linda Collinge-Germain claims that there are only three manifestations of the narrator's subjectivity in Hemingway's positively skeletal and excessively objective short story—and that one of them isn't even clearly illustrating Nick Adams's point of view, since it could just as easily be George's. I might acknowledge how integral this extremely limited subjectivity is, in terms of why this story operated as a filmlike blueprint, and as a hard-boiled progenitor of film noir. Rather than speak here of a subjective and perspectival viewpoint, instead, the extreme limitedness of "The Killers" and its inherent objectivity parallels the demarcated limits of an objective camera lens—objective, first because of its mechanical nature, if we borrow from one of the central ideas of André Bazin's *What Is Cinema?* Bazin argued that the camera offered a model of an automatic world, and thus photography and cinema derive an advantage from man's absence. This concept is distilled in Bazin's etymological reading of the French word for lens—*objectif*—thus revealing the objective nature of the photographic at the level of language (13).

More specifically, *The Killers* continues to fulfill this objectif because the film adaptation borrows Hemingway's iceberg theory as its own structuring principle. Siodmak faithfully translates the Hemingway story into the film's prologue, lasting approximately the first 10 percent of its runtime. The rest of the film centers around how invented character Jim Reardon (Edmond O'Brien), a life insurance agent, solves the mystery of the Swede's life dealings and ultimate demise. Operating as the quintessential noir detective, Reardon interviews a series of people who had known the Swede, and thus the story's structure turns he who has already perished in the opening sequence into an object of discourse already past. Orson Welles revolutionized this same flashback narrative structure in *Citizen Kane* (1941); after the death of Charles Foster Kane, a reporter named Thompson hopes to deepen the understanding of the media magnate by figuring out the meaning of his final utterance, "Rosebud." After hearing the stories told by those who knew Kane, including people like his ex-wife and business manager, the film crystalizes Kane only as object of discourse, a sphinx without a riddle. From beginning to end, the film version of *The Killers*—paying clear homage to Welles's film—exhibits the Swede as passive. Indeed, he is rendered so with finality when murdered by the killers in the opening sequence, yet none of the flashbacks that make him the object of discourse recuperate any sense of the Swede as a person. The audience learns that he sacrificed any supposed principles to protect femme fatale Kitty Collins (Ava Gardner), that he throws a fight before an injured hand forces him out of the boxing ring, and that he became the stooge of the robber gang, double-double-crossed by leader Colfax (Albert Dekker) and his paramour-turned-wife, Kitty.

While the film adaptation may have used the author's writing techniques as representational strategy, Hemingway's theory of omission allowed him to develop what Zoe Trodd calls a "camera-eye aesthetic" in his fiction that was explicitly multi-focal, thus asserting the existence of numerous "angles" (8). As did Dickens, Hemingway "rendered in prose a series of filmic wide-shots and close-ups," sometimes using a cutting technique to rapidly move back-and-forth between scenes, characters, or images (6). Indeed, British linguist Roger Fowler suggests that Nick Adams, the narrator in "The Killers," "occupies a definite viewing position, like a fixed camera" (Bordwell 8–9). Siodmak imparts his own modernist/expressionistic aesthetic in the film adaptation, correlative to the original story's minimal details and to Hemingway's own equivalent style, uses a multifocal omniscient perspective, and a fixed camera that mimics the position of Nick Adams's definite viewing position in the original text.

Film noir was a post facto label for a series of World War II–era American films that displayed a certain "darkness" in both tone and visual components. The label emerged thanks to French critics who, in Paris during the summer of 1946, watched a series of American films which, according to Raymond Borde and Étienne Chaumeton's *Panorama du Film Noir Américain,* shared "a strange and violent tone, tinged with a unique kind of eroticism" (17). So, the noir was borne of this initial French critical interest that linked the films of the period, such as John Huston's *The Maltese Falcon* and Billy Wilder's *Double Indemnity,* with the hard-boiled literature, or pulp fiction, coming from American writers such as James M. Cain and Raymond Chandler.[2] But many consider Hemingway the true father of the hard-boiled tradition that inspired noir, and one of the only hard-boiled writers to be living in and writing from Paris in the 1920s, which only strengthens this cultural lineage. Film critic Nino Frank coined the term *noir* to describe a particular cycle of crime dramas marked by a psychological darkness in the same year as the release of the Robert Siodmak–directed adaptation of Hemingway's "The Killers"—a conveniently timed coincidence perhaps, yet at least one that forces us to recognize this film adaptation as one of the most important noirs in the very year noir became a thing.[3]

I use the word *thing* to describe noir here for a variety of reasons. First, there's simply no consensus on what it is. Janey Place and Lowell Peterson, for instance, use the term *movement,* in consideration of noir as characterized by a homogeneous visual style that can often cut across genres. *Genre* itself can mean many things, possibly demarcating a way to group films by similar conventions, or by similar intentions. Film scholar Robin Wood sees noir as "occupying an indeterminate space between a style and a genre," while others regard it as a "hybrid" or "generic field," something "which defies classification (16). For Thomas Elsaesser it's a "conceptual black hole" and critic Steve Neale, being quite the nihilist, "denies that it ever existed" (Park 2).

But first, back for a moment to Hemingway's iceberg theory and its natural relationship with the traditional use of chiaroscuro in film noir. The noir style emerged largely from the intersection of hard-boiled fiction and the German

Expressionist movement, which focused on developing filmic compositions that were particularly unstable, "designed to unsettle, jar, and disorient the viewer" (Place and Peterson 68). The suggestive power of Hemingway's minimalist narration in the short story finds itself companion to, or perhaps even inciter of, the "visual dissonances" that constitute noir. Delphine Letort suggests that noir's classic stylistic elements, such as canted camera angles and unbalanced shot compositions, were "able to stylize the hidden forces pervading Hemingway's writing" (54–55). The suggestive power of Hemingway's theory of omission is echoed in the film adaptation through its expressionist lighting. Film noir made great use of chiaroscuro lighting; borrowed from the Italian word meaning light–dark and developed by painters like Rembrandt and Caravaggio, *noirs* built visual composition around small points of light and therefore offer meaning in and even as shadow.

In his book *Hemingway and the Movies,* Frank Laurence suggests that light is "the essence of the aesthetic and chemical properties of film, whereas light is only incidental to the descriptive and symbolic possibilities of literature, though the symbolic possibility is shared with film" (202). Indeed, Hemingway eschews

Fig. 1: When the killers drive into town at the very beginning of the film, the chiaroscuro effect creates an overwhelming darkness that threatens the small area of artificially lit road mediated through their windshield, resembling icebergs in a sea of darkness. (Robert Siodmak, *The Killers,* 1946, Universal Pictures)

Fig. 2: Small islands of artificial light cast the eponymous killers deeper into dark silhouette when they arrive in Brentwood, New Jersey. (Robert Siodmak, *The Killers*, 1946, Universal Pictures)

almost all description in his short story, save for a few details about Nick walking to and from the Swede's boarding room under "the arc light," an important structural component in the story that also reads like screenplay directives. Even more, Hemingway repeats "bright boy," usually to describe Nick, no fewer than twenty-five times in the story. A slight on Nick's masculinity and affirmation of his adolescent naivete, Hemingway's conspicuous and copious use of the word *bright* connects with his seeming occupation with the mise-en-scène lighting he describes in his story that presages the quintessential noir cinematic scenery of the 1940s: in particular, night-for-night lighting. The short story opens as it grows dark, a streetlight flicking on outside; later, as Nick runs to warn the Swede, "the arc-light shone through the bare branches of a tree" (220). Returning to the lunchroom, "Nick walked up the dark street to the corner under the arc-light," as if he's already a character in an ex-ante *noir*, where "small areas of light seem on the verge of being completely overwhelmed by the darkness that now threatens them from all sides" (Place and Peterson 67).

Author Aldous Huxley claimed Hemingway created meaning within the white spaces of his writing, those spaces left open to vast interpretation and, equally, to the endless possibilities of film adaptation. Film images create meaning, according to Soviet montage theory, by acting as building blocks that acquire signification in the act of *juxtaposition* (to borrow Lev Kuleshov's keyword), *conflict,* or *collision* (Eisenstein's preferred terms). Theoretically speaking, montage theory suggests that film technique, rather than reality, generates the emotions of and effects on the spectator. Soviet filmmaker Vsevolod Pudovkin outlined five principles of relational film editing used to enhance the viewer's understanding of the story: leitmotif, or the reiteration of theme, would usually involve the repetition of a shot, sequence, or motif to create an important visual code. Take, for instance, the repeated visual motif of the Swede's hand in Siodmak's film (Figs. 3 and 4). As one can see in Fig. 3, Sidomak's carefully composed shot exhibits Swede's limp, open hand the moment he gets murdered by the killers, a visual manifestation of his failure to control his fate, his failure to take his destiny into his own hands. Fig. 4 shows the doctor examining his injured hand after he fails to throw his right to win the boxing match. A career in boxing means a literal earning of one's keep with one's own two hands; an injured hand implies the destruction of a career that casts Swede as the central, masculine object of the audience's gaze. Rather than embody a hard work ethic or the equivalent, instead, the film's leitmotif of hand imagery offers the spectator a characterization of the Swede as passively external from both his environment and any semblance of control over it.

To return, *thing* might be a fitting word because of noir's lack of central identity, but some of its crowning features illustrate an essential refusal of subjectivity, too. In her seminal work defining film noir through its chronotopes, Vivian Sobchak reminds us that *absence* is film noir's structuring principle. What she calls "lounge time" is structured by spatiotemporal structures and spaces like the cocktail lounge or the hotel room, which threaten the traditional function, security, and very outward identity of society, as well as temporal continuity and relative cohesion. The spaces of *The Killers*—hotel rooms, bars, roadside diners, boardinghouses—are equally characterized as other, and without familial connection, "all refuse individual subjectivity and intimacy" (143). In flashback, we see the Swede in the boxing ring—an equivalent to the betting parlors or horse-track references in Jacques Tourneur's *Out of the Past*—that is, spaces where aimless time is spent, and money is spent aimlessly as well.

The boxing ring is equally important within Hemingway's short story and to Hemingway himself, who told Josephine Herbst, "My writing is nothing, my boxing is everything," a statement that suggests, according to J. Lawrence

Fig. 3: Opening preamble: shot of the Swede's hand falling limp on his bed post, after the killers shoot him. (Robert Siodmak, *The Killers*, 1946, Universal Pictures)

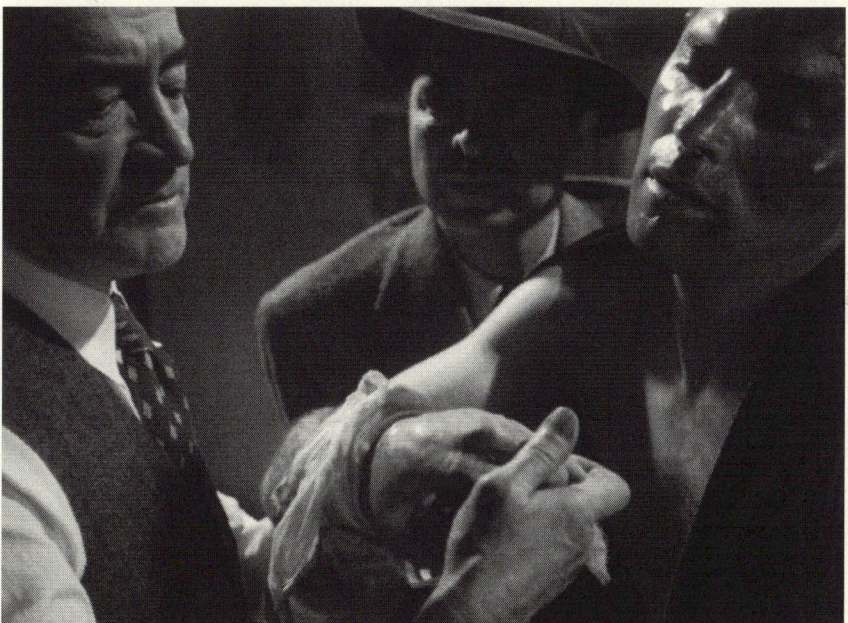
Fig. 4: In flashback, shot of the Swede's hand after he fails to throw his right and loses the match. (Robert Siodmak, *The Killers*, 1946, Universal Pictures)

Mitchell, "an almost pathological need to assert his manhood" (7). Since his teenage years, Hemingway would invite friends over for sparring sessions, posed for pictures imitating the poses of championship boxers like John L. Sullivan, and, ever "a convincing raconteur," boasted of his boxing exploits with professionals (8).[4] Somewhere in the scant details of the short story we learn that Ole Anderson had been a heavyweight prizefighter; his landlady knows he "was in the ring," an acknowledgement she makes to contrast with his being a nice gentleman, and a worthy explanation for his being longer than his boardinghouse bed. Seemingly an occupation that affirms masculinity and strength, in both the short story and film adaptation of *The Killers* boxing only serves to highlight the schism between activity and passivity—fighting and giving up—built into the Swede's character.

A common component of the noir film is a male protagonist, or central figure, whose well-being has been endangered by a desirable but dangerous spider-woman, a femme fatale who usually functions as an obstacle to the male quest. Often, but not always, the world of the film attempts the restoration of order through the eventual destruction of this erotically manipulative woman. Classic Hollywood films often rely on the objectification of female characters; in "Visual Pleasure and Narrative Cinema," film theorist Laura Mulvey established contemporary feminist film theory by arguing for the gendered nature of Hollywood narrative cinema, where visual compositions are "ordered by sexual imbalance" and "pleasure in looking has been split between active/male and passive/female" (715). Noir films often fall squarely into this coding of women for their *to-be-looked-at-ness,* as Mulvey calls it, or as objects of the male gaze. *The Killers* offers an extremely blatant example of this when the Swede, alongside his date, Lily, meets Kitty Collins, sitting at the piano in a private club.

The scene offers a particularly excruciating example of the woman as object of the male gaze, the Swede's eyes magnetically attached to Kitty while Lily's are watching him watching. Kitty soon breaks into song to further solidify herself as the center of the entertainment or the spectacle herself. Positioned in the foreground, Kitty wields the control over Swede's gaze, just as she will over his actions in the film's diegetic near future.

Yet, when paying attention to the visual depictions of the Swede in and around the boxing ring, one notices that he's constantly in a swooning pose, akin to the famous one of Ava Gardner used in marketing materials for the film. Even more specifically, his eyes are often closed in these shots or staring up into the heavens as if he's given up—and he has. He is rendered passive

Fig. 5: Laura Mulvey's *to-be-looked-at-ness* on all too full and flagrant display. (Robert Siodmak, *The Killers,* 1946, Universal Pictures)

as a boxer, forced to throw the fight, and he can't throw his right because of his damaged hand. Boxing, a supposed spectacle of male prowess, instead renders the Swede's useless *to-be-looked-at-ness* and, in effect, positions him as feminized. In "Womanliness as a Masquerade," Joan Rivière offers the performative function of womanliness as a mask for women who wish for and/or to exhibit masculine traits, to prevent anxiety and possible retributions of the opposite sex. The reverse is true in *The Killers,* according to Delphine Letort, who proposes that boxing is "part of a masquerade that encodes masculinity" in the narrative: "Hemingway and Siodmak decode the masquerade of maleness while drawing the portrait of men who try to perform their masculinity, turning their life into a spectacle" (60, 59). In his work *Hemingway's Theaters of Masculinity,* Thomas Strychacz argues that Hemingway emphasizes a "*theatrical representation* of masculinity," transient and subject to abrupt change, his characters' "codes of manhood" themselves staged—all of this supported, seemingly, by the author's own penchant for extravagant performances in life.

This mirage of masculinity only fortifies the nothingness of Ole Anderson as a subject within the film. He has no fight left in the ring, both in boxing and in life: at the end of Hemingway's story as with the beginning of the film's, he flatly affirms no fewer than four times in varied repetition, "There ain't anything to do" (221). The American film noir protagonist, much like the Hemingway hero from which it drew, is someone to whom something is done.

Rendered passive definitively, as the hitmen draw closer the Swede is also out of time, a commonality within the bleak tableaux of noir films: a man fated to die. Siodmak expands the short story by means of the flashback structure common to the construction of noir films, which introduces a "reversed temporal order that creates the past as the site of the fiction" (Turim 170). Stylistic traits of noir further help create "the figuration of a filmic otherness" with which Hemingway's story was already imbued (170). The most notable scenic detail Hemingway uses here is the mirror that runs along the back of the counter in Henry's lunchroom. Max, the more aggressive of the two hitmen, repeatedly looks in the mirror rather than at the people to whom he speaks. Sitting at the counter, Max "didn't look at George but looked in the mirror." "'Well, bright boy,' Max said looking into the mirror" instead of at Nick; in fact, "Max looked into the mirror all the

Fig. 6: The doctor checks the Swede's badly injured hand after the boxing fight, the Swede, looking lifeless, eyes closed and occupying a center position in the four-shot, a composition that suggests he is being controlled and overwhelmed from all sides. (Robert Siodmak, *The Killers,* 1946, Universal Pictures)

Fig. 7: Buttoning up the Swede now that his boxing career, emblematic of his will and worth, has been destroyed. (Robert Siodmak, *The Killers*, 1946, Universal Pictures)

time he was talking," a spectator of his own masculine spectacle (217). Mirrors feature prominently in the film adaptation as well; the lunchroom mirror, loyally replicated in the opening scene, allows for a complex visual composition that doubles the characters into their reflections and complicates the direction of their glances, Increasing the tension created in the literary medium. Siodmak amplifies the notion of doubleness and/or the double-cross by using mirrors, most notably in the mise-en-scène of the final shootout scene at the Green Cat Nightclub. A mirror frames the main room as the camera enters, thus causing spectatorial confusion over whether we are looking at an image, and mirrors action occurring behind characters, thus offering multifocal perspectives that find theoretical locus in Hemingway's short story.

Formally, nowhere is the inability to control time, or one's one fated position, more clearly illustrated than in the film's flashback scene of the Prentiss Hat Company robbery, committed by the Swede and the gang of thugs led by big Jim Colfax. In an exceptional example of long-shot cinematography, perhaps only trumped by Welles's opening sequence of *Touch of Evil* (1958), the viewers watch the scene materialize on screen as the insurance company president reads a newspaper story reporting the caper. Robert Porfirio argues that this scene functions as the germ for the entire development of modern caper films, having a grand effect on the stylistics of later filmmakers like Steven Soderbergh. But the timing of the scene changes from beginning to end: at first, the company president reads the words in the newspaper, and the camera captures and displays the images for the viewer somewhat simultaneously (the holdup men suddenly appear). But soon, the temporality shifts, as if someone is winding the hands of the clock faster. If you remember, the clock, and whether it is correct, is a crucial part of Hemingway's story which, coincidentally, begins around 5:20 P.M. and ends approximately at 7:30—a suitable length for a feature film. "Oh, to hell with the clock," one of the hungry killers proclaims in frustration over whether it's still lunch or just now dinnertime (215). Indeed, the clock operates as a signal of disruption and the site for the reversibility of meaning; actions, events, and other human behaviors may be kept rational and regulated by the tables of time, while alternatively, time—like one's past, or one's fate in the future—can never be escaped (Letort 58).

Soon, the men committing the robbery fall just behind the timing of the man narrating their actions in the film, giving the impression that they are captured by a fatedness within the scene, or even *of* the scene as spectacle, and thus overall, within the story. Like "each step of the holdup," this scene is carefully planned, the "clinical detachment of the narrator" and the camera's omniscient and objective perspectives reinforcing the negative existentialism of the film and the alterity of man, especially of Ole Anderson (Porfirio 181). According to Dana Polan, negative existentialism, a common characteristic of 1940s noirs, demonstrates an environment radically external to a character's self, values, and personality, negating the power of free will or the ability to control one's fate.

In *Being and Nothingness,* Jean-Paul Sartre writes how if one were to examine the "room of someone absent" "the very traces which he has left can be deciphered as traces of him only within a situation where he has been already posited as absent" (26). Every image "demands a negation," at least as "a nihilating withdrawal of consciousness in relation to the image apprehended as subjective phenomenon" (26). Though Sartre only makes mere mention of how our own feelings of being from past to present emerge "like images from a magic lantern," much of his existential thought can be applied to *noir* film/theory. Particular to *The Killers,* the Swede operates as a manifestation of Sartre's notion of "being-for-others," predicated on the visual component of *"being seen"* by the Other, or "other people and our awareness of them" (Brevda 334). The Swede doesn't see; he is only seen by others, by nature of the flashback structure of the film. Sartre's forms of being betray his "'criminal love' for the tropes of noir," according to William Brevda, who puts it even more succinctly that for Sartre, "*cogito ergo* noir" (333).

Hemingway uses "objective correlates" to symbolize his characters' internal states of mind, which, in turn, translate into the cinematic images used to construct the film adaptation (Letort 58). This process of external symbolization in relation to one's past and its traces equates to another famous thinker's own iceberg theory—Sigmund Freud. While Hemingway's theory suggests the writer's desire to communicate only somewhat explicitly, in terms of implicitness more directly, Freud's topographical model of the mind often got explained through an iceberg analogy. While what we see and acknowledge is that which is conscious—the tip of the iceberg above the surface of the water—unconscious mental processes and repressed desires fall below the surface and remain at depths. Freud largely invented the study of psychoanalysis with his publication of *An Interpretation of Dreams,* wherein he discovers that the real significance of

Fig. 8: The famous first shot of the Swede, resigned to his imminent death, in which the lighting is manipulated to make his face appear entirely blacked out, a symbolic evocation of him being a non-subject. (Robert Siodmak, *The Killers,* 1946, Universal Pictures)

dreams, their latent content, is concealed, translated into the manifest content, or outward symbolic projections, experienced in the dream. Notably, Freud's study was published in 1899, in the same decade in which the first films were being shown by the likes of the Lumière brothers in Paris; indeed, dreamwork and film work bear striking similarities on a variety of theoretical levels. "Freud's remarks on art bear a striking similarity to Hemingway's on fiction" in terms of the artist's task being to veil the unconscious (Johnston 70). In fact, Hemingway's own loss may have inspired his theory of omission as a defense mechanism. In 1922, an entire suitcase of all his prior written manuscripts and typescripts was stolen, a shock that took him months to recover from (69).

In his study on the villainy of the camera, William Rothman suggests that "at the heart of every film is a truth we already know: we have been born into the world and we are fated to die" (347). In this sense, *The Killers* epitomizes film theory on a meta-level scale. There is a lot we can learn through it. And also, nothing at all.

Appendix: Discussion Questions

1. What specific elements of Hemingway's short story are particularly visual, and in what way(s) do they get adapted into the film? In the reverse, are there any elements of the 1946 film that you find compellingly literary?
2. How might you explain the relevance of the insurance agent and investigation that structures the film adaptation? Is there a logical or theoretical imperative in your reading of the short story that would make this a smart or particularly relevant choice? Explain.
3. How does Kitty Collins get portrayed in the film version of the story, and what does her addition lend to the expansion of the narrative that fits (or doesn't) Hemingway's original short story?
4. How would you adapt Hemingway's short story into film for a modern audience?
    a. Stylistically, what choices might you make when adapting the story into a color film or television series? Without the expressive quality of black and white, what other ways might you visually express the content of the story in cinematic adaptation?
    b. What elements would you choose to keep or to change, and why? How might you modernize Hemingway's original story depicting hitmen in 1920s Chicago?

Notes

1. Charles Dickens, one of the most acclaimed and popular Victorian writers, lived concurrent with the development of precinematic technological developments such as the daguerreotype, the stereoscope, and the phenakistiscope but died before the earliest motion sequences—like those British photographer Eadward Muybridge developed with his zoopraxiscope—were created. For more on Dickens and the relationship between his writing and the cinema, see G. Smith, and for more on Dickens and film adaptation see Glavin.

2. Film noir earned this label because of its resemblance to the *série noire*, a French publishing imprint established in 1945 that mainly published Anglo-American hard-boiled crime fiction.

3. In his 1946 naming of the *film noir* category, Nino Frank cites four particular movies: *The Maltese Falcon* (1941), *Laura* (1944), *Murder, My Sweet* (1944), and *Double Indemnity* (1944).

4. For a fuller history of Hemingway's boxing exploits and, equally important, his boxing stories—like the one about how James Joyce would treat him like his bodyguard, which he told a *Time* magazine correspondent in the 1950s—see Mitchell.

Works Cited

Bazin, André. *What Is Cinema?* Vol. 1. U of California P, 1967.
Borde, Raymond and Étienne Chaumeton. "Towards a Definition of *Film Noir*." *Film Noir Reader*, edited by Alain Silver and James Ursini, Limelight Editions, 1996, pp. 17–25.
Bordwell, David. *Narration in the Fiction Film*. U of Wisconsin P, 1985.
Brevda, William. "'Is There Any Up or Down Left?' Noir and Existentialism." *Soundings: An Interdisciplinary Journal*, vol. 89, nos. 3–4, 2006, pp. 321–46.
Collinge-Germain, Linda. "The Aesthetics of Revealing/Concealing in 'The Killers' by Ernest Hemingway and Its Adaptation by Robert Siodmak." *Journal of the Short Story in English*, vol. 59, Autumn 2012, pp. 93–105.
Eisenstein, Sergei. *Film Form: Essays in Film Theory*. Harcourt, 1977.
Frank, Nino. "A New Kind of Detective Story," *L'Écrán Français* 61, Aug. 28, 1946, pp. 8–9.
Freud, Sigmund. *The Interpretation of Dreams: The Complete and Definitive Text*, translated and edited by James Strachey, Basic Books, 2010.
Genette, Gérard. *Narrative Discourse: An Essay in Method*. Cornell UP, 1983.
Glavin, John, ed. *Dickens Adapted*. Taylor & Francis, 2017.
Hemingway, Ernest. "The Killers." *The Complete Short Stories of Ernest Hemingway: The Finca Vigía Edition*. Scribner, 1987, pp. 215–22.
Johnston, Kenneth G. "Hemingway and Freud: The Tip of the Iceberg." *Journal of Narrative Technique*, vol. 14, no. 1, Winter 1984, pp. 68–73.
Laurence, Frank M. *Hemingway and the Movies*. UP of Mississippi, 1981.

Letort, Delphine. "The Writing of a *Film Noir:* Ernest Hemingway and *The Killers.*" *Screening Text: Critical Perspectives on Film Adaptation,* edited by Shannon Wells-Lassagne and Ariane Hudulet, McFarland, 2013, pp. 53–65.

Mitchell, J. Lawrence. "Ernest Hemingway: In the Ring and Out." *Hemingway Review,* vol. 31, no. 1, 2011, pp. 7–23.

Mulvey, Laura. "Visual Pleasure and Narrative Cinema," in *Film Theory and Criticism,* 7th ed., edited by Leo Braudy and Marshall Cohen, Oxford UP, 2009, pp. 711–22.

Out of the Past. Dir. Jacques Tourneur. Perf. Robert Mitchum, Jane Greer, Kirk Douglas. RKO Radio Pictures, 1947. Film

Park, William. *What Is Film Noir?* Bucknell UP, 2011.

Place, Janey and Lowell Peterson. "Some Visual Motifs of Film Noir." *Film Noir Reader,* edited by Alain Silver and James Ursini. Limelight Editions, 1996, pp. 65–75.

Plimpton, George. "The Art of Fiction XXI: Ernest Hemingway." *Paris Review,* Spring 1958, p. 88.

Polan, Dana. *Power and Paranoia: History, Narrative and the American Cinema 1940–1950.* Columbia UP, 1986.

Porfirio, Robert G. "*The Killers:* Expressiveness of Sound and Image in Film Noir." *Film Noir Reader,* edited by Alain Silver and James Ursini, Limelight Editions, 1996, pp. 177–87.

Pullman, Philip. "Dickens and Pictures." *Dickensian,* vol. 108, no. 486, 2012, pp. 13–15.

Rivière, Joan. "Womanliness as a Masquerade." *Female Sexuality: The Early Psychoanalytic Controversies,* edited by Russell Grigg, Dominique Hecq, and Craig Smith, Routledge, 1999, pp. 172–82.

Rothman, William. *The Murderous Gaze.* Harvard UP, 1982.

Sartre, Jean-Paul. *Being and Nothingness.* Washington Square P, 1992.

Smith, Graham. *Dickens and the Dream of Cinema.* Manchester UP, 2003.

Smith, Paul. "Hemingway's Early Manuscripts: The Theory and Practice of Omission." *Journal of Modern Literature,* vol 10, no. 2, 1983, pp. 268–88.

Sobchak, Vivian. "Lounge Time: Postwar Crises and the Chronotype of Film Noir." *Refiguring American Film Genres,* edited by Nick Browne, U of California P, 1998, pp. 129–70.

Strychacz, Thomas F. *Hemingway's Theaters of Masculinity.* Louisiana State UP, 2003.

Trodd, Zoe. "Hemingway's Camera Eye: The Problem of Language and the Interwar Politics of Form." *Hemingway Review,* vol. 26, no. 2, 2007, pp. 7–21.

Turim, Maureen. *Flashbacks in Film: Memory and History.* Routledge, 2013.

Wood, Robin. "*Rancho Notorious* (1952): A Noir Western in Color," *Film Noir Reader 4,* edited by Alain Silver and James Ursini, Limelight Editions, 2004, pp. 261–75.

Rhythmic Cycles in *The Sun Also Rises, For Whom the Bell Tolls,* and *The Fifth Column* and Their Film/Theater Adaptations

Jean Jespersen Bartholomew

In Hemingway's *For Whom the Bell Tolls* (1940), there is a marvelous, yet sometimes puzzling chapter opening that discusses a merry-go-round and a wheel. The wheel likely refers to Robert Jordan finding himself back at the point of beginning in his relationship with Pablo, which throughout the book is a strange and fascinating one. Jordan is resolving at the start of chapter 18 to no longer play games with Pablo, to studiously answer his queries as he would anyone else's, rather than try to outmaneuver the tough Spaniard whom he now knows is very smart, a chess master of sorts, albeit a burned-out one (230). Further gamesmanship-type maneuvers, Jordan concludes, will only result in more rides on an elliptical, unsettling wheel, one that in its egg-shaped orbit promises only more upset and disorientation. "No one would choose to ride this wheel," he adds (230).

That same wheel, cycling from beginning to end in the narrative, represents other threads of Hemingway present in many of his stories but specifically and strongly in the two other works to be examined here. *The Sun Also Rises* (1926), for instance, includes two scenes, near the beginning and the end, with Jake Barnes sitting uncomfortably confined in the car or horse carriage (again, with wheels) with a woman—Georgette and later Brett in the beginning of the novel, and Brett again at novel's (and film's) end, in a cyclical ride on wheels going nowhere: Jake's condition is not going to improve, and his taut relationship with Brett is going nowhere as well. At a certain point he could "shut his eyes without getting the wheeling sensation," and it's good news when "the world is not wheeling any more" (118). While the latter refers most directly to alcohol, that metaphorical spinning, cycling sensation or mention of wheels in Hemingway often points to a world out of balance, when the universe controls the spin and man is sometimes just there for a brief ride doing the best he can.

In its own version of an "Isn't it pretty to think so?" ending, *The Fifth Column* (1938) similarly spins from pretend housekeeping by the two main characters living in two adjacent hotel rooms at play's beginning to the sad realization at play's end that any thoughts of a white picket fence for the pair are inevitably specious in Philip's line of work, especially in the middle of war. Room 109, belonging to journalist Dorothy Bridges, has on its door the sign Hemingway displayed on his own room door at the Hotel Florida, "Working, Do Not Disturb" (1), in the first of several small flips between biography and fiction operating oh-so-close to one another in the play. Here Bridges is the journalist, perhaps not a great one, with Philip next door, more involved in intrigue, the spotting of traitors, and the like. Man and woman set up to play house in war at the beginning; traveling full circle, man and woman at the end discuss a real house, a real life, but it's going nowhere, not happening. Philip gives up on the white picket fence (much as the highly politically involved Gellhorn would head into World War II early on sans husband). Dreams of domesticity in *The Fifth Column* die largely because Philip—whose job is partially to identify and send people to their deaths for being part of the Fifth Column—has already gone full circle and is into the war too deep: "I've been to all those places and I've left them all behind" (90). Philip, too, has been around the wheel. This one is presented as an ellipse in style and in content, masterfully evoked in the play, with scenes of humor and near-normal banter and details repeatedly, suddenly, and rhythmically crashed in upon by shells hitting nearby rooms and creating total discord in the Madrid streets. This is a discord musically represented by a piano mazurka in minors that Hemingway deliberately invokes for sensory impact. If one had to select an ellipse of pain in music one couldn't do better than Chopin's *Mazurka in C Minor, Opus 33, No. 4*. Anyone who thinks *The Fifth Column* is a weak work probably hasn't listened to that music, nor imagined it accompanying a shelling that might at any moment result in one's death. The dissonance is piercing as the music rolls from relative innocence to harsh tragedy.

The disintegration of Philip's white picket fence, in turn, parallels Robert Jordan's frequent and persistent statements that while his relationship with Maria is very real, and she clearly is more his woman than anyone else has been or will be, he nevertheless cannot afford a wife in his dangerous lifestyle (not any domestic life for him, he decides at more than one point, even before he is trapped by gunfire and certainly after). Neither the books nor the films fail to highlight the irony of these full-circle starts and endings, and Hemingway runs the characters in all three of these works full around in a predictable, unsettling way once the pattern is seen.

This sense of cycling through the wheel (present also in the performed play and films) is but one of many surprising but clearly relevant threads of parallel connection that scholars and students can discover in the three works set side-by-side, perhaps in a course such as Hemingway Seminar: Spain. In this case, the threads are very clearly seen in start-to-finish framing in both the written and film or play versions. But that is just the beginning of the incredible Hemingway art created by the artist in Spain that we may share with students. Hemingway skillfully dives in and out of fairly in-depth, historically related segments (Golz in *For Whom the Bell Tolls;* the treatment of spies in *The Fifth Column*), point-counterpoint balance between light and dark (the furs and caviar *in The Fifth Column* versus sudden shelling); the lovemaking in *For Whom the Bell Tolls* countered by realistic and very grim depictions of death. Visual and sensory images of opposites guide the way in this artistic weave.

A Country Runs through It: Spain

Moreover, the primary relationship of all three works is that they all largely or totally deal with Spain during its time of greatest upheaval in the twentieth century—the Spanish Civil War (or the years leading up to it). In *The Sun Also Rises,* Hemingway presents a seemingly innocent 1920s Spain, full of bullfights and festivals, as compared to ten years later. The 1920s Spain that Hemingway had so loved provided a canvass for characters who had it all in friendship but gave it away in self-made complications (Brett), or in secrets eating away well behind more light-hearted scenes (Jake, Mike, Cohn, others). How Spain is drawn and created in the novel and in the film are worthy of comparison. They highlight Hemingway's descriptive mastery.

Director Henry King resorts to grand—even aerial—views of Paris in the *Sun Also Rises* film to attempt to match Hemingway's descriptive power: not opening with Robert Cohn, as the book does, but with beautiful overhead shots of Paris itself. Sam Wood's *For Whom the Bell Tolls* comes closer to matching Hemingway's start to that novel with Jordan surveying the bridge for the initial scene just as in the novel. The theater version of *The Fifth Column* should follow Hemingway's dialogue and prompts directly, as plays by masters usually do, but of course set design and casting could vary with each production, open to some creativity, perhaps by students themselves staging the play. In any play, the act of artistic creation reaches out to the viewer, the directors, and the actors to complete. Because of that highly creative element, always changing and changeable, *The Fifth Column,* regardless of flaws, remains the most dynamic, yet to be discovered, yet to be maximized of Hemingway's works. How might students stage it or film it? Challenge them and find out.

The two later works, set in a Spain ten years hence from *The Sun Also Rises* (late thirties rather than twenties), both deal heavily with the serious aspects and complexities of the Spanish Civil War, to which Hemingway and his then partner Martha Gellhorn were both very dedicated to "the Republic." The civil war was a prequel to World War II in their view, given the involvement by Hitler and Mussolini with Franco. In the text, of course, Jordan, Pablo, Pilar, Anselmo, General Golz, and the rest of our main *For Whom the Bell Tolls* characters side together in disheveled fashion to fight a somewhat nebulous air and artillery foe. We know we are in Spain, but Hemingway assumed readers knew more about the Spanish Civil War than twenty-first-century students likely know.

Hemingway was present primarily as a reporter during the Spanish Civil War, and both he and Gellhorn lobbied the Roosevelts repeatedly for more official American involvement, which never came. Volunteers did come to Spain and the Republic's aid (more than fifty nations in all) due to the efforts of many, and Robert Jordan's odd transition from Spanish instructor in Montana to bridge blower fits that paradigm. It is explained by way of mentioning Jordan's earlier visits to Spain, his knowledge of the land, and a solid knowledge of engineering, but again, without more history preceding the reading, students may remain somewhat lost as to exactly why Robert Jordan from Montana is there, and especially as a volunteer. History and background are needed—a must—before reading the book or watching the film.

Basic Course Plan and Summary

Thus, it makes sense that in any Hemingway seminar devoted to these three works, one might well begin with *The Sun Also Rises,* since it is the earliest and the easiest in terms of length and, arguably, the amount of background history needed. It is placed in prewar France and Spain, well before Hitler or even Franco became a household name. Hemingway was eager to knock his first major novel out of the park, even seeking advice from his friend F. Scott Fitzgerald. Fitzgerald made many suggestions, especially in chopping the beginning to create a faster jump into the story, making the Sean Hemingway version of the novel a good choice for study, since it refers to those changes. My classes usually follow the reading of that novel with the absorbingly colorful film of the same name, directed by Henry King (1957), and then the two longer Hemingway works from the Spanish Civil War of the late thirties: *For Whom the Bell Tolls* (along with the film) and *The Fifth Column,* perhaps also including some of the related short stories headquartered in Spain (often Madrid) of that same period—"The Denunciation," "The Butterfly and the Tank," "Night before Battle," and "Under the Ridge" (*Complete Short Stories* 420–28, 429–36, 437–59, 460–69). Films and/or other visual presentations for all three larger works provide valuable illumination, as might film documentaries about the period, some of which are quite well done. The changing history and situation of Spain, from carefree to very dark, and the shifting concerns of Hemingway's characters in Spain, from a focus on love, friendship, and drinking (*The Sun Also Rises*), to dominance of war and code (both *The Fifth Column* and *For Whom the Bell Tolls*) allow readers to gain clarity via layering of knowledge and use of contrast in novels, play, and films.

If there is time, yet another film for primary inclusion would be from the eyes of Hemingway in Spain via his own documentary, since Hemingway and Joris Ivens created *The Spanish Earth* to influence the Roosevelts and other power players to come to the aid of the Republic. If so, including at least portions of *Hemingway's Second War: Bearing Witness to the Spanish Civil War,* Alex Vernon's painstakingly researched, seminal text on the making of *The Spanish Earth* is useful as well for background on the relationship between Hemingway and communist cofilmmaker Ivens and also for awareness as to what was real versus "creatively enhanced"—possibly a significant amount.

As a play and an infrequently read work, *The Fifth Column* garners increased student interest if it is put to life via readers theater, in a theater or theaterlike situation as Hemingway envisioned. Students may be assigned rotating parts every several pages or so, given that certain characters seem more popular for vocalizing and some characters also have more lines. One student might be assigned to investigate and provide sound, such as to resemble shelling sounds at the hotel. Allow three to five days of class time, depending on length of your class and whether one presents the entire play or primarily key portions (recommended), with discussion of the play in between scenes. The parallels and connections between the play's main characters and the real-life Hemingway and Gellhorn grab student interest, right down to the interesting flips on who has the room sign as mentioned earlier, or Hemingway's tongue-in-cheek critique via the play of Gellhorn's fashion interests. Film version creation could for classes with film majors, or add in simple set design (diagonal or slightly akimbo grey boards with a "Working, Do Not Disturb" sign?) for the reading, or consider a class encompassing screenplay writing and transposing *The Fifth Column* into a workable screenplay. This also could work very well as a senior capstone project.

Film treatment as a discussion point can readily be achieved for *The Sun Also Rises* and *For Whom the Bell Tolls,* since previous, quality filmed versions (see later discussion) exist for both. Students seem to really enjoy both of these (share the films only after reading quizzes), as well as the readers-theater version of *The Fifth Column.* Handled creatively, this can be a scintillating class.

Each of these works will be dealt with in turn and in more depth in the following sets of materials, with a resource listing that may allow design of a variety of courses as based on one or all three of the works. Students may reach toward literary, historical, screenplay, film, or cultural research projects of their own, perhaps culminating in oral presentations to cap the course in more typical fashion and to pique interest in numerous smaller areas that might not be covered otherwise, from Spanish war poets to Spain's colorful, often propagandistic war posters.

The Sun Also Rises

This book is a wonderful opening to any Hemingway seminar, as it invites discussion as well of writers such as Scott Fitzgerald and of Hemingway's 1925 parallel group of friends who really did go down to the bullfights in Spain. It captures the flavor and times of a very popular period and place in history: France and Spain, the 1920s, and of all the Hemingway novels, this one is almost certainly fully completed by all students and appeals to them from many current contexts and parallels to today's world, thus assuring a good start to the course. The novel is easily and interestingly augmented by a plenitude of materials relevant to the period, from classic jazz recordings (highly recommended at the start of class a time or two) to film, art, style, and architecture research work about that period as well, perhaps leading to brief student reports, oral or written, on other players from Hemingway's 1920s world (Stein, Anderson, Fitzgerald, and many others [see appendix]).

The Sun Also Rises also invites relevant comparison of the way the novel exists for us today in academia with the way the novel *was*—for example, the opening with its edits considered, some of which Fitzgerald suggested versus Hemingway's original. Further, it clearly is a good starting point, given chronology of the works, for discussing the development of Hemingway's style. Besides the mentioned Hemingway proclivity for framing a story; stylistic, thematic, character development; and organizational discussions also abound with *The Sun Also Rises*. Simply having students sketch the geographical movement in the novel is productive. This allows them to see the building blocks in the novel as Hemingway may have seen them and to analyze his artistic use of geographic movement. Emotions and growth, plateaus of each character's development can also literally be line graphed using a time base for character ebbs and flows and to cut away at theme development.

In my courses, we always thoroughly examine and discuss or dissect text prior to any showing of the film, so as to prevent students from leaning on the film for all knowledge of Hemingway. This way, too, the film is more of a reward after the more academically challenging novel. I typically break the film into two or three evenings, sometimes more if any in-class time is utilized for this purpose. Planning this ahead and viewing the film two or three times closely proximate to viewing it with the students is very useful, since asking the students pointed questions to compare and contrast will aid them in seeing how film and novel formats work. They also will begin to see possible weak points in the film relative to the novel, or even vice versa.

I also ask students to mark their novels as they are reading when they spot places that are obviously going to be difficult to transfer to film, then, after seeing the film, we see how well they predicted those portions and how the filmmaker handled or perhaps largely ignored the issue—or how the screenwriter or director left out the long line or deliberately overemphasized a certain scene. Having students read all of the written work with some concern for how it would transfer to film makes film discussions much more interesting.

One of the ways for students to track the novels or play and the films effectively is keep a side-by-side journal of the two types of filtering. Part of the journal can be for comparisons of the major characters as presented in the novel and then as presented in the film. "Which characters are most faithfully replicated in the film?" I ask them. "Which characters are dropped way back, changed, or even all but eliminated in the film version?" Did that (addition or omission) make sense, and why?" "Did the filmmaker make any bad calls in presentation or cutting or augmenting?"

The same, of course, can be done with individual scenes, having students discuss whether certain scene losses improved or weakened the film versus the novel. Are some aspects simply too complex or subtle to translate from writing into film? (Consider the fishing scene and the oblique references to evolution. Or consider the easy entrance and exit of some support characters, most notably Harris.) Which aspects are more forcefully conveyed by film? Students find it illuminating that a typical screenplay is only 100 to 120 pages, with wide margins, which helps them understand the cuts.

In what ways is the film not well done? While my students tend to be happily surprised by the film in terms of its depiction of early-twentieth-century Spain and the feel for its culture and festivity, one aspect students nearly always complain about is the age of the actors, especially an aging Tyrone Power as Jake. Is this a valid critique that some of us gloss over, many of us being older than the characters? Compare the famous photo of Hemingway and friends in Pamplona to the characters as seen in the film. Are they similar in age and deportment or vastly different? Was the director and producer's decision to go with big names from the golden age of film a good decision or not? Many believe the casting of Robert Evans as the bullfighter was a major mistake, one the owners of the film insisted on (perhaps a student will want to research that story). Ask students whom they would cast today if a remake were to be made. Also, what changes would they make to the script, if any? Any course emphasizing screenplay might ask the students to write a new screenplay covering one portion or even the entirety of the novel.

Essayist Kelly DuPuis, in the special feature "Hemingway in Film," included with the DVD version of *The Sun Also Rises,* notes that the final film version may have leaned toward presenting characters as *types* rather than as real people. He seems to believe that if intended by director or actors, this was a mistake and one making the film much less real. To these points, perhaps ask students whether Ava Gardner, Tyrone Power, and Errol Flynn, apart from the age issue, create definite types, and if so, whether they fail in creating and bringing to life Hemingway's characters as real people. Did filming *The Sun Also Rises* thirty years after the novel was published affect its presentation, on this issue or any others? All are good discussion points. Additionally, a comparison of the actual film script, even just a few pages, with the same section from the novel, is an interesting classroom exercise that can be done with any novel or story that has been transformed into film. Having some of Hemingway's own words on the classroom walls as posters can remind everyone of a *point of creative beginning* belonging with Hemingway's written word.

For Whom the Bell Tolls

The bell tolls for thee. Spain could be anywhere. Hitler's wars could be happening today. The townspeople whom Pablo prods to their deaths in the square are far more similar to himself and Pilar than they are different from them. Pilar knows this. If that message isn't clear in this great novel by Ernest Hemingway, then nothing is. However, before students are prepared to receive the message of universality in this very specifically grounded political tale of nearly lost Spanish history and death, it's important to note that this work perhaps more than any other by Hemingway requires significant historical background and knowledge prep. Otherwise, readers may become very confused or left in the dark on the political background, even as they resolve to keep reading.

THE HISTORY

I usually set the groundwork for studying *For Whom the Bell Tolls* by preceding it with two or three sessions devoted to the history of the Spanish Civil War, including reading assignments and a possible documentary or two. This is time well spent, especially since it also will apply to the third work in the seminar, *The Fifth Column* (1938).

Depending on the venue and course level, many students likely will not even know there was a twentieth-century Spanish Civil War or when it occurred relative to the world wars, let alone be able to adequately describe the players and why that war was important. This is unfortunate, but it is one area of history Hemingway helps us remedy. Of course, we now echo Hemingway's early recognition that the Spanish war was indeed a prelude to World War II, involving as it did three major axis players (Hitler, Mussolini, and Franco), all of whom supported the Franco-led rebellion in Spain, along with the Roman Catholic Church (for complex reasons, which students may wish to research). Educators may also wish to share that some artists, such as popular painter Salvador Dali, stood among the friends of Franco—which is certain to cause some consternation. These areas can be covered by lecture or small student reports if time permits. Students fire up exploring such often undiscussed issues as Dali's friendship with Franco or why Hitler felt compelled to destroy Guernica (one might include in the discussion Picasso's painting by the same name), or the self-sacrificing yet odd presence of so many American volunteer nurses in Spain (see the award-winning documentary *Into the Fire: American Women in the Spanish Civil War* [2002], by Julia Newman with many insights from Martha Gellhorn, Dorothy Parker, and Eleanor Roosevelt).

KEY AREAS OF SPANISH CIVIL WAR HISTORY
FOR DISCUSSION OR LECTURE

Basic definitions assist understanding. Who were the Loyalists and the Republicans? (They were on the same team: both against Franco and his Nationalists). Why is a Spanish Republican very different (as in, the two have no relationship) from an American Republican? Who are the Nationalists and the Rebels? (They are both pro-Franco and pro-fascism.) Clarifying ahead and making lists of supporters on each side opens everyone up to read the book more knowledgeably without confusing terms getting in the way.

Typical questions to expect or to ask: Why did neither the United States nor Britain engage in this war on the side of democracy and the people (the Republic) versus a thinly disguised practice war for Hitler? (Answer: This was primarily because of costs and also fear of being engaged in any upcoming wars in a then much weakened state. There was also fear of being seen on the wrong side at the end, especially if one's team lost.) What was the Spanish history leading up to the war, and what provoked Franco to challenge the elected government? Why were Ernest Hemingway and others, especially Martha Gellhorn, convinced that this war needed to be won to block a larger war sure to involve Hitler? Why did Hitler, and to some extent Italy's Mussolini, as well, lend so many supplies and staffing to the Franco effort, and how much of did they lend? Why did Hemingway gradually change his very early neutral-to-positive views of Mussolini, and where is this documented?

At what levels and why were so many American volunteers involved in the war effort, as well as volunteers from other nations? How many were artists and why were poets and writers engaged in fighting? How was Britain's George Orwell involved, for example, and how did his involvement as a volunteer in the war differ from Hemingway's? (One presentation option I have often encouraged students to explore is the involvement in Spain by other outside artists and writers besides Hemingway, since there are so many. And, by the way, I ask them to discover, which artists or writers were in some fashion involved with Hemingway while in Spain?)

How did the war end? What type of leader was Franco in the aftermath? (He was a very cruel dictator.) How many records of the pre-1940 period in Spain and the cause and times of the Republic were saved versus destroyed throughout the remainder of the twentieth century? Why were they destroyed? What repositories for the truth exist today? The Library of Congress, Brandeis University, and the University of California, San Diego, are a few places with major holdings of art and posters. The Association for the Recovery of Historical Memory (in Spanish: Asociación para la Recuperación de la Memoria Histórica)—winner of the 2015 ALBA/Puffin Award for Human Rights Activism—is an important group seeking to restore the truth of Spain's history during and after the war and the heartless reign of dictator Franco. Franco apparently buried and destroyed as much truth as he could (Burnett). Other places exist for rebuilding truth from over a half century of lies and destruction by Franco.

If there is room for one assigned outside text related to history, I would suggest Helen Graham's *The Spanish Civil War: A Very Short Introduction* (2005), with other excellent possibilities available.[1] Additionally, a rudimentary and satisfactory lecture regarding the basic history can be prepared utilizing the Graham text alone. As noted, I also like to punctuate this section (and later portions of the novel) with a few excellent documentary films about this war.

One of the most helpful exercises I have students engage in near the *beginning* of the *For Whom the Bell Tolls* unit is to prepare an artistic bookmark that lists the groups forming the Republic on one side and the Rebels with Franco on the other. This is a final check to be certain that they understand the participants in the two multifaction groups that engaged in the battle. To many students, *the Republic* sounds old-fashioned and *the Rebels* sounds slightly more grounded in new thinking, the exact opposite of what is, to most minds, closest to the truth.

Furthermore, the Spanish Republicans, who had been duly elected in the run up to Franco's rebellion against those elected, were very *liberal,* so liberal as to likely be viewed as socialistic or communistic in today's climate, certainly left of centrist left. But they had been elected to rule, and Franco was engaged in a fascist attempt at a coup to win dictatorship within Spain. To most of the people within Spain, an evil fascist dictator was worse than a dream of far-left liberalism and shared farms, plenty of food, and the possibility of everyone working together toward shared goals. So it was that many of the people fought for the Republic.

One area of further confusion is the Soviet involvement. A widespread misperception about Hemingway and about the Spanish Civil War overlap here. Hemingway did not advocate the Russian system, but he deeply appreciated the Soviets officially showing up to fight for the Republic. An article he wrote on his hatred of fascism is an important one to share with students, "Fascism Is a Lie," which was published in June 1937 in the communist-leaning magazine *New Madrid*. Here he clearly opined, "It looks as though we are in for many years of undeclared wars." He also was sarcastic about writers who did not put finding the truth in those wars up front, even though becoming involved enough to find the real *truth* was inevitably *dangerous,* he admitted. Finally, he offered that there is only one way to "quell a bully [referring to Hitler, Franco, and Mussolini—all fascists], and that is to thrash him." Soviet support for the Spanish people was forthcoming against the bully Franco, whereas American support was not, and at the time Hemingway and many others viewed any of those willing to fight for the Republic as useful and quite honorable. Hemingway and Martha Gellhorn had begged the Roosevelts (Eleanor was Martha's close friend) for more official American support, but none was forthcoming. The Soviets, however, supplied materials, advisors, and soldiers. For Hemingway, the Russians were on the right side at the right time, and the US government was not.[2]

Without formal American or British support, the strange coalition of volunteers from over fifty nations fighting for the Republic would likely have been completely doomed quite early *except* for the Russians, and, as it ended up, by 1938 it was doomed anyway. Hemingway's own writings with regard to fascism and/or communism make for a good topic for student reports (albeit a difficult one), perhaps using material from *By-Line* and other nonfiction works.

History is implicit in much of Hemingway. In Spain during this complex war, we both realistically and credibly have a Robert Jordan showing respect for the orders of General Golz (who admittedly had changed his originally Russian name). The Spanish people, the informally present Americans and Brits, the French, the Communists (including some who were French), and the Russians (sent by Stalin but heavily representing the Trotskyites who unknowingly were being sent to slaughter), comprised much of the ragtag band of the real fighting Republic. In many ways, the Republic imploded on itself with lack of organization and modern planes and equipment, not to mention unfortunate intrusions via various fifth columns sent or established by Franco or his primary supports, Hitler and Mussolini.

THE NOVEL, *FOR WHOM THE BELL TOLLS*

A character study journal for *For Whom the Bell Tolls* is a good assignment suggestion, given the number of important characters introduced in the narrative. Hemingway rolls them out relatively slowly, starting with the memorable visual of Jordan surveying the bridge. Each is given a highly visual and distinctive look, voice, even accent, and personal character that mark this as a book in which Hemingway worked very hard to create credible characters, and successfully so, establishing them all as unique individuals. A discussion of the ways Hemingway makes each of these characters have appeal and likeability is usually lively.

Place is similarly important. Artistically inclined students might be encouraged to illustrate their journals or even be allowed a small amount of latitude for an artistic project or accompaniment to a presentation. The mountains, caves, rivers, and meadows as Hemingway describes them are truly beautiful, and some of his excellent text might accompany any such art projects.

Theme is not subtle in this work. Life is harsh. For some, life is harsher. Love is a value the second it is felt, but in war it's a fragile flower. Fighting for freedom is worth anything else, almost everything else. All war is ugly, and for many, war causes deterioration of code and value. (In which characters does this happen? Does it happen with Pablo? How does Pablo change? This is a good query for debate. It assuredly does not cause deterioration for Robert Jordan, who acts always within the Hemingway code. Is love defeated for him or not?)

Hemingway, as usual, uses place to facilitate plot. There are three primary locus points, a triad, if you will: the bridge, the cave, and El Sordo's cave, plus a few minor ones. Hemingway rotates his characters from place to place, often slowing events down for tension just when we are wondering what will happen from a previous thread. Even climbing and descent are useful to the novel's movement. The exceptions to this rotational setting approach include deliberate slow-downs that are so slow as to seem like slow motion, such as for the killings in the plaza by Pablo and others, and extreme slowdowns are also reflected in his style at the points of lovemaking and being with Maria. Scenes involving Maria sometimes include sentences from Hemingway running more than a page, not the simple style he is known for. Does slow motion simulate intense feeling?

Style merges with content. With Pablo, Hemingway deliberately slows to a level of tedium to make us, his readers, watch and watch and watch, listen and listen and listen. War is hell, Hemingway says loudly and overwhelmingly.

Those on the other side of the war, here on the ground, are like neighbors. They were simply on the wrong side, perhaps standing mostly with the Catholics. In another village, they would be on the right side. Even some Republicans behaved badly, because war makes everyone behave badly. A great discussion can occur about why and how Hemingway slows down plot in the plaza chapter and how he gives details for each person killed, no matter how long it takes. Why does he do this? Students often think that chapter was a mistake. Under what understanding or with what intent might it be considered successful?

Hemingway takes a huge risk here, I think, and may have been misunderstood for having done so. Here, Pablo, in his old assertive leadership role, had led the charge to identify and quickly punish those who had worked in any way for Franco or who were fascists. Pablo emphasizes the fascists as hateful and murderous, with a nihilistic philosophy, just as Hemingway viewed fascists in real life, yet knowing that many of the people killed on the other side were similar to him. In this chapter, person after person is vividly described in some detail, and then run between two lines to the cliff where each is then summarily tossed over the cliff. This is a wrenching chapter, and Hemingway's style in dragging it onward, along with its companion treatment in the film, are worthy of any time spent. Hemingway builds steadily to the killing of the priest and uses the word *mob* repeatedly near the end of the chapter, suggesting a vivid understanding of mob mentality and how quickly it can develop. "Did you like it, Pilar?" Pablo later asks about the cliff killings. "No . . . except for Don Faustino [a major fascist]. I did not like it." But Pablo liked "all of it" except for the priest (131). Major, animated discussions ensue over this one. Ask: does mob mentality play out in the world today?

Count the deaths in this chapter, and it is not even a small percentage of those similarly treated cruelly in all of Spain, usually by the fascists, but, in this case, without regret by the Republic via Pablo. All might seem like good people on a given day in a normal world. This is an important facet to underscore for students regarding just what war does: even when it's necessary, everything spins to destruction.

THE FILM, *FOR WHOM THE BELL TOLLS*

The filmed version of *The Sun Also Rises* may partially fail (even if it is often enjoyable) because its actors were chosen to play types, not to portray individual people so much. Is this true in *For Whom the Bell Tolls?* (Most students will perceptively (and, I think, correctly) say "no"). *For Whom the*

Bell Tolls was filmed earlier than *The Sun Also Rises,* in spite of falling later in historical chronology. Did the time of filming affect the quality of the film or the approach to filming? Students may also wish to place both of these films in the context of the directors' other works, perhaps for a special project or presentation.

How is the important chapter about the plaza killing in *For Whom the Bell Tolled* handled in the film? Could it be handled better in a future film version? Should one replicate the length of that book chapter in the film, percentagewise?

Similar questions accompany Maria: on film there is no way to effectively share Hemingway's more than page-long sentences about Maria and little way to express all of the emotion and what has happened, except for the joyous mischief clearly present in Ingrid Bergman's eyes. How else did the director use the properties of film to convey these intimate scenes?

Similarly, Hemingway resorts with amusement to "unspoken thee" and "unspeakableness" to express swearing in the novel, which also evokes questions and discussion among students regarding censorship. How is this handled in the film? What could have been done differently in the film or (or novel) today? What would the impact be?

With this novel, because it is quite long, unlike *The Sun Also Rises,* I usually show segments of the film at appropriate junctures intermingled with the reading. So we might read up to El Sordo's cave scene, for instance, and then watch the film to that point. This also helps students absorb the broad range and number of characters present in this longish work.

A great discussion here can revolve around these questions: How does Hemingway's *style* in the text transfer to film? How does it *not* make it into film? Are there particular elements of his style and content that would be lost in any film? Such as Robert Jordan's inner thoughts? Or do the monologues work? In what other ways did the director attempt to compensate? Could he have done better? How?

COMPARE AND CONTRAST

I typically have students prepare a list of comparison points between the novel and the film, as part of their journals or even as out-of-class take-home quizzes or exams. These can be differences in the areas I mentioned earlier: characters and fullness of character description, sections left out in the film, use of place, adherence to written descriptions both of character and place, and theme (are any themes in the novel missing in the film?). Are attempts to emulate Hemingway's style in a different medium successful or unsuccessful—such as direct replication of dialogue or the addition of oral intonations? Since Hemingway goes against his own short and simple style in certain passages, however, how does the film address that important shift in cadence of Hemingway's words? Does it?

Generally, students find, and I concur, that the film version of *For Whom the Bell Tolls* is reasonably accurate, or at least representative, in portraying what it does try to depict from the book. The characterizations, particularly of Pilar and Pablo, seem naturally evoked in both the book and the film, with the film director frequently relying on verbatim dialogue and skillful casting to do so. "That *is* Pablo!" the students will joyfully say.

All in all, this is one film that is unlikely to ever be filmed better than the original was, and my students have usually voiced that conclusion also. Gary Cooper and Ingrid Bergman and even those with minor roles are credible and top acting talents, still recognized as Hollywood giants today. The film featured the novelty of starring Hemingway's close friend, Cooper, which isn't happening again, since Cooper and other Hemingway acquaintances are gone. A remake of *The Sun Also Rises*, however, might be wonderful and be an improvement, given its possibly weak casting, with the caveat that there will be few better Bretts than Ava Gardner. Rarely does one see eighteen-year-old young men in shock and awe over the beauty of an older, previously unknown (to them) actress—most likely the desired effect for Brett. However, Tyrone Power seems even more defeated than Jake Barnes would have been, and, according to my students, he appears twenty years Jake's senior, according to my students. For them, *The Sun Also Rises* casting is uneven.

Hemingway's and Jordan's motley crew in the mountains of Spain appropriately represents a range of backgrounds and *types*—in both the novel and the film. While these types may emanate largely from the Spanish people, unique aspects creep into even the abbreviated film characterizations, from gypsies with great humor to a Spanish instructor from Montana. Most students find the *For Whom the Bell Tolls* film running closer and more meaningfully related to the novel than does the film version of *The Sun Also Rises*. Interestingly, Paramount's success with the former have led to overconfidence with the latter, filmed in the late fifties by 20th Century Fox and a glamor-hungry Darryl Zanuck, using many stars all but past their prime , and not necessarily bothering to match ages as Hemingway presented them. Nevertheless, Ava Gardner and Errol Flynn, highlight and even save the film, for many students, through highly stylized portrayals of their roles, but at a cost.

Would students change the *Sun Also Rises* script, and why? If *For Whom the Bell Tolls* were redone, who could one cast from today's available actors that could conceivably be better? That's always more than a good, lighthearted ten minutes on which to end a Friday!

The Fifth Column

If as an instructor you've covered the Spanish history element with *For Whom the Bell Tolls,* that may suffice here for background before directly launching into this play, focused on Madrid and its environs during the Spanish Civil War. However, one could do *The Fifth Column* (1938) as a short standalone course, with a stage production (at least a very small one) or perhaps a prelude to a screenplay and then filming of same if students have access to film equipment. (This might even be included in a class on videography.) I've also included it in a course on spy literature, complete with Spanish Civil War history, Cold War history, and World War I history. (The other works in that course include *The Spy Who Came in from the Cold* [1963] by John le Carré and *The Thirty-Nine Steps* [1915] by John Buchan as well the nonfiction *Writer, Sailor, Soldier, Spy* [2016] by Nicholas Reynolds about Hemingway signing up to spy for the Russians after Spain.) Whether Hemingway, like his main character in *The Fifth Column* was an active spy at any time (even Reynolds concludes that *active* is not the operative word), I find this play underused and infrequently staged for all of its layers of intrigue. It is historically fascinating with regard to Spain and Hemingway biography. It is one of the few Hemingway pieces to display his sense of whimsy and humor (in the middle of war, no less), and I've happily placed it in a few of my other courses with excellent results.

One might add into history elements for *The Fifth Column* some coverage of the history of spying in the Spanish War. Like so much of that war, spying was a complicated business. There were spotters in many of Madrid's bars, seeking to identify and turn in to authorities any known fascists who might carelessly visit a bar or some other establishment that could be watched. (See also and perhaps share with students the Hemingway short story "The Denunciation" [*Complete Short Stories* 420–28].) Spies lead to counterspies and, well, there you have *The Fifth Column.*

A fifth column is a behind-the-scenes, somewhat invisible group of people who want to blend with the opposition and want to appear to be part of one side but are really part of the other. Students of course typically find this whole aspect a draw into the material. In Spain, there were certainly Franco-inspired fifth columns operating within the Republic and vice versa. Identifying those posing as one's own was important, if it could be done. This is Philip's real job in *The Fifth Column*. Could errors occur in identification? Of course, they might. Could the situation be both tragic and comic? Of course, it could. So it is in Hemingway's play.

This play is tragicomedy. Humor and puns abound, yet at its core it follows a sometimes spy-writer who is doing his best to contribute to the Republican effort and who in the end sacrifices his own dreams of a homelife. Modeled a bit after Hemingway's location in Madrid at the Hotel Florida, the apartment next door in this hotel is occupied by a young woman, Dorothy, in the fashion of Martha Gellhorn, yet a woman much more insipid and comically inspired than was Gellhorn. One can imagine Hemingway and Gellhorn both laughing over some of the inside jokes, digs, and comical allusions to their own lives.

The fun begins, and the humor truly shows itself when students begin giving vocal drama and character to the voices of *The Fifth Column*. I have probed this play with students by way of readers theater from chairs (even rotating characters among the actors for better line distribution and for all to experience the different characters) up to staging the play or even partial filming with screenplay of one act. There are identifications and misidentifications in the play, and there is a bit of Shakespearian, wrong-door comedy in the mix. Hemingway takes jabs at the Gellhorn character, Dorothy (notably for purchasing fox tails during the austere Spanish War, similar to the fur adornment Gellhorn wore in a photo taken in roughly the same period next to an admiring Hemingway), but the writer also pokes fun at his own alter-ego character, Philip.

Limited mostly by the now defunct Hotel Florida for the action (although a bit of it is outside in the streets or countryside), Hemingway texturizes this play with sound (such as shellings and music), vivid characterizations, and caricatures (such as the Moroccan prostitute with a very heavy accent but otherwise a comic Judy Holliday or Goldie Hawn in spirit). Don't miss the opportunity to let students rotate the characters, as some are more enjoyable to play than others, and students can also be responsible for sound effects, from background sounds of bombs zinging by or planes coming in, to the playing of a sad and discordant but variably paced Chopin *Mazurka in C Minor, Opus 33, No. 4* (magnificent, really—I suggest the Arturo Rubinstein version). Hemingway chose the piece wisely. It captures the turn of the wheel, and the minor chords echo the elliptical spin of that war and its inevitable turn back to terror.

During the play, the war deteriorates, full of cloak and dagger and interrogation, but war is not over at play's conclusion. However, here there is no future for love, just as in *The Sun Also Rises* and *For Whom the Bell Tolls*. War kills love, at least for its dedicated fighters. Philip does not die waiting for the fascists as Robert Jordan had, but he knows death is always just a stone's throw away and he sends the Dorothy character packing at play's end (just as Jordan had threatened to leave Maria at the "coastal home" in Spain, but then he dies instead). In this case, when Dorothy asks Philip about where they should go as a pair, he somberly opines, "We won't go anywhere," with oblique yet clear significance (90).

The play must be *heard* to be appreciated, ideally with some detail of Hemingway's Spanish Civil War relationship with Gellhorn included with the historical background. I don't think quietly reading *The Fifth Column* shows that aspect at all clearly. It needs to at least be vocalized by a variety of persons taking on the various characters. Students enjoy it, learn from it, surprisingly laugh a lot in spite of serious underpinnings, and have plenty of questions about Hemingway and Gellhorn. Unlike Pablo's or even Jake's wheel, the omnipresent yet iceberg wheel in *The Fifth Column* is at times a friendly, lighthearted flirtatious one juxtaposed against the occasional intrusions of death, with the serious parts camouflaged by culture and random bits of autobiographical jabbing and humor. For that reason alone—Hemingway's deft, cyclic, almost musical weaving between lightheartedness and catastrophe not present in quite the same way anywhere else in his work—the play is worth inclusion somewhere in a Hemingway curriculum.

New York City's Theater Guild presented the play briefly in 1940, less than two years after it was written but after the war was over, in a heavily rewritten version, one that did not please Hemingway and which garnered bad reviews. While critics enjoy raking it, negative critique creates a negative bandwagon effect, and it was a short run. Those bad initial reviews have echoed and magnified through time. The play came back again in original form in the United States only for a short run, in 2011 at New York's Mint Theater. Once the Spanish Civil War was over, remembrance of the conflict and interest in any plays about it also was at a nadir. The Russians have kept this play alive as a staged presence over time and have given it the most showings as well as the most positive reviews.

The Fifth Column might enjoy local revivals and awaits young writers to prepare a screenplay or filming in future here in the United States, at least in a college setting. Perhaps some historical lecture or brief documentary might precede any theater presentation for context. The lack of knowledge on that war, sadly, may make the play *seem* irrelevant today, when the opposite is true. War is always with us. So is humor and the irony of human lives.

Perhaps Hemingway created the play to put us on the wheel and to allow us, via immediacy and multisensory experience, to feel the elliptical ride of war and its power against love and the fine points of human culture. A foxtail wrap or a tin of caviar means little next to Guernica or bombs going off next to one's hotel room.

To experience that disruptive elliptical cycle of life when war is involved, *The Fifth Column* requires the full experience and the original play in Hemingway's words, not a botched, rewritten, non-Hemingway version (as was staged in New York in 1940). Nor will mere quiet reading by armchair critics who aren't even aware of the importance of its musical inclusions ever do the play justice. True, it includes comedy. But those attending the play (should it again be produced) who prepare with knowledge, an open mind, and ears and heart to listen will come away better for having ridden Hemingway's cyclical wheel of inevitably distorted life in war, a surrealistic wheel that becomes at its core *The Fifth Column*.

Such a course as this seminar on Hemingway's Spain may assist in illuminating a triad of significant Hemingway works about a country he so loved and that, as a world-class writer and in all ways open to him, he struggled valiantly to save.

Appendix: Student Projects and Classroom Ambience

Classic jazz from the twenties lends itself well to open a class hour or be used for a project; it is easily available via Internet and might include a variety of suggested period-specific artists. Saxophonist and clarinetist Sidney Bechet (consider playing "Ghost of the Blues" [1924], "I'm Through; Goodbye" [1928]; "Shag" [1932]; and "Egyptian Fantasy" [n.d.]). Anything by Duke Ellington from this period will work well to illustrate twenties jazz; so will works by Cab Calloway, especially "Zaz Zuh Zaz" ([1933–34] if possible, share the film-clip version—students love it); Jimmy Dorsey's "Sidewalk Blues," "Stockholm Stomp," "Hurricane," or "Black Bottom Stomp" (multiple recording dates); and Josephine Baker and Her Orchestra, such as "Then I'll Be Happy" (1927). Please note that Baker's voice is notably clearer on most of the later recordings of the early works. Each of these jazz artists spent time in Europe, some choosing to live there. A good sense of the Jazz Age from can also be gained by watching PBS's *The Jazz Age* or Burns's *Jazz,* both documentaries including vintage footage.

Spanish music relevant to period and setting for the three texts is readily available. *Musica de raza* style was extremely popular, as was the Spanish operetta style *Zarzuela.* Cuban and South American music were arriving on the scene; music and dance included the Argentine tango. A few specific Spanish musical artists of note are Maria Cervantes, Sindo Garay, and Benny More, with a variety of individual pieces easily available online (i.e., on Spotify). Additionally, *Spain in My Heart: Songs of the Spanish Civil War* (Appleseed 2003) is a useful album

Visual artists of note include Hemingway's beloved Cezanne but also Matisse, Breton, and Dali (friend to Franco) with a special nod to exploring Dali's *Guernica* and Picasso's well-known painting by the same name (both of which portray one of the worst bombings of the Spanish War, which was instigated by Hitler). Consider a look at Jan Bishop's *The Steins Collect,* which includes many of the artists Hemingway would have seen in his visits to Gertrude Stein's salon.

Poster art in Spain, especially that used for propaganda, makes an excellent special project. The University of California has many holdings of Spanish Civil War poster art, some online, and the Merrill C. Berman Collection is available online.

European photographers of the time included Berenice Abbott and Man Ray, both friends of Stein.

Style and fashion might capture student interest. Pauline Pfeiffer was a fashion model in Paris when Hemingway met her. Coco Chanel is one obvious cultural research choice in this field, especially since she was a cultural influence beyond fashion (promoting and helping to establish Stravinsky, for example), but Paul Poiret and others are also worthy of study.

Philosophy matched the innovative levels of modernist art; consider Simone de Beauvoir and Jean-Paul Sartre's existentialism. Political philosophers in Spain during this time included Primo de Rivera, Gil Robles, and Isaac Puente.

Architecture was reaching new heights. Jazz Age architects included Walter Adolf Gropius and Le Corbusier, known for new simple and sleek lines. This simplicity echoed Hemingway's style with words.

Buildings and gathering places in which Hemingway actually lived or wrote include the Hotel Angleterre, the Stein salon, Sylvia Beach's bookstore, and jazz clubs (Chez Bricktop, the Moulin Rouge, and Le Grand Duc in Paris).

These are all possible topics to explore. Cafes or bars such as La Closerie des Lilas and the Café les Deux Magots work very well for student research emphasizing influence of place and gathering points, exploring the culture of the period, plus Hemingway's use of such places in his life and writing. In Madrid, the Florida Hotel, Las Ventas, and the Cerveceria Alemana were Hemingway haunts; the latter two remain available to visit.

Other writers from twenties with modernist influence and/or effect on French or Spanish culture include Joyce, Fitzgerald, Dos Passos, Anderson, Malraux, Tzara, Pound, Koestler, and Orwell (the latter two participated in the Spanish Civil War). Poets of the period include Paul Fort and Langston Hughes, and outstanding Spanish poets include Federico Garcia Lorca, who was killed during the war, and Miguel Hernandez Gilabert, who died in prison after Franco placed him there with a lengthy sentence after the war, at the beginning of his dictatorship.

This list is meant to provide a "research ideas" starting-point collection for teachers and students looking into the effects of the major cultural shift and milieu surrounding Hemingway, his characters, and the historical events present in the three works at hand.

Notes

1. Additional recommended volumes on the history of Spain during this period include works by Paul Preston, Stanley Payne, and Adam Hochschild.

2. The intricacies of Russian involvement in Spain are treatises unto themselves (or again, research projects for students), but part of the matter can be explained via the representative experiences of writer George Orwell, whom students find very interesting, if one wishes to use him as a model for those complications. Orwell was nearly killed as a volunteer fighting for the Republic by other Republic fighters, because he was in a Trotsky-dominated fighting unit. Non-Trotsky Russians more loyal to Stalin were at one point shooting at Orwell's unit (essentially friendly fire of the deliberate kind). Stalin had sent many Trotsky supporters to fight for Spain's Republic, because he wanted Trotsky supporters dead anyway and never planned to allow them to return to Russia. The deliberate friendly fire from Stalin's supporters was a bizarre part of that game plan, and Orwell was caught in the middle in a unit he had simply been assigned to. Meanwhile, Stalin gained more sympathizers in the Republic for sending so many fighting bodies even though they came from two groups that hated each other back home in Russia.

Works Cited

Hemingway Works Related to Spain and This Hemingway Seminar

Hemingway, Ernest. *By-Line: Ernest Hemingway: Selected Articles and Dispatches of Four Decades,* edited by William White, Scribner's, 1967.

———. *The Complete Short Stories of Ernest Hemingway: The Finca Vigía Edition.* Scribner's, 1987.

———. "Fascism Is a Lie." *New Madrid,* June 22, 1937.

———. *The Fifth Column and the First Forty-Nine Stories.* Scribner's, 1938

———. *For Whom the Bell Tolls: The Hemingway Library Edition.* Scribner's, 2020.

———. *The Sun Also Rises: The Hemingway Library Edition.* Scribner's, 2014.

Histories and Articles

Bishop, Jan. *The Steins Collect: Matisse, Picasso, and the Parisian Avant-Garde.* San Francisco Museum of Modern Art and Yale UP, 2011.

Burnett, Victoria. "Families Search for Truth of Spain's 'Lost Children,'" *New York Times,* Feb. 28, 2009, A12.

Graham, Helen. *The Spanish Civil War: A Very Short Introduction.* Oxford UP, 2005.

Hochschild, Adam. *Spain in Our Hearts: Americans in the Spanish Civil War, 1936–1939.* Houghton Mifflin Harcourt, 2016.

Newman, Steven. "Ernest Hemingway and the Spanish Civil War." *Medium,* June 4, 2018, medium.com/@stevenewman.newman/ernest-hemingway-and-the-spanish-civil-war-c37d3e1399af. Accessed 20 Jan. 2019, page discontinued as of 18 Mar. 2024.

Payne, Stanley G. *The Collapse of the Spanish Republic: Origins of the Civil War.* Yale UP, 2006.

———. *Fascism in Spain, 1923–1977.* U of Wisconsin P, 1999.

———. *The Spanish Civil War.* Cambridge UP, 2012.

———. *The Spanish Civil War, the Soviet Union, and Communism.* Yale UP, 2011.

Preston, Paul. *A Concise History of the Spanish Civil War.* HarperCollins, 1996.

———. *The Spanish Civil War: An Illustrated Chronicle, 1936–39.* Grove, 1986.

———. *The Spanish Civil War: Reaction, Revolution, and Revenge.* W. W. Norton, 2007.

———. *We Saw Spain Die: Foreign Correspondents in the Spanish Civil War.* Skyhorse, 2009.

Reynolds, Nicholas. *Writer, Sailor, Soldier, Spy: Ernest Hemingway's Secret Adventures, 1935–1961.* William Morrow/Mariner, 2017.

Vernon, Alex. *Hemingway's Second War: Bearing Witness to the Spanish Civil War.* U of Iowa P, 2011.

Films, DVDs, and CDs

For Whom the Bell Tolls. Adapted from a novel by Ernest Hemingway. Dir. Sam Wood. Perf. Gary Cooper and Ingrid Bergman. 1943. Universal Home Video, 1998. DVD.

The Good Fight: The Abraham Lincoln Brigade in the Spanish Civil War. Dir. Noel Buckner, Mary Dore, and Sam Sills. Perf. Studs Terkel. 1984. Kino Lorber Films, 2008. DVD.

"Hemingway on Film." Special feature in *The Sun Also Rises,* film adapted from a novel by Ernest Hemingway. Dir. Henry King. 1957. Special feature interviews with Kelly DuPuis and Charles Oliver. 20th Century Fox Home Entertainment, 2007. DVD.

Into the Fire: American Women in the Spanish Civil War. Dir. Julia Newman. First Run Features, 2002. DVD.

Jazz. Dir. Ken Burns. Narr. Keith David, PBS, 2001. DVD.

The Jazz Age. Narr. Fred Allen. 1956. Shanachie Entertainment, 2003. DVD.

Spain in My Heart: Songs of the Spanish Civil War. Appleseed Recordings, 2003. CD.

The Spanish Earth. Prod. and dir. Ernest Hemingway and Joris Ivens. 1937. Reel Vault, 2015. DVD.

The Sun Also Rises. Adapted from a novel by Ernest Hemingway. Dir. Henry King. 1957. 20th Century Fox Home Entertainment, 2007. DVD.

Teaching Hemingway's *The Sun Also Rises* as Novel and Film

Donald A. Daiker

According to Hemingway scholar Joseph Flora, *The Sun Also Rises* is "a novel consistently ranked among the masterpieces of twentieth-century American literature, the novel critics regularly judge Hemingway's greatest" (131).

So, when a widely acclaimed director, producer, and screenwriter collaborated with five of Hollywood's most experienced and talented actors to make a film version of *The Sun Also Rises* closely based on the novel, the result was sure to be a rousing critical success, right? Wrong! When the film was released in 1957, it was met with less than approbation, and its standing has not improved in the ensuing years.[1] Although Hemingway had approved the script of the film (Jividen 81), he is reported to have walked out twenty-five minutes into its screening, calling it "pretty disappointing and that's being gracious" (Buchwald 5). He is said to have commented, "Any picture in which Errol Flynn is the best actor is its own worst enemy" (Jividen 81).

But Errol Flynn, once Hollywood's leading man, after triumphs in films like *Captain Blood* (1935) and *The Adventures of Robin Hood* (1938), was hardly the only asset of *The Sun Also Rises,* the movie. It was directed by Henry King, who had earlier successfully adapted Hemingway's highly praised short story "The Snows of Kilimanjaro" (1952) to screen. Seven of King's many films earned nominations for the Academy Award for Best Picture. The movie script of *The Sun Also Rises* was written by Peter Viertel, a well-regarded novelist who had earlier cowritten the script for the multi-award-winning *The African Queen* (1951) and who thought Hemingway's story "ageless" and "fascinating in its impressions of Europe after World War I" (Schallert F1). Viertel would later write the script for Hemingway's *The Old Man and the Sea* (1958). The film was produced by movie mogul Darryl F. Zanuck, once the powerful head of 20th Century Fox, who had earned a Best Picture Academy Award for *All About Eve* (1950) and would be nominated for *The Longest Day* (1962).

For the role of Jake Barnes, the novel's narrator and protagonist, Zanuck chose Tyrone Power, although his first choice had been Gregory Peck, who starred as the dying writer Harry in *The Snows of Kilimanjaro*. Like Flynn, Power had won fame in swashbuckler roles and romantic leads, but he had moved on to make films like *The Razor's Edge* (1946), *Nightmare Alley* (1947), and the popular *Eddy Duchin Story* (1956). Susan Heyward had been cast as Jake's love interest Lady Brett Ashley, but when Hemingway insisted on Ava Gardner, Zanuck went out and got her. Gardner said, "Lady Brett Ashley is the most interesting character I have ever played" (Schallert F1). For supporting roles, Mel Ferrer, who had appeared in *War and Peace* (1956) with his wife Audrey Hepburn, was chosen to play Robert Cohn, Jake's rival for Brett's favors. Eddie Albert, who had been nominated for a Best Supporting Actor Award in *Roman Holiday* (1954), which starred Peck and Hepburn, was cast as Jake's best friend and traveling companion, Bill Gorton. According to film critic Gene D. Phillips, the five formed "an incomparable cast of first-rate actors" (133).

Why, then, despite its eminent director, screenwriter, producer, and star power, is the film generally considered a critical failure? This was the central question I posed to the sixteen adult students who had registered for my mini course, "*The Sun Also Rises* as Novel and Film" in the fall of 2018. Offered through Miami University's Institute for Learning in Retirement, the course met for seventy-five minutes on five consecutive Tuesdays. Here is our schedule:

ERNEST HEMINGWAY'S *THE SUN ALSO RISES* AS NOVEL AND FILM

Class 1: *The Sun Also Rises* (novel), book 1, chapters 1–7.
          The Sun Also Rises (film), the first 35–42 minutes.
Class 2: *The Sun Also Rises* (novel), book 2, chapters 8–14.
          Pay special attention to chapter 14.
          The Sun Also Rises (film), the next 35–40 minutes.
Class 3: *The Sun Also Rises* (novel), book 2, chapters 15–18.
          The Sun Also Rises (film), the next 35–42 minutes.
Class 4: *The Sun Also Rises* (novel), book 3, chapter 19.
          The Sun Also Rises (film), the final 30–40 minutes.

Class 5: *The Sun Also Rises* (novel), reread your favorite scene or two.
The Sun Also Rises (film), rewatch your favorite scene or two.

At our initial class meeting, after forming a circle and introducing ourselves, we began discussion with my request that, going around the circle, everyone offer a brief comment of any kind about the novel, the film, or the two together. Several students volunteered that the actors were too old for their parts in the film. They singled out Tyrone Power, who at age forty-four was playing Jake Barnes, who is probably in his early thirties in the novel.[2] It is several years since the end of World War I, where Jake had been an airplane pilot "flying on a joke front like the Italian" (25). Apparently, he had been shot down by Austrian antiaircraft fire, rescued, and brought to a hospital in Milan to recover from his wounds. There, he learns that while he still experiences sexual desire, he has no direct means of satisfying it because his penis has been shot off.[3] The other male leads in the film were also older than viewers expected: Errol Flynn, playing Mike Campbell, was forty-eight; Mel Ferrer, as Robert Cohn, was forty; and Eddie Albert, as Bill Gorton, was fifty-one. Among the leads, only Ava Gardner was the age of her character, Brett Ashley: thirty-four.

Another student, who had obviously watched the film closely, said she had found it self-contradictory. She called our attention to the opening narration that set the film in Paris in 1922: "We were part of that spectacular lost generation of young people who continued to live as if we were about to die." She asked if we remembered that line from the novel. Yes, we said, the novel's first epigraph is "You are all a lost generation" (xxv). But no one could remember a line about living "as if we were about to die"—and that's because the novel includes no such line, not even close. Moreover, in both the novel and the film, Jake Barnes, the narrative's primary voice, leads a rather traditional, un-Bohemian life: he has a full-time job as the director of an international press service; he dresses in a suit and tie (at least in the film), every morning he goes to his office, where he works a seven-hour day; and he lives in a comfortable, multiroom apartment with (in the film) a lovely view of Paris. He also keeps careful track of his funds; he has, in current terms, approximately $25,000 in his checking account. Moreover, nothing Jake says or does in either the novel or film suggests living as if "we were about to die." Jake is cautious rather than risk-taking: when danger threatens in a potential fight with Robert Cohn, an experienced boxer, Jake defuses the situation with humor and an apology (32). When Cohn had earlier asked Jake, "Do you know that in about thirty-five years we'll be dead," Jake became angry, as his swearing indicates: "What the hell, Robert. . . . What the hell?" (9). Thus, in no way does Jake, of either the novel or film, live as if he were about to die.

Several omissions in the film's opening scenes in Paris suggest that its director did not really understand Hemingway's novel.[4] For instance, King omitted Jake's key statement that "it is very important to discover graceful exits" (9). The novel focuses on a series of graceful and graceless exits, culminating in Robert Cohn's graceless exit at the end of book 2 and Jake's graceful exit from Brett in the novel's concluding pages. King does include Jake's telling Robert that "going to another country won't help" (the novel reads "doesn't make any difference" [9–10]), but he skips what follows: "I've tried all that. You can't get away from yourself by moving from one place to another. There's nothing to that" (10). King fails to understand that Hemingway's novel is about Jake's search for sustaining values at a time when traditional values no longer hold. It is those traditional values that Jake challenges when he reflects that the "Catholic Church had an awfully good way of handling" situations like his: "Not to think about it. Oh it was swell advice. Try and take it sometime. Try and take it" (26). None of these lines appear in the film, perhaps to avoid offending the Catholic Church, perhaps because King does not understand the centrality of Jake's efforts to live well despite his sexual incapacity.[5] For Jake, living well encompasses concern for others: "I try and play it along," Jake says of his injury, "and just not make trouble for people," another key statement not found in the film (26).

If King excludes several thematically important novel passages from the film, he also unaccountably adds lines—often clichés—*not* found in the novel. For example, when Jake and Brett are first alone in the film, Brett tells Jake that in regard to their relationship, "nothing ever changes" and continues, "You said one day I'd hate you. I wish I did." None of these three sentences, or their equivalents, appears in the novel. When Brett later asks, "How are you, Jake?" he responds, "I could be worse. I could be dead." Not only are these words never spoken in the novel, but in their self-pity they are totally uncharacteristic of Jake. Robert Cohn is often self-pitying—"I guess it isn't any use. . . . I guess it isn't any damn use," he laments in his last novel scene (155). But Hemingway's Jake is more likely to confront pain and disappointment with humor—"That was funny," he says of the liaison colonel's revelation of his wound—rather than self-pity (25). The makers of the *Sun Also Rises* film, therefore, seem not to have misunderstood Hemingway's Jake Barnes completely.

Furthermore, King seems not to have recognized the importance of Count Mippipopolous in the novel, where he serves as a positive model for Jake. The count is the only character in book 1 who has learned how to "enjoy everything so much" (50). He enjoys good food, good wine, roses, buying and serving champagne, spending money, cigars that draw, Napoleon brandy, watching Jake and Brett dance, and of course, Lady Brett herself. But in the film, the count is reduced to a comic character who overspends wildly, indulges his protegee, Zizi, and fails to seduce Brett. Hemingway's count chooses not to dance—"I would do it if I would enjoy it," he says (52)—but in the film he dances awkwardly beside Brett. Perhaps King made what seems like a gratuitous change to add action to an otherwise static scene—or to keep Ava Gardner on the screen longer.

Just as every male character in the novel finds Lady Brett beautiful and even irresistible, so Jake Barnes is liked by all. That's one point, one of my students observed, that King got right. In both the novel and film, the prostitute Georgette finds Jake likeable in a world that is otherwise "expensive and dirty." "You're not a bad type," the novel's Georgette says. "We get on well" (14). The film is even more explicit: "I like you, Jacob. You're a nice man." When Jake and Georgette arrive at a restaurant, his friends call excitedly to him with invitations to join them (14). King is also faithful to the novel in depicting Jake's generosity with money. In the opening scene, we see Jake tipping a cab driver, and he later leaves so much money for Georgette to get home that Zizi quips that she must live in Marseille. What my students also liked about the film is the instrumental music that accompanies Brett and whose familiar lyrics accurately describe her feelings for Jake and his for her: "You do something to me / That nobody else can do."

During our second class, which focused on the first half of book 2 and the corresponding film scenes, my students were most surprised by how much of the novel King just passed over completely, perhaps because they involve little physical action. Chapters on end, including Jake and Bill Gorton's pleasantly uneventful train ride from Paris to Bayonne, are skipped. So are the relaxing times that Bill and Jake enjoy at a small inn in the remote Spanish village of Burguete.

One highlight of their stay is the warm friendship that Jake and Bill develop with the Englishman, Harris.[6] The few days Harris spends with Jake and Bill rank with the best experiences of his life: "I say, Barnes. You don't know what all this means to me . . . Barnes. Really, Barnes, you can't know. That's all" (104). I asked the class why they thought King excluded Harris from his film. We decided that

King simply does not recognize the vital importance of friendship in Hemingway's novel.[7] In the novel, Jake and Bill enjoy friendship with Basque peasants during their bus ride to the Irati River and at a posada stop where they happily buy drinks for each other (85). Hemingway underscores Jake's close friendship with Bill in many ways but principally through their frank, painful discussion of Jake's off-and-on-again relationship with Brett (99). Jake's final image of Bill is the "empty" train tracks that signal both Bill's departure for Paris and Jake's sense of loss at his leaving (186). In the film, where no such scene appears, King further devalues the theme of friendship by emphasizing Bill's drinking, turning him into a womanizer, and relegating him to comic scenes with Mike Campbell, a bankrupt drunkard.

Perhaps King's most troubling omission is the fishing scene on the Irati River. For each of the five days Jake and Bill spend in Burguete, they walk from their inn to the Irati to fish for trout, each catching a half-dozen good-sized ones on a typical day. But King reduces five days and two-and-one-half chapters to a mere thirty seconds on a stream hardly large enough for a dozen fish.

According to Phillips, the brief scene "comes across as a routine fishing trip out of *Field and Stream*" (126). What King fails to consider is Hemingway's setting up Jake's experiences in Burguete as a marked contrast to those in Paris. In Hemingway's Paris, Jake is guided by time and the calendar: he gets to work by nine and at exactly "eleven o'clock" leaves for a press conference; he makes an appointment to meet Brett "at the Crillon at five"; and during a taxi ride with the prostitute Georgette, they notice "the New York *Herald* bureau with the window full of clocks" (29, 24, 13). But time seems to have stopped in Burguete. Jake even asks Harris, "What day of the week is it?" and Harris observes, "Wonderful how one loses track of days up here in the mountains" (101). Sleep comes easier in the mountains, too. In Paris, Jake had experienced nights "when you could not sleep," but in Burguete Jake sleeps soundly and wakes fully rested in the morning (25, 89–90). The "stop-and-go" traffic signals of Paris are of course unnecessary in peaceful Burguete with its one road and "no side-streets" (12, 87).

But what most distances Hemingway's Burguete from Paris is the absence of conflict. In Paris, conflict is everywhere. Cohn threatens to beat up Jake over Brett; Cohn is repeatedly insulted by his mistress, Frances Cline; Harvey Stone calls Cohn a "moron" and "case of arrested development" until Cohn offers to "push [his] face in"; Brett causes "a row" when she arrives, drunk, at Jake's apartment at half-past four in the morning; and Georgette causes "a frightful row" at a dancing club (36, 26, 23). By contrast, serenity reigns in the Spanish countryside. At Burguete there are "families sitting in their doorways," playful goats, week-old Spanish newspapers, and fish that can't wait to be hooked (87). Nearby is the peaceful "monastery of Roncevalles," protected from conflict with the outside world by its height of "twelve hundred metres" and its "gray metal-sheathed roof" (87). Nor is there conflict for Jake, because "there was no word from Robert Cohn nor from Brett and Mike" (100).

Because King seems not to have recognized Hemingway's pattern of alternating locations, shifting from sites of conflict to sites of comfort, he moves much too quickly from Paris to Pamplona (another site of conflict, because Brett reappears there along with her lover, Robert Cohn, and her fiancé, Mike Campbell). But the film's Pamplona sequence, which lasts approximately seventy minutes, more than half the film, does capture many of the important elements of the novel: pageantry of the fiesta with parades of dignitaries, music, bells, fireworks, squares and balconies crowded with revelers; Jake's continuing friendship with Juanito Montoya, proprietor of the Hotel Montoya, where Jake, Bill, Brett, Cohn, and Mike stay; the open hostility between Cohn and Mike, which both Jake and Bill try to allay; and, most prominently, scenes of bullfighting. Those film scenes include the running of the bulls from their cages into the arena, where—as Jake explains to the others—they are picked up and calmed down by the steers. They include the introduction of Pedro Romero, the young bullfighter who performs brilliantly in the bull ring. Outside of the ring conflict reigns, reaching its height when Cohn knocks out both Jake and Mike and then brutally beats up Romero, leaving him unconscious on the floor of his hotel room.

An unconscious Romero—that's one of the several things King changes in Hemingway's story. In the novel, Cohn cannot knock out Romero. No matter how many times he slugs him, the bullfighter will not stay down: "He kept getting up and getting knocked down again. Cohn couldn't knock him out" (161). So, unlike in the film, Romero emerges as the moral victor in the fight and with the heroic status that King denies him. King additionally fails to identify Romero as Jake's tutor and exemplar.

King also changes the relationship between Jake and Juanito Montoya. In the novel, Jake's introducing Brett to Romero costs him Montoya's friendship—perhaps forever. Thus, when Jake checks out of the Hotel Montoya, he pointedly observes, "Montoya did not come near us. One of the maids brought the bill" (184). But in the film, Jake and Montoya make up—perhaps because King is fond of happy endings and neatly tied packages. Their last meeting is one of apology and forgiveness. "I feel badly," Jake says, and Montoya responds, "It's not your fault. That is life." When Montoya then says, "See you next year" and Jake replies, "You can count on it," it's clear that in King's world, unlike Hemingway's, there need not be serious consequences for bad behavior. In the novel, a Spanish man running with the bulls is gored and killed, but in the film, no one dies (157–58).

Once again, students noticed what King omits, and these omissions from the Pamplona sequence are especially significant. Most important, King entirely ignores the meaning and value that Jake attaches to bullfighting—as does Hemingway. Whereas Jake helps Brett understand bullfighting as a metaphor for confronting whatever threatens to wound and perhaps destroy you, King sees it primarily as "spectacle" (134). Whereas Jake contrasts the purity of Romero's bullfighting with the "faked" bullfighting of Marcial and Belmonte, neither of Romero's rivals so much as appears in the film (134). Whereas Hemingway carefully distinguishes between the dangerous "terrain of the bull" and the safe "terrain of the bullfighter," King dismisses the distinction (171). Whereas Hemingway shows through Romero's bullfighting that mistakes and defeats can be rectified by positive action—in the bull ring Romero "was wiping all that out now. Each thing that he did with the bull wiped that out a little cleaner"—no such statement emerges from the film (175). For King, bullfighting is bullfighting, pure and simple. But for Hemingway, bullfighting offers, among other things, a demonstration of living "life all the way up" (9).

When the fiesta is over, Hemingway's Jake spends a day in Bayonne, France, before leaving for San Sebastián, Spain. What attracts him to San Sebastián is that it is not Paris or Pamplona; it is not an arena of conflict. "It would be quiet in San Sebastian," Jake thinks, especially since he will arrive "before the season opened" (187). Jake anticipates "wonderful trees along the promenade above the beach," "many children sent down with their nurses," and listening to "band concerts under the trees" at night (187).

But King, not recognizing the novel's pattern of alternating settings, sends Jake not to restful San Sebastián, Spain, but to luxurious Biarritz, France, an elegant seaside resort long known for its high fashion and royal clientele. In a beach scene that lasts just a minute, Jake is shown retrieving a young woman's beach ball and then receiving a telegram from Brett beseeching him to come to Madrid. Once again, what King fails to incorporate from the novel is telling. He omits all mention of Jake's return trip to Bayonne, his ambivalent feelings about reentering Spain, his gaining an hour in doing so, his establishing order in his hotel room, his encounter with the bicycle racers, and, above all, the strenuous swimming and purposeful diving that illustrate Jake's attempts to strengthen himself in preparation for the summons from Brett that he anticipates will arrive soon.

In response to Brett's two identical telegrams beseeching him to come to Madrid—there is only one in the film and no evidence that Jake sends one in return—Jake telegrams thßat he will arrive the next day. What is missing in the film is any kind of acknowledgment that Jake is learning and growing. There is nothing at all in the film that suggests the self-knowledge—and determination—of this key paragraph from the novel:

> That seemed to handle it. That was it. Send a girl off with one man. Introduce her to another to go off with him. Now go and bring her back. And sign the wire with love. That was it all right. I went into lunch. (192)

Here is Jake at his most honest and forthright: for the first time, he owns up to his culpability in Brett's relationship with Cohn ("Send a girl off with one man") and with Romero ("Introduce her to another to go off with him"). But also for the first time, Jake fully understands—and takes responsibility for—what he has done and what he is doing: "That was it all right." But the closing "I went into lunch" implies that Jake will move beyond his mistakes of the past, and that's exactly what he does when he meets Brett in Madrid. But none of this is suggested or implied in King's film.

When Jake arrives at Brett's bedroom in the film, he is visibly angry. "You're short of funds. Is that it?" he asks Brett, and eventually he extends a wad of bills which she accepts. But in the novel, Jake is not angry at all. He is calm and controlled, seeming to sympathize with Brett as she explains, crying and shaking, why she has had "such a hell of a time" with Pedro Romero (194). Both the film and the novel end with the same image of Jake and Brett in a Madrid taxicab, but the concluding lines are vastly different. The novel ends with Jake's answering Brett's "Oh, Jake. . . . We could have had such a damned good time together" with "Yes. . . . Isn't it pretty to think so?" (198).

By contrast, the film ends with Brett's "Oh, Darling, there must be an answer for us somewhere," and Jake's answering "I'm sure there is." In the film, Brett snuggles up to Jake and he rubs her hand tenderly as they almost kiss. But in the novel, there is no snuggling or handholding or near kissing: that Brett rested "comfortably" against Jake is one clear sign that Jake's passion for Brett is no more. King may have wanted his film to end on an upscale note, but that was surely not Hemingway's intention.

For many readers of *The Sun Also Rises,* chapter 14 is most important. Hemingway signals its importance by placing it at the very center of the novel, and he sets it apart from all other chapters because it lacks dialogue of any kind. The significance of this chapter lies in its presenting Jake's—and Hemingway's—philosophy of life and definition of morality. Jake's philosophy is optimistic: he believes "you could get your money's worth" of life's enjoyments because "the world was a good place to buy in" (119). For Jake, immorality consists of "things that made you disgusted afterwards," which means that morality is defined by what makes you happy afterwards.[8]

When Jake feels disgusted with himself, purposely getting drunk, after he makes it possible for Brett and Romeo to sleep together, it's a sign that he has behaved immorally. When at the end of the novel he feels "fine" for having rescued Brett in Madrid, it's a sign that he has acted morally. Judging from the film version of *The Sun Also Rises,* King has either not understood—or considered important—Jake's/Hemingway's philosophy of life and definition of *morality.* If he had, he might have considered using a narrative voice like Joanne Woodward's in Martin Scorsese's brilliant film adaptation of Edith Wharton's *The Age of Innocence.*

While overaged actors may help explain the critical failure of *The Sun Also Rises* as film, an even more cogent reason is its superficiality. That superficiality is revealed in the series of clichés that mar the film from beginning to end: Cohn's "Why haven't I seen her [Brett] before"; Brett's "You said someday I'd hate you. I wish I did"; Cohn's "She was the only woman who made sense to me" and, later, "What have I done?" and then, about to return to Paris and Frances, "I only hope I'm not too late" and "People always want what they can't have"; and Montoya's "That is life." My students couldn't understand why Viertel replaced Hemingway's masterful dialogue with clichés like these.

The film is superficial in failing to show that the structure of the novel—its alternating geographies, movements from arenas of tension and conflict (Paris, Pamplona, Madrid) to arenas of peace and comfort (Bayonne, Burguete, San Sebastián)—provides a yardstick for measuring Jake's growth in understanding, control, and resolution. That resolution emerges clearly as Jake's train ride to rescue Brett reaches its final destination: "The Norte station in Madrid is the end of the line. All trains finish there. They don't go on anywhere" (193). These lines do not appear in the film, but in the novel, they register Jake's determination to end, once and for all, his romantic relationship with Brett. The final image in the novel—the "mounted policeman in khaki" whose raised baton slows the taxi and presses Brett against Jake—is likewise absent from the film and a further sign that King misses the deeper symbolic meanings of Hemingway's text.

Not understanding Hemingway's deeper meanings, King also left out thematically important details. For example, in the novel when Jake arrives in Madrid to find Brett in bed and her hotel room "in that disorder produced only by those who have always had servants," the details indicate that Jake has come to understand his subservient role as Brett sees it (194).

But in the film, Brett is up and dressed neatly, and her hotel room looks relatively tidy, so Hemingway's suggestion that Brett relies on Jake and others to clean up her messes is missed. The film had earlier failed to include the concluding line of the chapter in which, thanks to Jake's intercession, Brett and Romeo leave the café for his bedroom: "A waiter came with a cloth and picked up the glasses and mopped off the table" (149). Only later will Jake be obliged to help clean up that mess. He knows how to do so because his own hotel room, which we never see in the film, is the model of neatness and order in the novel: "I unpacked my bags and stacked my books on the table beside the head of the bed, put out my shaving things, hung up some clothes in the big armoire, and made up a bundle for the laundry" (188).

Teaching the Hemingway novel alongside the Zanuck/King/Viertel film helps us better understand and appreciate the novel's nuances and subtleties, many of which are either ignored or rejected in the film. To take one final example, the novel's concluding pages focus on two key Madrid scenes, both locations chosen by Jake, the first in the bar of the Palace Hotel, the second in Botin's, "one of the best restaurants in the world" (197). Neither scene appears in the film, which means that we do not get to see Jake's control of his relationship to Brett, his humor, his gusto in eating "a very big meal," and his enjoyment of wine. "I like to do a lot of things," Jake tells Brett. Nor do we get to hear Jake's final, conclusive words before leaving Botin's: "I'll finish this"—which he does in dismissing Brett's heartfelt invitation to contemplate the might-have-been by labeling it "pretty," appealing but false (198). Instead, the film gives us a taxicab riding into the setting sun as a biblical voice proclaims that "One generation passeth away and another generation cometh, but the earth abides forever. The sun also rises."

The film highlights the limitations imposed by the strict movie code enforced between 1934 and 1968. Known as both the Hays Code, after Will H.

Hayes, a devout Catholic and president of the Motion Picture Producers and Distributors of America from 1922 to 1945, and the Breen Office for Joseph Breen, the administrator Hays appointed to enforce the code in Hollywood, they were a set of industry-imposed guidelines for all motion pictures. The Hays Code prohibited graphic or realistic violence, profanity, suggestive nudity, sexual persuasions, and rape. Its first "general principle" is that "no picture shall be produced that shall lower the moral standard of those who see it. Hence the sympathy of the audience shall never be thrown to the side of crime, wrong-doing, evil, or sin" (Mondello). In part because of the Hays Code, not only are all references to the Catholic Church and all anti-Semitic comments eliminated from the film version of *The Sun Also Rises*, but so is the profanity that Hemingway considered essential. When his editor, Maxwell Perkins, asked if he could cut down on the profanity, Hemingway wrote, "I never use a word without first considering if it is replaceable" (*Letters* 97). When Perkins asked a second time, Hemingway responded, "I reduced so much profanity when writing the book that I'm afraid not much could come out" (107). Thus, when Bill Gorton asks if Jake has ever been in love with Brett, Jake says, "I don't give a damn anymore" and swears three more times, clearly indicating that he is "sore" that Bill has broached the subject, although he tells Bill otherwise (99). In the film, he just says, "I'm all right. I'm all over it now."

When Perkins specifically objected to Brett's "I'm thirty-four, you know. I'm not going to be one of these bitches that ruins children" (195), which has become one of the most frequently quoted passages from the novel, Hemingway responded forcefully: "But in the matter of the use of the word 'bitch' by Brett—I have never once used this word ornamentally nor except when it was absolutely necessary and I believe the few places it has been used must stand" (*Letters* 97). The film's sanitized version is "I'm not going to become one of those women who ruins children." At the same time, the film elevates Romero's age from eighteen in the novel to twenty-two, which means that he is no longer a child to be ruined. Of course, the film completely ignores the novel's scene in Jake's Paris bedroom where he and Brett attempt intimacies just short of intercourse (45).

The code did not require happy endings but, as Jill Jividen writes, "Hollywood tended to manufacture happy endings in order to please audiences" (81). So, at the end of the film, virtually everyone is happy: Mike anticipates reviving his finances on the French Riviera; Bill is happily headed back to Paris and then America; Cohn and Jake have made up, and Cohn heads to Paris to make up with Frances; Montoya has accepted Jake's apology and will warmly welcome Jake back to the Hotel Montoya next year; and Romero has gracefully escaped from Brett's clutches. Jake and Brett may not be happy—they are not smiling the last time we see them on screen—but there is at least the possibility that they may be able to find "an answer" to their dilemma, that the sun may rise for them.

Teaching *The Sun Also Rises* as novel and film offers students the opportunity to consider critical questions about the many differences between the two forms, which include language, structure, character development, and theme. These contrasts highlight the novel's superiority, helping to explain both why *The Sun Also Rises* as film was a critical and popular failure and why *The Sun Also Rises* as novel ranks among the world's best.

Notes

1. As of August 18, 2022, the Rotten Tomatoes audience score is a lowly 38 percent, while the Internet Movie Database scores it higher, at 6.2/10.

2. Jake's age is never stated in the novel, but we know that Brett, who seems to be about Jake's age, is thirty-four (195).

3. Hemingway told George Plimpton, "I wondered what a man's life would have been like after if his penis had been lost and his testicles and spermatic cord remained intact." Quoted in Meyers 190.

4. I assume that director Henry King is responsible for all decisions except the script, which is writer Peter Viertel's domain.

5. My students remarked that King also excludes the novel's half-dozen anti-Semitic slurs, including Jake's comment that Cohn "had a hard, Jewish, stubborn streak" (9). The film never explicitly identifies Cohn as Jewish.

6. Harris is the name of the American soldier who greets Jake in front of the New York Herald office building in Paris in the film's opening scene; no such scene appears in the novel.

7. In his earlier fiction, especially Nick Adams stories like "The End of Something," "The Three-Day Blow," and "Cross Country Snow," Hemingway celebrates friendship in his warm depiction of Nick's relationship with his Michigan friend Bill and his European friend George. Nick's friend Bill is not Bill Gorton, although each character seems to be modeled upon Bill Smith, Hemingway's best summer friend.

8. In *Death in the Afternoon,* Hemingway writes, "So far, about morals, I know only that what is moral is what you feel good after and what is immoral is what you feel bad after" (4).

Works Cited

Buchwald, Art. "The Great Feud of Mr. Hemingway and Mr. Zanuck." *Los Angeles Times,* 29 Nov. 1957, p. B5.

Flora, Joseph A. Review, *Reading Hemingway's* Across the River and into the Trees, by Mark Cirino. *Hemingway Review,* vol. 36, no. 2, 2017, pp. 131–34.

Hemingway, Ernest. *Death in the Afternoon.* Scribners, 1932.

———. *The Letters of Ernest Hemingway.* Vol. 3: *1926–1929,* edited by Rena Sanderson, Sandra Spanier, and Robert Trogdon, Cambridge UP, 2015.

———. *The Sun Also Rises: The Hemingway Library Edition.* Scribners, 2014.

Jividen, Jill. "Cinema and Adaptations." *Ernest Hemingway in Context,* edited by Debra A. Moddelmog and Suzanne del Gizzo, Cambridge UP, 2013, pp. 76–85.

Meyers, Jeffrey. *Hemingway: A Biography.* Harper & Row, 1985.

Mondello, Bob. "Remembering Hollywood's Hays Code, 40 Years On. *All Things Considered,* NPR.org, Aug. 8, 2008, https://www.npr.org/2008/08/08/93301189/remembering-hollywoods-hays-code-40-years-on.

Phillips, Gene D. *Hemingway and Film.* Frederic Ungar, 1980.

Schallert, Edwin. "Hemingway's 'Sun Also Rises' Filmed After 30-Year Wait." *Los Angeles Times,* 2 June 1957, F1.

Visual Values

The Success and Failure of Hemingway's Ethics in Film

Sean C. Hadley

It is well known that Ernest Hemingway often considered the film versions of his work to be little more than source of incomes. His famous "you throw them your book, they throw you the money" mentality toward the arrangement suggested that his skepticism of Hollywood ran deep (qtd. in Phillips 6). Except for 1958's *The Old Man and the Sea*, Hemingway never even sat through an entire screening of any movie adaptation of his writing (Phillips 147). This disdain arose from more than a mere matter of misinterpretation. Critics often misunderstood his works, and in some ways, this characterized his literary life to the point of normalcy. Hemingway may have been annoyed or put out when readers could not see beyond, to the iceberg below the surface, but he could handle it. Still, the Hollywood problem persisted. Even when he was directly involved, as with *The Old Man and the Sea* featuring Spencer Tracy, the film just never quite hit the right notes. What is it about Hemingway's writing that made making film adaptations so difficult? *The Macomber Affair* turns an otherwise jarring but beautiful story into a sappy forbidden-romance film. And perhaps the worst of all, the film of *The Sun Also Rises* takes a complex character in Jake Barnes and turns him into a detached chain smoker. Students do not need much guidance to recognize these problems, but they often attribute them to issues such as historical location or shoddy workmanship. One of the goals in pairing Hemingway's writing with films ought to be helping students move beyond such a superficial understanding.

The astute student quickly observes that part of the issue in adapting Hemingway's work is his iceberg theory of writing: "If a writer of prose knows enough about what he is writing about he may omit things that he knows and the reader, if the writer is writing truly enough, will have a feeling of those things as strongly as though the writer had stated them" (*Death in the Afternoon* 192). While this method works in Hemingway's writing, it does not translate to a movie screen with any precision, and thus the director often fills in what is omitted, for the sake of the audience. Perhaps even more important, the actions of the characters Hemingway creates exist as something other than mere violence or heroics; the movement of Hemingway's iceberg is one of moral value as well as activity, for the two things cannot be separated in Hemingway's work. If students are provided with a framework to handle concepts specific to Hemingway, they may better understand the necessity a character's moral activity, in addition to the virtue of Hemingway's narrative arcs. There are multiple sources for such a guide, but Aristotle's *Poetics* stands out as, I would contend, the best. Using the philosopher's outlines of tragedy and comedy, the moral formation embedded in Hemingway's fiction becomes clear, especially when compared with the lack of these virtues in the film adaptations. Thus, students trained in this method recognize elements of Hemingway's moral action and then can explain why attempts to capture this on the big screen fall so far off the mark.

The Benefits of Adaptations

Adapting a story for performance is as old as the Greek theater. Aeschylus, Sophocles, and Euripides built their literary careers on taking stories told by others, reimagining them as stage performance, and then putting that performance on display for the ancient Greeks to watch with wonder. Even the concept of giving awards for performed adaptations finds its root in the Grecian past, and this is mirrored in the present-day obsession with winning an Oscar.[1] Those who had read the great Greek tragedies or the various treatises that were penned contemporaneous with them easily recognize these patterns. But for many students, this comes as a small revelation. The result of this gap in understanding means that the teacher must lead the student to such connections, simultaneously shattering the erroneous notion that Aristotle is nothing more than a stuffy old philosopher. Once you have them through that transition in their thinking, however, often it is the student who will begin to find patterns that follow Aristotle's schema.

It helps, of course, that the original audience of the *Poetics* was Aristotle's students. The format lends itself readily to critical thinking and analysis, which is why it remains one of the most valuable tools for students today. By recovering this helpful lens, students learn to recognize common elements in good storytelling, while becoming better judges of the visual performance that often preoccupy their theatrical focus. Aristotle stakes his claim on the idea that each genre contains basic components and that two of these elements are most important, with plot ranking first and spectacle falling to the bottom (37–38). If a student tends to watch a movie on the sole basis that it is made by their favorite director or it stars their celebrity crush, then they will find such analysis cumbersome. But it does not take too much prodding for them to see the merit in Aristotle's argument. Take, for instance, the idea that character development is secondary to plot. If the emotional state of the character drives the story, the movie becomes slow and tepid. But, if the plot drives the story, and the character is developed outwardly from that action, then a sense of time is restored that fits the narrative. *The Sun Also Rises* illustrates this well, as do virtually all of Hemingway's short stories. Spectacle, the dependence on flash or surprise instead of action, may dominate the movie world in many respects, but it is not hard to identify how the spectacle-driven movie fails. Ask students to compare *Gladiator* (2000) and *Transformers* (2007), and this issue becomes clear. Students ought, then, to examine source material and begin to explore why changes are made. Any adaptation of a story that makes drastic shifts, in plot or spectacle specifically, must justify these changes through the execution of the story.

Aristotle's notion of *mimesis,* imitation that aims to produce in the mind a focus on metaphysical or "higher" things, reinforces a key aspect of the genre of tragedy (44). The point is a simple one: stories teach ethics. Thus, the tragic tale is also the one that encourages the audience to imitate right moral behavior.[2] The tragic tale prompts action in the audience, confronting the viewer with a moral decision. As the German philosopher Hans-Georg Gadamer observes, "moral knowledge, as Aristotle describes it, is clearly not objective knowledge— i.e., the knower is not standing over against a situation that he merely observes; he is directly confronted with what he sees. It is something that he has to do" (362). Though dramas, operas, and the like continue to be performed across the world today, the advent of film brought an unexpected change to the cultural interpretive realm. For the first time, people separated by thousands of miles could participate in a shared performative experience. This brings what Alasdair MacIntyre calls "the Sophoclean dramatic encounter," to a larger community (163). The complication arises because in such a drama, "it is not simply the fate of individuals . . . it is the individual in his or her role" who represents the entire community (163). Moral formation still comes in the same way, as actors and actresses perform on screen at the behest of a director, but for the first time it is something presented as a series of options. A student might spend the weekend watching the latest horror flick, which advertises its bloodiest scenes, or they might choose a romantic comedy, where everything works out just right in the end. Either way, it is up to the audience to pick the moral formation they will imbibe. The pairing of Hemingway and film helps students wrestle with the choices that directors make, on the one hand, but also helps provide them the critical faculties to question those choices, on the other.

Looking at Specifics

What follows are a few observations that demonstrate the value of using Aristotelian categories to explore film adaptations of Hemingway's work.[3] For each of the two examples, only one scene is compared, but it would not be hard to extrapolate similar conversations using the guided questions provided at the end of this essay. The challenge has been to select a pivotal moment from each text and movie combination which will illuminate just what I aim to communicate with my students. Some students will not take these tools seriously, even if they use them well for assignments and discussions. But as with the development of any skill, repeating the action over and over again might just make it stick.

The Sun Also Rises

There are many approaches to Jake Barnes and his friends.[4] But, however one interprets it, there can be general agreement that it is fundamentally a story about values (Stoneback 103–4). This is made clear in the famous "values scene" involving Brett, Jake, and Count Mippipopolous. Hemingway's careful navigation of dialogue and unspoken tensions force readers to think for themselves. What does the Count mean when he says, "You must get to know the values" (50)? Whatever he means, this single utterance propels Jake through the rest of his pilgrimage, coloring the relationship of Montoya to his American friend, as well as shaping the important scene of Jake's prayer in Pamplona (78). Without this scene, much of Hemingway's moral claims, especially about the nature of relationships, would be impossible to navigate. After all, some people have "being a bitch" instead of God, while other have God "quite a lot" (197). Such a scene would surely play an important role in film adaptation of this seminal American novel.

So how does the movie shape up compared with the key scene described? If one looks only at the values scene, the viewer might readily surmise that the film adaptation is some entirely independent work that happens to have characters of the same names. Coming off a flashback, which is not in the novel in the same way as King portrays it, Jake, Brett, and the Count find themselves in a mess of a scene. The Count is far from the boisterous, lovable figure found in the novel, appearing for a touch more than three minutes in Jake's apartment (compared with the seven pages of conversation of the novel: 43–50). Never once do the characters even use the word *values!* And this singular omission undermines any moral development for the rest of Jake's journey. Praying in Pamplona becomes Brett's business, not Jake's. Brett's notion "to behave decently again" replaces the original story's "being a bitch" (2:08:30). King omits Jake's moral transformation entirely, and replaces it with a subtle ethical choice by Brett. This leaves many students often scratching their heads, asking "why?"

Though the movie is a letdown and confirms much of Aristotle's criticisms, it is not a total loss. King's aims, focused clearly on a redemptive view of Jake and Brett, are made clear in this scene and accentuate later moments that differ from the novel. Thus, the movie fails on an interpretive level more than an aesthetic one. This is an excellent place to go back to Aristotle, highlighting the value he places on diction (38–39). By altering the speech of the characters in this fashion, King guts the scene of its moral import, which he fails to replace with anything of similar value. It digresses into a sappy moment of unsatisfied romance, replacing a transcendent notion of love with a subpar earthly notion built around wanting what one cannot have. Hemingway's novel does not advocate a departure from the physical but recognizes the role the metaphysical plays in the life of any character. King's film misses this, and his changes to the action and speech of the characters show how his vision falls short. If only he knew his Aristotle!

The Macomber Affair

Another prime example is Hemingway's great short story "The Short, Happy Life of Francis Macomber."[5] The tale begs to be adapted to the big screen, containing all of the elements that make for a Hollywood success. It is undoubtedly some of Hemingway's best action writing and manages to avoid the sort of spectacle that Aristotle loathed. Beyond that, the story of Francis Macomber acts as a sort of moral guidebook. It suggests that even with the competing values systems of the hunters, the native trackers, and the American elite, there is a commonality among them that transcends particular actions. Key to this development is the conversation between Macomber and Wilson in the early part of the story (9–12). Though it establishes that Francis Macomber is a coward, it also invites the reader into his remorse, his grief, his fear. Even Robert Wilson, whose observations create a framework for the reader, struggles to fully understand Macomber. The scene ends with Margot's return, but not before Wilson notices how Macomber's blue eyes revealed his "hurt" over the lion (12). With the reappearance of his wife, though, the moment of masculine humility is over. This scene, and how it is interpreted, colors the rest of the story and tends to push readers toward a conclusion about Mrs. Macomber's fatal shot (27). Through a combination of thought and dialogue, key elements in Aristotle's theory, Hemingway puts the reader into a position of evaluation: either Francis Macomber is a worthwhile human being or he is not. And the reader has to figure it out. The film, however, takes a more aggressive approach.

Most students will express skepticism simply at the title of the film adaptation. *The Macomber Affair* removes all doubt about the focus of tension in the film and subsequently warns the intuitive reader that Hemingway's point did not affect the director's interpretation as much as one might have hoped. Consider the same scene after Margot's departure to her tent. Instead of continuing to talk with Wilson, revealing the conflict Macomber feels over his actions through his remorse and subsequent gratitude to the white hunter, director Zoltan Korda stages a fight scene. Macomber brutally abuses a servant boy, and then the gunbearer, Kongoni, taking all of his pent-up anger out on two innocent bystanders (48:20–49:00). Even Gregory Peck (as Robert Wilson) gets in a couple of good licks before the moment is over. Students commonly cringe through this scene, sometimes even vocalizing their shock at the departure from the original material. Korda's shift suggests a focus on action rather than diction, in line with Aristotle's theory. But this action creates spectacle, not plot movement. Turning Macomber into an egotistical jerk hardly constitutes improving on such a concise chronicle.

Unlike *The Sun Also Rises*, this film primarily serves as a caution to future filmmakers. While the flaws of King's movie relate to interpretive issues, Korda's problems stem from a failure to grasp the text and its moral importance. And when that moral meaning is ignored, or so misunderstood as to be left out, the only way to fill the visual space is with spectacle. Despite the claim that the film adheres closely to the source material, Korda's focus on the action and emotional spectacle forces him to add unnecessary scenes.[6] Hemingway's story is the life of a man from birth to death, even if that life is a short one. These archetypal notions resonate with *Oedipus Rex* and *The Bacchae,* exploring how an individual's development and change brings danger and discord. But Korda's film comes across more like an embarrassing satyr play, reducing human virtues to an adulterous affair and a nonsensical sacrificial moment. When Margot Macomber walks out of the final scene, her departure is not met with the same sort of applause that one expects at the closing of *Casablanca.*

Conclusion

Bearing in mind that "what you see beyond" only goes beyond "when you know," films create a tricky situation (Hemingway, *Selected Letters* 780). The temptation of the teacher is to give the student everything, from background context to editorial disputes, controversies, writer involvement, and more. But this often hampers the student's ability to genuinely assess the film. For every film I offer I use in class, I aim for the student to answer a single question: "Does this film offer a valid, or even better, interpretation of the written source's story?" Aristotle's theory is wonderfully built for inquiry because it does not demand the viewer know the author's intentions or cultural context. All that is necessary is to understand the parts of the story. And if a student can do that, then their interpretive skills will take them far beyond the American literature classroom.

Appendix: Discussion Questions

I suggest using a two step-approach when prepping students to watch *The Sun Also Rises* and *The Macomber Affair*: first, assess the students' understanding of the written work (through a quiz or discussion), and second, go through a list of questions for the students to consider as they watch the film. The questions might be reviewed aloud or simply given as a handout at the start of the movie. Though there is something to be said for taking a film as it is, without any prep work before viewing, the nature of using the films in this way means that a teacher ought to help students orient their minds. If they approach these films as if they were going to see a Michael Bay film in IMAX, it is doubtful that any positive moral formation will take place. The sample questions found below reflect some of the additional themes that are covered in the classroom, even if they aren't mentioned in the essay per se.

The Sun Also Rises
1. Contrast the opening narrations from the film and the movie. How is the narrative affected by the shift from opening on Robert Cohn and opening on Paris?
2. How does the novel shift the focus away from the title-bearing epigraph toward the quote from Stein? Why do you think King does this?
3. In the novel, Jake tells Georgette that he is "sick," but in the movie he tells her that he was "hurt in the war." How does this change the dynamic between them?
4. Throughout the film, World War I plays a large part in the changes the director makes. How does this affect Jake's portrayal? Is it true to the spirit of the novel?
5. How does the jump from Paris to Spain redirect the plot of the story in the film? Does the initial arrival in Pamplona and subsequent ride to Burguete seem necessary to Hemingway's story?
6. Mike Campbell does not appear in the film until marker 53:15 (and he is noticeably not Scottish). Yet, Hemingway considered Flynn's portrayal the highlight of the film. Does this hold true in your experience? Explain, remembering what Aristotle says about characters.
7. How does the scene with Mike's lost check add to Flynn's portrayal?
8. Why does King have Robert leave only after Romero passes out, leaving out the proud threat found in the book?
9. The only time Jake enters a church in the movie is when he follows Brett in and watches her while see prays. How does this make both of their characters different than in Hemingway's novel?
10. By the end of the film, everything has been fixed. Jake and Robert are friends again. Mike repents of his bad behavior. Montoya forgives Jake for his friends. Brett and Jake even ride off into the sunset (sunrise?) together. Is the movie then a tragedy, like the book, or a comedy?

"The Short, Happy Life of Francis Macomber" and *The Macomber Affair*
1. The movie begins with the end of the story. How does this tilt the viewer toward a certain understanding of Robert Wilson and Margot Macomber? Remember the importance of in media res to both Hemingway and Aristotle.
2. How does the reporter's presence at the airport create a sense of sympathy for Margot Macomber?

3. Peck portrays Wilson as in love with Mrs. Macomber. How does this change the moral code that Hemingway ascribes to white hunters?
4. When Francis Macomber and Robert Wilson first meet, Wilson warns against bringing Mrs. Macomber. Does this foreshadowing work, given that there is no real "reveal" anymore?
5. The film includes far more scenes with animals, and of more variety, than what is found in the story. Does this add to the moral dimension of hunting and ecological concerns?
6. Is there a significant difference between watching Macomber bolt like a rabbit and reading about it? Is this an example of spectacle or character?
7. Why does the director include the scene showing Mrs. Macomber's target practice?
8. How does Mrs. Macomber's declaration, "I hate you," change the final conversation with her husband? Why do you think Hemingway eschews such blatant statements in the story?
9. Mrs. Macomber gives the appearance of self-sacrifice. Does the film portray her as a stronger or weaker character than the story version? How does this affect the story?
10. *The Macomber Affair* focuses more on Wilson than on Macomber. At the end of the film, do you think this makes for a better story? Why or why not?

Notes

1. I give students a brief overview of the life of Sophocles so that they understand Aristotle's comments better. Due it's accessibility, I often have them read Griffith and Most.

2. Though the idea of tragedy is sometimes treated as dependent on the fall of the primary character, Aristotle's work is descriptive rather than prescriptive. *Oedipus Rex* might represent the perfectly executed tragedy, but not all tragedies are *Oedipus Rex*. If the key aspect for understanding the tragic is the fall of the moral center, then something such as *Alcestis* or *The Eumenides* misses the mark by a wide margin. That does not seem what Aristotle has in mind, which I suggest means some other criteria marks the tragic story (namely, Aristotle's earliest standard, the portrayal of humanity as better than they are in reality). See Halliwell's translation of the *Poetics*, 32–33.

3. There are many good translations out there that make the *Poetics* accessible to students. The one I find best for those who have little to no experience with literary theory is Leon Golden's edition, which is, unfortunately, sometimes hard to find. If your students must acquire their own books, I suggest using the Stephen Halliwell translation, which I have used throughout this essay.

4. King's film is easy to come by, available in physical DVD formats and digital as well. The 1984 version, by James Goldstone, is almost impossible to find. And that is probably for the best.

5. It can be a challenge to find a copy of this movie. Amazon and eBay sometimes have the DVD for sale from a third party, but the price can range anywhere from $15 to $50.

6. Gene Phillips argues that the movie adaptation is "by and large a serious and faithful rendition of the story," adding that given the length of the source material, the screenplay needed to be changed to meet length requirements (96–98). Even if timing is the issue, which seems dubious, the significant alterations of actions and dialogue certainly disqualify the movie from the "faithful rendition" category.

Works Cited

Aristotle. *The Poetics of Aristotle*. Translated by Stephen Halliwell, U of North Carolina P, 1987.

———. *Poetics: A Translation and Commentary for Students of Literature*. Translated by Leon Golden, commentary by O. B. Hardison Jr., UP of Florida, 1982.

Gadamer, Hans-George. *Truth and Method*. 1975. Translated by Joel Weinsheimer and Donald G. Marshall, Bloomsbury Academic, 2013.

Griffith, Mark, and Glenn Most. "Introduction to Sophocles," in *Sophocles I: Antigone, Oedipus the King, Oedipus at Colonus*. 3rd. ed. U of Chicago P, 2013, pp. 1–4.

Hemingway, Ernest. *Death in the Afternoon*. 1932. Scribner's, 1995.

———. *Selected Letters: 1917–1961*. Edited by Carlos Baker, Scribner's, 1981.

———. "The Short, Happy Life of Francis Macomber." *The Complete Short Stories of Ernest Hemingway: The Finca Vigía Edition*. Scribner's, 1987, pp. 5–28.

———. *The Sun Also Rises: The Hemingway Library Edition*. Edited by Seán Hemingway, Scribner, 2014.

MacIntyre, Alasdair. *After Virtue: A Study in Moral Theory*. 1981. U of Notre Dame P, 2007.

The Macomber Affair. Dir. Zoltan Korda. Perf. Joan Bennett, Reginald Denny, Jean Gillie, Gregory Peck, Robert Preston. United Films, 1947. Film.

Phillips, Gene D. *Hemingway and Film*. Frederick Ungar, 1980.

Stoneback, H. R. *Reading Hemingway's* The Sun Also Rises: *A Glossary and Commentary*. Kent State UP, 2007.

The Sun Also Rises. Dir. Henry King. Perf. Eddie Albert, Mel Ferrer, Errol Flynn, Eva Gardner, Tyrone Power, 20th Century Fox, 1957. Film.

Part II

The Middle Years

A Thrice-Told Tale

To Have and Have Not and Adaptation Studies

Kirk Curnutt

Between 1944 and 1958, Hollywood produced three versions of Hemingway's fourth novel, *To Have and Have Not* (1937), that could hardly depart more from their source material or differ from one another.[1] Tinsel Town's interest in this hard-boiled proletarian tale of a Key West charter boat captain–turned–rum-runner/human smuggler named Harry Morgan who is crushed economically by the Great Depression and ensnared in Cuban political upheaval is all the more striking for a specific reason: *To Have and Have Not* is considered one of the two worst novels the writer published in his lifetime. (Only *Across the River and into the Trees* [1950], which, as I write this in 2022, is just now enjoying its first silver-screen adaptation, is drubbed as routinely and as fervently.) Nearly sixty-five years after its final studio film version tanked at the box office, *To Have and Have Not* continues to hold the record for the most major-studio adaptations of any Hemingway work. *A Farewell to Arms* (1929) was twice filmed for the cinema, first in 1932 and then in 1957, while *The Sun Also Rises* (1926) was the subject of another (1957) adaptation and a two-part 1984 television broadcast. Among the myriad Hemingway works that have made it to the screen, whether fondly remembered (*For Whom the Bell Tolls* [1943]), tepidly received (*Islands in the Stream* [1977]), or quickly forgotten (*The Garden of Eden* [2008]), only the 1946 and 1964 adaptations of the 1927 short story "The Killers" (*Collected Short Stories* 215–22) approach Hollywood's three versions of *To Have and Have Not* for how broadly they depart from their inspiration.[2]

Compounding the curiosity of this cinematic attraction to a less-than-favorably remembered novel is that all three versions have complicated, if not checkered, production and reception histories. The initial two adaptations are mainly discussed for their places in their makers' oeuvres. The first and lone version to retain Hemingway's title, directed by Howard Hawks and distributed by Warner Bros., was a major moneymaker in 1944–45, despite receiving mixed-to-negative reviews. Today it is remembered mostly for its star power. It marked the first onscreen pairing of Humphrey Bogart and Lauren Bacall, whose erotic chemistry is so potent it overpowers the plot and turns Hemingway's gritty tone into sexy melodrama. Also ensuring critical interest in it is the fact that William Faulkner cowrote the screenplay (extensively revising original drafts by Jules Furthman), thus offering an irresistible example for critics to plumb how novelists turn their talents to screenwriting. Hawks scholars generally rank *To Have and Have Not* somewhere in the upper third of the director-producer's filmography, far above his first Faulkner collaboration, *Today We Live* (1933), but far below the quintessential 1940s efforts that surround it, including *His Girl Friday* (1940) and *The Big Sleep* (1946), the latter of which also features a script coauthored by Faulkner.[3] Yet, the movie is also widely viewed as a poor man's *Casablanca* (1942) for its pragmatic decision to eschew Hemingway's shoot-'em-up storyline and Gulf of Mexico setting to borrow shamelessly from the patriotic plot and tone of Bogart's most famous classic.

Through an odd coincidence, the second version of *To Have and Have Not*, *The Breaking Point* (1950), was directed by Michael Curtiz, who just happened to have lensed *Casablanca*, thus ensuring further comparison to that landmark movie. While most critics consider this version superior to Hawks's, for more than a half-century, *The Breaking Point* was mostly known as a "lost" classic rather than a film-buff favorite. That is because in the months before it was to have enjoyed a wide, heavily promoted release by Warner Bros., its star, John Garfield, was slandered as a Communist sympathizer, and the studio, fearing scandal, let movie flop in theaters before burying it deep in its vault (Johnston 112). Only since the mid-2000s has it even become available to most viewers, thanks to film-festival revivals and a well-researched and annotated DVD release in the celebrated Criterion Collection.

The third version, dubbed *The Gun Runners,* is often dismissed as a generic B-movie with little to recommend it—I note that my colleague James Plath, in the essay that follows this one, says it is "has been so panned that it's not recommended for classroom use." When *The Gun Runners* does garner discussion, it is usually because its director, Don Siegel, helmed the 1964 version of *The Killers* (and the first *Dirty Harry,* seven years after that).[4] The film also garners attention because it was the first (albeit humbly inauspicious) release from what became the behemoth Seven Arts Productions company, an independent producer that by the late 1960s was so prolific and profitable it acquired a controlling interest in Warner Bros. from no less than the studio's legendarily tyrannical chieftain, Jack Warner. (This is why late 1960s classics such as Steve McQueen's *Bullitt* are billed as Warner Bros.–Seven Arts Productions.) Otherwise, *The Gun Runners* is remembered mostly as a vehicle for the often-leaden acting of World War II hero–turned–movie star Audie Murphy and a scene-stealing villain turn by Eddie Albert, the venerable character actor who had portrayed Bill Gorton in the 1957 adaptation of *The Sun Also Rises* and would later find a profitable niche in such television escapism as *Green Acres, Switch,* and *Falcon Crest*.[5] This final version has not been—and probably will not be—the beneficiary of a handsome Criterion Collection edition.

For the past few years, I have employed these three versions in my introductory creative writing class to initiate students into adaptation studies. About a decade ago, aspiring authors at Troy University began asking me to incorporate screenwriting into our syllabus, eager to learn about the medium with which, for better or worse, they are more familiar and inclined toward than print. For a while I resisted these entreaties, insistent that because most novices are insufficiently familiar with the technical vocabulary of fiction, they needed to focus first on discerning the nuances of free, indirect discourse; second-person storytelling; "camera-eye" objectivity; and other forms of narrative perspective before tackling a whole other artistic genre with its own vocabulary. As I worked to complete a 2017 reader's guide to *To Have and Have Not* that included an appendix on the three adaptations, however, I reconsidered my reluctance, seeing in these wildly different films a potential heuristic for recognizing how characters and plot sequences can be extracted from a novel or story and completely transformed by recontextualizing them in another. I won't say the two weeks of class time we devote to this exercise transforms students wary of Hemingway's reputation for pugnacity and He-Man truculence into lifelong fans; nor does it soften my conviction that these movies are all three flawed in sometimes beguiling, sometimes baffling ways that have less to do with their regard (or lack thereof) for the novel than to the challenges and compromises each production faced as it reconfigured a text contrived to protest the perilous economic situation of 1937 into its own political time. What the experiment accomplishes is to teach the students that no theme or plot exists solely within the formalist world a film creates on the screen. Rather, a screenplay—as is true of any text—always allegorizes its own era. Encouraging beginning writers to think about this can help them appreciate the implications of any characterological or plot choice they might make.

As a theoretical framework for this exercise, I offer classes a quick primer on adaptation studies. At first students find the concepts we go over frustrating and confusing—not because the criticism isn't accessible but because it unsettles many of the uninterrogated assumptions they have about the relationship between a literary text and its film version. As I try to reassure them, scholars who write in the discipline share their disconcertment. Only in the past fifteen years or so has adaptation studies developed into a theoretically rigorous and creative field. Indeed, one of the first things I like to do when discussing how literary narratives transmute when translated from page to screen is to assign students Thomas M. Leitch's 2003 essay "Twelve Fallacies in Contemporary Adaptation Theory," a rallying cry for redefining the relationship between literature and film that helped advance the field by inspiring such subsequent efforts such as Christa Albrecht-Crane and Dennis Ray Cutchins's *Adaptation Studies: New Approaches* (2010), Yvonne Griggs's *Bloomsbury Guide to Adaptation Studies* (2016), and Leitch's own *Oxford Handbook of Adaptation Studies* (2017), to name but three.

After considering Leitch's fallacies, students find many of their ingrained measures and indicators for evaluating adaptations rewired. For starters, they begin to question the host–parasite relationship between the source material and the adaptation, which privileges the former as "original" and the latter as derivative. As Leitch writes, "It is much easier to dismiss adaptations as inevitably blurred mechanical reproductions of art than to grapple with thorny questions of just what constitutes originality" (16). As an example of how we interrogate this notion of originality, I make the case to classes that *To Have and Have Not* is arguably the least innovative or groundbreaking of Hemingway's fiction in terms of authorial invention: rather than break with the norms of, say, war literature or domestic realism as canonical efforts from the 1920s such as *In Our Time* (1925) radically did, this novel so overtly mixes two popular genres of the 1930s—proletarian literature and pulp fiction—that the narrative conventions and styles of each are readily identifiable. As I suggest to students, this obeisance to genre may render the text less unique or singular, but it affords adapters far more freedom in terms of fusing other elements of protest and noir traditions, whether in literature or film. From this perspective, once we jettison the often knee-jerk inclination to declare "the book is always better"—a claim for which *To Have and Have Not* sets a fairly low bar—we can more fully appreciate correspondences between literary fiction and a film adaptation as intertexts rather alterations that, no matter to what degree they change the initial iteration, need not be appraised as an outgrowth or a byproduct of the text on which they are based.

The critical reputation of *To Have and Have Not* actually helps underscore the need to question this scholarly tendency to favor literary forms over cinematic ones, a prejudice that seems almost inevitable when critics approach the subject as specialists in a specific author such as Hemingway. At best, one can argue that *To Have and Have Not* is really a novel only in name; at worst, one can dismiss it as an inchoate hodgepodge. Rather than invent a storyline unified by a distinct beginning, middle, and end, Hemingway, feeling pressured to produce a novel almost seven years after the blockbuster success of *A Farewell to Arms,* infamously compiled two previously published short stories alongside a third section that was hastily conceived and poorly executed. Part one, subtitled "Spring," was first published in *Cosmopolitan* as "One Trip Across" in April 1934 (20–23, 108–22). In it, Harry Morgan survives a shootout in Havana between a dictator's assassin squad and violent revolutionaries, gets ripped off by a tourist, kills a Chinese smuggler paying him to dump a boatload of undocumented immigrants at sea, and then must decide whether his alcoholic first mate, Eddie, can keep the murder secret or whether Harry must dispose of him too. (The story ends inconclusively on that question). In part two ("Fall"), which appeared in *Esquire* in February 1936 as "The Tradesman's Return" (27, 193–96), Harry and another mate, Wesley, have to dump a cargo of illegal booze off the Key West coast after a gun battle with Cuban police that costs Harry his arm, while their boat is pursued by an ambitious federal agent. In the third part ("Winter"), which Hemingway failed to sell as a short story to either *Cosmopolitan* or *Esquire,* a destitute Harry is pressured into running Cuban terrorists back to Havana after they rob a Key West bank to fund their revolution. Both he and his new mate, Albert Tracy, die in the process while rich tourists frivolously cavort across the island, oblivious to the plight of the working class whose labor serves their inanity. Needless to say, there is a lot of plot in *To Have and Have Not* that can't be packed into a single film's two-hour running time.

Students thus understand immediately that Hawks and the producers that followed (Jerry Wald for *The Breaking Point* and Clarence Greene and Herbert E. Stewart for *The Gun Runners*) needed some principle of selection to determine which plot strands might make for the best possible movie, both aesthetically and commercially. A useful first step for this exercise, then, is to invite classes to imagine they are screenwriting teams tasked with winnowing down Hemingway's profusive storylines and characters, much as Furthman first and then Faulkner were between 1942 and 1944, as Ranald MacDougall was in 1950, and as Daniel Mainwaring and Paul Monash in 1958 (although the latter duo had the benefit of working from an intermediary treatment by the then sexagenarian Ben Hecht, whose prolific career was in the process of winding down).

Requiring the students to work in teams is a way to emphasize filmmaking's collaborative nature. As we discuss, a fiction writer might produce a story or novel with little editorial input from a publishing company; one can say with certainty that *To Have and Have Not* could have benefited with more rigorous feedback in 1937 from Maxwell Perkins at Scribner's. Yet not even the most celebrated film auteur—a Martin Scorsese or a Quentin Tarantino, or a Howard Hawks, as we shall see—can exert total control over a production. Over the past two years, I have emphasized the collaborative aspect even more by having half of the class pretend they're members of a writers' room plotting the arc of a twelve-episode Netflix or HBOMax limited series instead of a two-hour movie. Students are often far less hesitant to debate the dramatic efficacy and cultural consequences of *potential* plot threads than they are the first drafts of fiction that they might individually bring to traditional creative-writing workshop sessions for peer evaluation.

As a prerequisite for the exercise, I naturally require students to read *To Have and Have Not* in all its 256-page glory. I doubt I will shock Hemingway aficionados by reporting that almost to a one they loathe it. Even English majors who want to identify with *The Sun Also Rises* or who appreciate the dramatic power of "Indian Camp" (*Collected Short Stories* 65–70) or the adroit switches of narrative perspective in "The Short Happy Life of Francis Macomber" (*Collected Short Stories* 5–28), right down to the lion's point of view, intensely dislike the novel. Part of their antipathy has to do with the rampant racial slurs against African Americans (seventy-nine uses of the *N*-word, by my count), Afro-Cubans, and Chinese peoples, not to mention the frequently deployed *bitch* to label female characters. The "One Trip Across" section is *To Have and Have Not*'s strongest, a self-contained masterpiece of suspense, but its background of the 1933 Cuban revolution, which unseated dictator Gerado Machado and launched the country into extreme chaos that paved the way for the rise of military strongman Fulgencio Batista, is a confounding ideological quagmire, without any clear-cut good guys to distinguish from the bloodthirsty villains. The "Tradesman" portion is a solid example of Depression-era protest fiction, but the novel had barely rolled off the printing presses in 1937 before its proletarian proselytizing fell out of fashion, and its rumrunning plot already felt old-fashioned four years after the repeal of Prohibition.[6]

At first glance, the third section is most problematic. As students are quick to recognize, its seventeen chapters are riddled with redundant scenes and sometimes embarrassingly repetitive dialogue that grinds its drama to a halt. In the opening section of part 3, for example, Harry Morgan bounces back and forth between Freddy's Bar, where he is forced, out of economic desperation, to conspire with the crooked lawyer Richard "Bee-lips" Simmons to ferry the terrorists, and his house, where his wife, Marie, frets about the dangers he won't share with her as he grabs a rifle and bullets to defend himself in case the journey goes wrong. In the course of six chapters (9–15), we enter Freddy's four separate times and the Morgans' home twice for conversations that feel wholly expository (91–141, a hefty chunk of text). That isn't even to mention that the contrast between the poor and the rich that the text's title promises is disproportional: the fatuous leisure class that was supposedly the target of Hemingway's ire makes only cameo appearances that feel entirely disconnected from Harry Morgan's struggle to feed his family as a charter-boat captain. Classes are typically surprised to learn that this asymmetry was the result of extreme chopping the author undertook on his original draft in summer 1937, just months before the book's publication. Hemingway claimed he ended up with more have-nots than haves for fear that the real-life people he'd based some of the latter on would sue him for libel. More likely, he amputated his manuscript for ideological rather than legal reasons.[7]

The more important point is that *To Have and Have Not* has all the ingredients of a great action-adventure or thriller; it just has too many of them, and the book often reads as if the author simply tossed its parts into a pot and cranked the stovetop to boil (as if that were the simple recipe for a potboiler!). As one film fan in a class put it, gleefully mixing her sports metaphors, the novel should have been a home run, but Hemingway punted. For many students, the idea that a "bad" or botched novel would ever inspire a Hollywood adaptation is bemusing. "Why bother?" and "What's the point?" are often the responses I receive after we review the novel's composition history.

To these replies, I offer an anecdote that Howard Hawks first shared with film historian Bruce F. Kawin in 1976, which quickly became film-studies lore. In

1939 Hawks and Hemingway were supposedly fishing together when, frustrated by the author's dismissive attitude toward Hollywood, the director defended his medium by insisting he could "make a [good] picture of your worst story . . . that god damned bunch of junk called *To Have and To Have Not*," a boast that seems even more audacious when one realizes Hawks couldn't be bothered to cite the title correctly (5–16). The claim reverses the values to which, according to Leitch, scholars trained in literature often unintentionally cling when analyzing adaptations—namely, the bias that as source material a novel *creates* while a movie version can only *imitate*. As classes evaluate *To Have and Have Not*'s mishmash of components, however, they begin to understand why producers went to the well not once, not twice, but three times: the integrants of the text can be recombined in innumerable ways to establish a throughline of plot that creates the structural unity for which Hemingway's tripartite form could never allow.

After they finish reading the novel, I ask students to whiteboard all the major plot points from the three sections, from the opening shoot-out in Havana all the way to the closing monologue of Harry Morgan's now widowed wife, Marie, left alone to raise their three daughters. Then I have each writing team separately pick the plot threads they believe can make for an exciting movie or limited-run series (without, for the moment, sharing their choices with other groups). Strikingly, as they soon discover after watching the three adaptations, they by and large zero in on the same parts the various screenwriters did decades ago. Although none of the Hollywood versions bother with the hero's amputation after the events of "Tradesman," students *love* the idea of a one-armed boat captain for a hero, recognizing, as Susan F. Beegel has documented, that Harry Morgan's lost limb links him to a long tradition of pirates, both historical and fictional, which seems perfectly suited to Key West's reputation for tropical corruption and lawlessness (107–28). They like the moral choice Harry must make between feeding and housing his family and breaking the law. And they like the relationship between Harry and Marie—although the bedroom scene in chapter 12, in which the husband, it is implied, uses the nub of his amputated arm to bring his wife to orgasm grosses them out (114). They appreciate the potential suspense that a smuggling story can generate, but they tend to shy away from the idea that even a hard-boiled hero would outright kill a villain like Mr. Sing to steal his money, as Harry does in the "One Trip Across" section (53–54). Quite often when asked which scene most strikes them as comparable to a movie they zero in on part 3's chapter 18, the single longest section (151–75). Here, the Cuban revolutionaries mow down Harry's first mate, Albert, in a hail of machine-gun fire and force "Cappy" (as they call Harry) to carry them to sea as their getaway driver. Once in international waters, Harry confronts the terrorists in a grippingly staged shootout that leaves them dead but Harry mortally wounded. "That would make a great movie," many of the students agree. They are not surprised, then, to discover that two of the three adaptations—*The Breaking Point* and *The Gun Runners*—climax with the shootout.[8]

As students select the plot elements they will arrange into the outline for a treatment, I discourage them from yet identifying their bank robbers or terrorists with a specific location or a political motive for the crime. They only learn the reason for this prohibition after they construct their story arcs, when I finally invite them to watch the three adaptations. Whether they binge them consecutively or spread them out over a weekend, they are typically surprised to discover how the plot strands remain so recognizable despite the adaptations being set in geographically varied locations. Hawks's *To Have and Have Not* shifts the action from Havana to the island of Martinique, one of the lesser Antilles and an overseas department of France, where the conflict is no longer between Machado's repressive regime and revolutionaries but between the Nazi-installed Vichy government and the French resistance. As if that political context did not echo *Casablanca* enough, the script calls for Harry to smuggle freedom fighter Paul de Bursac and his wife, Hélène, onto the island to launch a daring plan to free an ally from Devil's Island—about as blatant a lift of the former film's Victor Lazlo subplot as one might imagine.

The Breaking Point relocates its action to Southern California and substitutes Mexico for Cuba. This version is the only one to retain the Chinese smuggling plot with Mr. Sing (although Furthman also included it in his first draft for Hawks; for reasons I don't yet reveal to students, it was junked). Mr. Sing's inclusion, however, has the curious effect of bifurcating the script: the Bee-lips inspired lawyer, here named Duncan, first pressures Harry into the smuggling deal, then, upon hearing that the body of an unidentified Chinese man has washed ashore, blackmails the captain into supplying his boat as a getaway for a gang of thieves who rob the daily take of a local racetrack. The dual crime scenes supply credible causality to advance the plot, explaining why Harry allows himself to become an accessory to the heist, but they don't do much for the development of his character. Once the captain is inveigled in the robbery, Mr. Sing is never again mentioned, and Harry seems to have little anxiety about whether the authorities might pin the murder on him. As for *The Gun Runners,* it is the only adaptation that maintains the Key West–Cuba nexus (although it was filmed in California), but it contemporizes the conflict. The script is frustratingly light on particulars, but the revolution at hand is Castro's revolt against Batista, not the fall of Machado.[9]

I often devote an entire class session to mapping the differences and similarities of each adaptation as a way to illustrate another fundamental fallacy that Leitch identifies. Although student opinions vary as to which movie adaptation is most aesthetically effective, almost no one makes a case that Hemingway's novel is better than any of them—including *The Gun Runners,* at least in terms of dramatic cohesion. I like to point out how ingrained the particular assumption Leitch critiques is via the second half of Hawks's anecdote about the motivation behind his *To Have and Have Not.* When the director claimed he could make a good movie out of the author's worst book, Hemingway demurred, huffing, "You can't make anything out of that novel," inspiring Hawks to suggest a whole new premise: "You've got the character of Harry Morgan; I think I can give you the wife. All you have to do is make a story about how they met" (qtd. in Kawin 16). In offering this possibility, Hawks wasn't just proposing what we would come to call a prequel—he was jettisoning the very idea that fidelity to a novel should have any bearing on how we evaluate the adaption. To Leitch, fidelity is "a hopelessly fallacious measure of value because it is unattainable, undesirable, and theoretically possible only in a trivial sense. Like translations to a new language, an adaptation will always reveal their source's superiority because, whatever their faults, the source texts will always be better at being themselves" (160). The minute we ask how closely an adaptation follows the original, the privilege of "anteriority" dooms the film in question to pay tribute or homage to the novel as a precursor.

As a result, we as critical viewers may find ourselves lured unconsciously into the position of measuring the quality of an adaptation according to how it respects its umbilical connection to the source material, of asking whether a film is "any good" as a "preliminary, precondition, or a substitute for asking how [a script] works" within the logic of its own dramatic premises and necessities. We scholars may assume we are too discerning to fall into the trap of relying on fidelity to shape our expectations of a movie adaptation, but when I challenge them to list adaptations better than the text, students are often intrigued to find they generally struggle. They can name any number of movies that don't capture the power or beauty of their inspiration, but when I offer examples of films that are *more famous* that their source material, they often admit they didn't even know those works were originally novels. My favorite recent example is Walt Disney's *Bambi* (1942); few students today have ever heard of Felix Salten's 1923 novel, first translated into English in 1928 by the same Whittaker Chambers who twenty years later would later denounce government official Alger Hiss as a Communist, help propel Richard M. Nixon into the national spotlight, and usher in the McCarthy Red Scare. Even after a recent spate of reassessments after Salten's German-language original entered the public domain, they remain unaware of the book (Schulz).

While rejecting fidelity offers classes more freedom to assemble their plot parts, I nevertheless impart the reality that their prospective movie or series will still have to acknowledge its source material in some way—or, rather, acknowledge Hemingway as the author of *To Have and Have Not*. The reason has less to do with copyright—although we certainly explore the legal necessities of securing rights—than with branding. If there is any appeal to a new adaptation of the novel, it will almost certainly arise more from the ongoing reverence for the Hemingway legend than from any fond memories of the book. The two parallels we draw in class are to Jane Austen and to Stephen King. Perhaps the only thing these popular authors share is the value of their names as brands. Adaptations of their novels are guaranteed to draw the attention of their fervent fan bases, regardless of the marquee value of a cast or any auteur who imposes his artistic vision on a movie.

We thus spend further discussion time noting that all three *To Have and Have Not* adaptations are products of a period in which Hollywood regarded the Hemingway name as a box-office draw and centered much of its publicity efforts on his public image. As Mimi Reisel Gladstein has noted, the trailer for Hawks's version trumpets the novelist's "public persona" as "soldier of fortune" and "guide to an invigorating world of excitement" far more than it plugs Hawks's filmography or even the presence of Bogart and Bacall. Students often chuckle at what seems the irrevocably corny staging of the coming attraction, which features a spinning globe flashing "the locations for the most popular settings of Hemingway's novels and stories"—Spain, Italy, Africa, and France—with a typewriter superimposed on it, culminating in the declaration, "Ernest Hemingway takes you to the danger zone of the mid-Atlantic." As students recognize, this tagline borders on false advertising, for it implies that Hemingway had some voice in the movie (173).

This foregrounding of the author's name epitomizes another of the pitfalls of adaptation that Leitch argues literary critics ignore. Not only do source texts often distract attention from the internal requisites by which an adaptation must create its own dramatic logic and coherence, but "adaptations of the works of famous and prolific novelists are customarily measured not only against the novels they explicitly adapt but against the distinctive world or style or tone associated with the author in general" (164). In this regard, my creative writing teams are required to spend some time deciding what Hemingway "values" their versions of *To Have and Have Not* will promote. Many of them rightly catch that Hawks's film, despite its association with film noir (as James Plath also explores in his essay in this volume), isn't particularly Hemingwayesque, at least not as they picture his "distinctive world." The erotic electricity between Bogart and Bacall is nowhere to be found in the book, for example. Although Hemingway's dialogue crackles with hard-boiled repartee, none of Harry and Marie's conversations come anywhere close to the seductive innuendo of the first adaptation's most famous line, in which Marie tells Harry (or "Steve," as she insists on nicknaming him, an inside joke between Hawks and his wife): "You know how to whistle, don't you? . . . You just put your lips together and blow" (qtd. in Kawin 120).[10]

Hawks wrote this line specifically for Bacall's January 1944 screen test, uncertain whether the nineteen-year-old fashion model, who had never before acted, could carry a costarring role, especially alongside a major screen presence like Bogart. About as close as the Morgans come in Hemingway's text to the sensuality of the first adaptation is in their cringeworthy sex scene, in which Marie playfully asks, "Who's the best you ever did it with?" to which her spouse succinctly responds, "You" (113). In other words, their pairing generates little sizzle. Given Harry's taciturnity, I find students require a great deal of convincing that Hemingway meant for the Morgans' marriage to be recognized a loving, mutually supportive one, at least when compared to those of such "have" couples in the text as Richard and Helen Gordon. The core scene between that pair—a posturing, philandering writer and his bitter, also adulterous bride—quickly degenerates into proto–*Who's Afraid of Virginia Woolf* insults and recriminations over their connubial misery (182–92). All three sets of filmmakers were wise to avoid bringing the Gordons into the action, for the bourgeois discontent and hypocrisy they symbolize is all too ham-fisted and tedious in presentation.

That said, students struggle to define a purpose for Marie in their plots. Even after we discuss the novel's sympathetic portrayal of her in the penultimate chapter, a Molly Bloom–like stream-of-consciousness monologue in which she wonders how she will support her family now that her husband is dead (257–62), students remain dubious that domestic passion and devotion is truly a Hemingway value. Perhaps prejudiced by *The Sun Also Rises* and *A Farewell to Arms*, they are too accustomed to think of him as dramatizing the stoic endurance of isolated men instead of loving, if doomed, couples (such as Robert Jordan and Maria in *For Whom the Bell Tolls*).

The adaptations do little to reassure their doubts. Unlike Hawks's version, *The Breaking Point* and *The Gun Runners* offer their Marie characters, both renamed Lucy, little raison d'être other than to serve as beacons of spousal and maternal stability—as helpmates to rush home to, in other words. (Indeed, the end credits of *Runners* scroll over a shot of Patricia Owens beaming with relief as she spots her husband's ship returning to port, an image designed to reassure readers that the hero, renamed Sam Martin, survives the wound he receives in the climactic gun battle.) In both cases, these proxies for Marie are contrasted to gratuitous femme fatales clearly inspired by Hemingway's chief "have" temptress, Helène Bradley, who seduces and then ridicules the effete Richard Gordon in the novel (188–90). *The Breaking Point* devotes several scenes between Garfield's Harry and Patricia Neal's Leona Charles, a singer-cum-moll to one of his rich clients, even placing her on Harry's ship as a witness to Mr. Sing's murder. The point of her presence is never really clarified, however. It may be that screenwriter MacDougall invented her to serve as a "working girl" counterpart to Harry's charter-boat captain—both are employed at the whim of the rich—but in embodying illicit allure she seems something of a contradiction to Harry's dilemma: he is forced into crime by economic need, after all, not tempted into it. As Nathan Holmes notes, the most interesting scene featuring Leona is set in the movie's version of Freddy's Bar (dubbed Christian's Hut) when Phyllis Thaxter's Lucy Morgan unexpectedly arrives to intercept a flirtation between her husband and Leona. Summoning her there is none other than the establishment's bartender, who fears an inebriated Harry will violate his marriage vows. As Holmes writes, Lucy's arrival "punctures" the hard-boiled world that bars both here and in noir in general represent: "The domestic and cultural commitments [Lucy] represents unravel the bar's role as a counterdomestic world of its own. The fact that the bartender has called Lucy pulls the space out of the urban anonymity that marks most noir drinking establishments, placing it back in the realm of neighborly concern" (118). *The Breaking Point* may be unusual in this regard by emphasizing Harry's commitment to his family (far more so than the novel does), but that doesn't negate the fact that both Lucy and Leona are present mainly to shape Harry's heroic trajectory, not as agents of their own narratives (or even subplots).

As for the Helène Bradley figure in *Runners,* Gita Hall's Eva (nicknamed "the Swede" in the film, in honor of Hall's nationality; Seven Arts cast her hoping to promote the starlet as a "Swedish Greta Garbo") is given even less to do. Present mainly as arm candy to Albert's wisecracking weapons merchant Hanagan, she contributes most significantly by warning Murphy's captain that he can't escape the moral consequences of the crime he is forced into ("When they buy you for something," she says, "they buy you for everything"). Students generally love Bacall in Hawks's adaptation and want their Maries to share her prominence. The challenge, as they discover, is to find a viable function for the wife figure, a challenge Hawks evaded by imagining his *To Have and Have Not* as the story of how the Morgans first met.

As we watch the trailer for Hawks's version, students giggle at the line about Hemingway taking them to the "danger zone." (A few semesters back, one student even burst into Kenny Loggins's 1986 chart-topping hit of that name, the theme song to the campily macho Tom Cruise fighter-pilot movie *Top Gun.*) When I ask why classes find the action-adventure promised in the trailer as equally foreign to Hemingway's sensibility as the sultry romance, they will say they're inclined to think of Hemingway as a "literary" writer whose craftsmanship symbolizes the modernist belief in le mot juste and dramatic understatement. Action-adventure motifs such as fight scenes and shootouts seem the very antithesis of the vaunted iceberg theory, which implies that conflict should be omitted so the drama is only subtly inferred, requiring greater reader involvement with the text to discern the "thing left out."

Their resistance only rigidifies when I show them the over-the-top theater poster for *The Gun Runners,* which features a suspiciously buff Audie Murphy cocking his shirtless torso back to swing to butt of an automatic rifle, as if preparing to knock out the teeth of the film's villain, under the legend HEMINGWAY-HOT ADVENTURE.[11] Compared to this hyperbole, the taglines for various *Breaking Point* promotional posters are exercises in restraint, claiming the action comes "SCREAMING OFF THE PAGES OF THE HEMINGWAY STORY" to make for a "HIGH POINT IN HEMINGWAY EXCITEMENT". The exploitation of the Hemingway name generally confuses students and often leaves them uncertain not only of what authorial values the hero should uphold but how to convey it. To this, I offer what they initially take as a fairly shocking suggestion:

why not include a Hemingway-like character in their cast, a writer who struggles with how best to portray the working-class characters he writes about? Because they find the Richard Gordon character superfluous to Harry Morgan's story, classes will shrug at this possibility. Yet, they grow more amenable to the option when I reveal to them, via Michael S. Reynolds's *Hemingway: The 1930s* (1996), the fourth installment of his multivolume Hemingway biography (1986–99), that Hemingway toyed with doing just that. As Reynolds reveals, drafts of the third section of *To Have and Have Not* include references to a famous writer in Key West who has sold his literary soul. Known as "the Old Slob" (Reynolds 236; Curnutt 124), the character—who never appears in a scene but is talked about at several moments—captures the author's own worries in 1936 that his leisure-oriented lifestyle of fishing, hunting, and carousing had compromised his art, an anxiety expertly captured in "The Snows of Kilimanjaro," arguably his greatest single short story (*Collected Short Stories* 39–56). Plotting out a season's worth of story arcs for a hypothetical limited series, including a Hemingway-like character in the story fills at least some teams with metafictional intrigue.

In the half-dozen or so times that I've conducted this exercise, students have invented some very clever variations that cater to contemporary action-adventure expectations. Both *To Have and Have Not* and *The Gun Runners* include Harry's drunken mate Eddy from the "One Trip Across" section, albeit for comic relief rather than for the moral quandary of whether Harry can trust him to keep the murder of Mr. Sing quiet (60–64). Most classes, however, find the alcoholic shtick performed by Walter Brennan and Everett Sloane dated and tiresome and cut the character. Taking a cue from *Runners,* in which Sloane's dipsomaniacal mate (named Harvey instead of Eddy) stows secretly aboard the hero's boat to play a pivotal role in the climactic shootout, at least two teams in different semesters have proposed that *Marie* should sneak onto the ship to make her more central to the action—an excellent suggestion, in my view. Several teams recognize that Juano Hernández's Eddy character (called Wesley) in *The Breaking Point* adds an important racial dimension to that film and believe his role in their plots deserves expanding; almost unanimously they want him to at least survive until Harry's boat is out to sea instead of dying dockside. In some cases, students like that in *Breaking Point* Wesley and Leona are both present for the murder of Mr. Sing (even if Leona's presence is only decorative) and suggest transferring that triangle to the final battle with the robber-terrorists, making both Marie and Wesley central to the choreography of the shootout. None of the teams has ever felt comfortable with the

Chinese illegal-immigrant subplot and usually suggest changing it to some kind of drug-smuggling operation. The one time a student suggested making the Mr. Sing figure a trafficker of white sex slaves, female students groaned aloud in disapproval, several citing the farfetchedness of the 2008 Liam Neeson film *Taken,* in which a former CIA agent frees his daughter from just such a kidnapping/prostitution operation. One classmate promptly regaled us with Harry Morgan's potential recitation of that movie's most famous line, in which the steely Neeson promises the lead trafficker, "I will look for you, I will find you, and I will kill you"—still a popular Internet meme.

Very few of the teams assigned to map out a self-contained thriller include any of Hemingway's "haves"—they simply don't feel that within a potential 120-page script they have time to make a Hélène Bradley figure crucial to the plot. (As some even point out, neither did Hemingway). Meanwhile, teams mapping out a whole season of a potential series see in the Bradley/Gordon characters the blueprint for an ensemble show along the lines of such recent streaming-service critical favorites as HBO's *The White Lotus* or Peacock's *The Resort.* These are shows that, much like Hemingway was attempting, contrast the dignity of service-industry workers to the banal delusions and insular woes of the wealthy tourist class, usually ascribing their angst to economic entitlement, or what we might call "affluenza."

One semester, I even experimented with requiring teams to use as their "haves" the general outlines of the characters Hemingway introduces in his chapter 24, a veritable catalog of income-inequality corruption: a gay couple in which the younger "kept" man (Henry Carpenter) is about to be cut loose by his aging benefactor (Wallace Johnston); an unnamed grain broker about to be indicted by the Internal Revenue Service; a new-money family rich from a pharmaceutical enterprise aiming to raise its aristocratic stock by marrying off a daughter to a respected member of Yale's Skull and Bones secret society; and a washed-up actress, Dorothy Hollis, who serves as a mistress to a "professional son-in-law of the very rich" (241). Quite frankly, this requirement proved an absolute disaster. Students hated trying to create backstories within the confines of Hemingway's characterological outlines. Ostensibly, their resistance arose from their insistence that the novel's critique of the rich was tinged with homophobia, sexism, and class resentment. Yet, as we talked through how we might filter out some of Hemingway's more repellant prejudices (he impugns Carpenter and Johnston's masculinity, for example, by making the first a trust-fund baby and the second a pedophile), students discovered a deeper truth about creating a dimensioned dramatis personae: it is far easier to create "likable" working-class heroes whose striving we can cheer on despite their flaws than it is to create rich people who aren't flat, cliched stereotypes. As I tell students, I suspect that for Hemingway this, too, was a central lesson learned from writing *To Have and Have Not*.

To this point, classes have designed their plots according to formalist criteria: they reorder and combine scenes, revise and revamp characters, strictly to shore up dramatic logic and avoid dreaded plot holes. Only after their basic outlines are in order do I introduce the production background responsible for the three adaptations' most obvious successes and failures. Students usually struggle, for example, to understand why *To Have and Have Not* so blatantly apes *Casablanca*, even wondering how plagiarism charges were minimized. As I inform them, Jules Furthman's initial screenplay managed to preserve far more of Hemingway's novel than subsequent adaptations, even making space for the rumrunning plot of "The Tradesman's Return," in which Harry is wounded in the arm (although not badly enough to require amputation) as well as the Mr. Sing thread (although the smuggler, renamed Mr. Kato, is not killed but rather turned over to the police). The major difference is a romantic triangle, as the Marie and Helène Bradley characters vie for Harry's affection, and a striking change in tone from Hemingway's angry defeatism: as Kawin writes, because "Hawks had a temperamental objection to stories about, as he put it, losers," he demanded that Harry not only survive but thrive after his dealings with tourists and revolutionaries (26). As he summarizes, "by the middle of February 1944, Hawks and Furthman had put together a witty and elaborate script, telling the story of how Morgan and Marie might have met, and retaining from the novel Johnson's fishing trip [the tourist who rips off Harry], Mr. Sing/Kato's alien-smuggling operation, Morgan's arm wound, and the bank robbery, together with some commentary on [Cuban dictator] Machado and the coming revolution" (30–31).

Why, then, Martinique and World War II instead of Cuba in 1933? As students are shocked to learn, nearly $1 million had already been spent on preproduction, including sets and some secondary photography, when Nelson D. Rockefeller of the Office of the Coordinator of Inter-American Affairs suddenly objected to a script that might offend an important wartime ally such as Batista. Jack Warner was on the verge of pulling the plug when Hawks, calling on Faulkner, suggested the change of location to the lesser Antilles, using anti-Vichy government material Faulkner had developed for an unproduced screenplay called "The De Gaulle Story" (Kawin 32). *To Have and Have Not* was thus the product of a hasty political compromise, with Faulkner completing scenes only days before they were shot from March to May 1944. Hawks also allowed for a great deal of on-set tinkering with lines, which further changed the serious tone to acknowledge Bogart and Bacall's burgeoning real-life romance. That the movie is cohesive and affecting despite its obvious debt to *Casablanca* is a testament to the under-the-gun creativity of its director, screenwriter (Faulkner, that is; Furthman apparently contributed little after his initial draft), and cast. Even a cursory account of the production is eye-opening for students: it reveals to them that moviemaking is a fluid, dynamic process that may begin with the page but more often comes together during filming under stressful circumstances.

Other political considerations shade the subsequent adaptations. As I tell students, Hemingway's proletarian proselytizing in part 3 would have sounded suspiciously communistic by the late 1940s as the culture geared up for the House Un-American Activities Committee investigations that would eventually derail Garfield's career. MacDougall, Curtiz, and Garfield still wanted the script to have political bite, though, and thus conceived of this second Harry Morgan as a disgruntled World War II veteran struggling to make a living during a time of unparalleled economic advancement as the war industry shifted production capabilities to consumer goods and the government invested in education. The threat Harry feels to his livelihood, with his boat on the verge of repossession and his family and community pressuring him to seek employment outside of the charter-boat industry, is thus a symbol less of the Great Depression than of the postwar shift toward white-collar professions and the corporatizing of masculinity. The irony is that Garfield's Harry cannot make a living in his chosen field at a time when the tourist industry should be thriving. As Michael Civille writes, "This notion of a localized economic recession opposes the nationwide assumptions regarding the broader spread of postwar prosperity, bringing the harsh reality of working-class struggles to the screen" (8).

The displacement makes Harry far more sympathetic to the alienation of his African American mate Wesley, who in the novel is depicted as a coward whose lack of masculine resolve is directly attributed to his race: "Ain't no nigger any good when he's shot," Hemingway's Harry grunts at one point (87). That *The Breaking Point* was written and filmed as the civil rights movement gained traction (both with Henry S. Truman's integration of the armed forces and the NAACP's initial legal challenges to *Plessy v. Ferguson*) brings into prominence the social justice subtext of the movie by portraying Harry and Wesley's families as wholly integrated and mutually supportive, as united in a community. As Civille notes, "viewers are presented with a reasonable alternative to the tradition of American discrimination in an early scene, when Wesley drops off his son so that Lucy can take him to school with the Morgan daughters. Undermining pre–*Brown v. Board of Education* assumptions about segregated schools, the kids play together before going to class, further establishing a world of interracial equality" (9). Formally, Wesley's role in the action never rises to more than that of a supporting player, yet the presence of Hernández as Wesley foregrounds the implicit sociracial theme; the actor had won acclaim a year previously for portraying Lucas Beauchamp in the 1949 film version of Faulkner's 1947 novel *Intruder in the Dust*. In this regard, Harry's efforts to protect Wesley from any involvement in the bank robbery become a metaphor for white Americans' efforts to shield African Americans from the country's long history of racial abuse and exploitation. Yet the movie also issues a stern warning about the need to maintain white and Black working-class solidarity. This clarion call is issued in its final shot, perhaps its single most famous moment: when Harry is rescued and rushed to the hospital, where he will survive only if his arm is amputated, Wesley's son stands alone on the dock in a wide-angle shot, completely ignored, his father presumably forgotten by all but him, the last image before the credits roll. As Civille concludes, "by reinvigorating Wesley's spirit in the form of his orphaned son"—an important contrast to the callousness with which his dead body is tossed overboard at sea—"the filmmakers confront a recurring domestic issue [racism] while characterizing the evolution of white labor struggles in the United States as potentially orphaning the civil rights issue. This conclusion elevates the film from a white liberal attempt at acknowledging a social issue to a visionary work that warns audiences of the difference between the pretense of ambitious reforms and lingering American realities" (14).

Given the importance of this racial subtext, then, it's unfortunate that the racetrack robbery in *The Breaking Point* is so extraneous to the movie's political concerns, at least as compared to the issues of freedom fighting depicted in the novel and in Hawks's and Siegel's adaptations. Curtiz's gangsters come straight out of central casting and have absolutely no ideological connection to the theme of working-class struggle; they're strictly in it for the dough. Not unlike Leona's presence, their purely opportunistic criminality feels like a noir convention imported without being integrated in the skein of the filmmaker's reformist intentions. (As one student asked after viewing the film, "Why didn't they make Leona part of the gang?"—another compellingly creative suggestion).

Despite its reputation as hackwork—a fault mainly of the gruelingly quick twenty-day shooting schedule Seven Arts forced on Siegel and his production staff—*The Gun Runners* captures better than any of the other versions the tricky moral morass of political revolution that Hemingway aspired to mine in his novel (and which fascinated him throughout his career). In a brief exchange drawn from chapter 18 in which Harry and one of the young revolutionaries, Emilio, debate whether violence is ever justified in an insurgency (163–67), Audie Murphy's captain discovers that the Cuban terrorist Albert's mercenary brings along on the illegal weapons run, Juan (portrayed by Carlos Romero), is a fisherman who hopes to return to his humble living after Cuba's repressive regime is toppled. "When this is over," Murphy replies, "let's hope we'll both be fishermen again."

Despite this potential moment of empathy, the movie's own politics seem intentionally muddled. *The Gun Runners* was produced during an interval in the Cuban Civil War in which American support for Batista faltered due to the dictator's violent abuses, leading to a federal arms embargo that, without supporting the antigovernment rebels, impeded the military's ability to beat back the opposition. Seizing on the opportunity to gain leverage, rebel supporters began a steady smuggling trade of arms into the country, with headlines like "Cuban Gun-Runners Use U. S. as Armory, Customs Says" proliferating in American newspapers. But according to reports like these, funding for such operations came not from leftists but from moneys concealed by the regime of Carlos Saladrigas Zayas (Batista's predecessor, whom he ousted in 1952), seeking to reinstitute democratic but avowedly pro-capitalist reforms begun in the mid-1940s at the conclusion of Batista's previous reign. Although *The Gun Runners* depicts rebels as hearty ideologues, Albert's Hanagan is no Frank Sturgis, the future Watergate burglar who raised money to arm Castro in 1957 before teaching Che Guevera and other guerillas military tactics the following year (and then breaking with Castro after Batista's overthrow over the guerilla leader's Communist leanings). During the smuggling operation, Juan discovers that what are supposed to be boxes of automatic rifles are actually rocks and pipe, worthless junk Hanagan plans to pawn off on the rebels to steal their money. His goons then shoot the fisherman and toss him overboard (just as in Hemingway's novel the revolutionaries do Albert Tracy). In other words, rather than take sides in the civil war, the filmmakers make the villain an amoral opportunist—only in it, like Curtiz's gangsters, for the money. This twist seems to complicate unnecessarily the plot just as suspense is building toward the shootout scene with the hero, requiring Eddie Albert to go into exposition mode and detail every point of his plan as only bad guys in the movies do when screenwriters don't want viewers confused.

Reading the movie against the historical context of 1958, it feels as if Seven Arts were hedging its bets, unwilling to throw its lot in with either Batista or Castro.

Drilling down into this type of detail can sometimes leave students glassy-eyed, but I insist to them it's important information to know if they are to structure their plots to feel organic and not the product of external necessities or compromises dictated by politics. As an example of the ability make such choices, I offer them one more surprise. While Hollywood filmed three separate adaptations of *To Have and Have Not,* a fourth one actually exists, which few English-speaking scholars discuss. I had never heard of Nasser Taghvai's 1987 Iranian adaptation ناخدا خورشید, translated into English as *Captain Khorshid* until, in the middle of an online presentation to the Key West Art and Historical Society during the pandemic summer of 2020, I was asked what I thought of it. For a brief moment I was tempted to resort to the old academic trick of equivocating by saying I had not seen it . . . *lately,* but my fear of fibbing got the better of me. After admitting my ignorance, I discovered a description of this Farsi-language adaptation on the Wikipedia page for Hemingway's novel. (The moral: always read Wikipedia.) Striking about the film is how the elements of Hemingway that Taghvai transposes into his southern Iran setting "speak" despite the language barrier. My students can follow the plot despite their lack of fluency in Islamic and Persian culture, right down to the gripping, claustrophobic shootout scene on the captain's boat, in which the one-handed hero played by Dariush Arjmand dies. In effect, students' inability to understand the dialogue and their unfamiliarity with Iranian political history excuses them from worrying about narrative context. They can instead focus exclusively on action as a kind of pure pantomiming of plot and character. Many of them feel more sympathy for Captain Khorshid than they do the characters played by Bogart, Garfield, or Murphy, simply because his lack of options in the nameless gulf port populated by political exiles, roving criminals, and shifty merchants unfolds to them through gestures and facial expressions. The point is not whether Taghvai's adaptation is ultimately deemed "literal" or "loose"; the point is that the film offers students a chance to consider storytelling as communicating through the barest essentials possible—something Hemingway, with his insistence on embedding seven-eighths of the conflict below the surface, could surely appreciate.

Notes

1. There is always some debate in Hemingway studies as to whether we count *The Torrents of Spring* (1925) as a novel. For my purposes, I count *To Have and Have Not* as the writer's fourth novel, after *Torrents*, *The Sun Also Rises* (1926), and *A Farewell to Arms* (1929). If one prefers to say *Torrents* is more of a satire or burlesque than a proper novel, then *To Have and Have Not* is only his third.

2. A purist might argue that "The Killers" has also been filmed three times, for critics often refer to Soviet director Andrei Tarkovsky's 1956 twenty-one-minute experimental student film. This essay, however, concerns only full-length features.

3. *Today We Live* is loosely based on a powerful World War I story of Faulkner's, "Turnabout," which first appeared in the *Saturday Evening Post* on 5 March 1932 and was included in 1950's still-definitive *Collected Short Stories of William Faulkner* as "Turn About" (475–509). Faulkner wrote dialogue for the film and forged a friendship with Hawks during his first of several unhappy stretches working for Hollywood studios to generate income.

4. A decade and a half before *The Gun Runners*, Siegel also compiled the opening montage to *Casablanca*.

5. It should also be remembered that Albert was a two-time Academy Award nominee for best supporting actor, once before *The Gun Runners* (for 1954's *Roman Holiday*) and once after (for 1972's *The Heartbreak Kid*).

6. Prohibition was officially repealed on December 5, 1933, with the ratification of the Twenty-First Amendment to the Constitution, which did away with the Eighteenth, which outlawed alcohol sales beginning in January 1920. Internal evidence in "The Tradesman's Return" suggests the timeframe is fall 1934, roughly eighteen months after the spring 1933 setting of "One Trip Across." As I explain in my reader's guide, rumrunning continued for at least a few years after prohibition ended, as a means of avoiding taxes on alcohol (68).

7. The original manuscript of part 3 ends with a long chapter in which an ancillary character, Tommy Bradley, attempts to run dynamite to Cuba as a favor to his friend Roddy Simpson. Bradley is a globe-trotting adventurer with more than a passing resemblance to Hemingway. Accompanying him on the journey is the faux-proletarian writer Richard Gordon, based at least in part on John Dos Passos, whose friendship with Hemingway was then inexorably ending, due to disagreements over the Spanish Civil War. Typically, critics assume Hemingway cut this section because he feared either Dos Passos or Jane Mason, the woman on whom he based the novel's femme fatale, Heléne Bradley, would take him to court. A likelier suggestion is that the politics of this final portion, completed in January 1937, suddenly contradicted the insistence Hemingway began to voice during his first trip reporting from Spain that March through May. His advocacy on behalf of Spanish Loyalists (the left-leaning Republican government, fighting for its life against a nationalist insurgence led by General Francisco Franco) now clashed with Tommy Bradley's drafted sarcastic commentary on the futility of political action. Thwarting Bradley and Gordon's dynamite run is a squall that sends

them retreating to Key West, where Tommy's boat promptly sinks in the marina. Nature is a "good old ambushing bitch," Tommy decides, and laughs—whereupon the draft unceremoniously ends. Such a sardonic conclusion would have infuriated the circle of antifascists with whom he was working to support the Loyalists. In particular, at the same time he was readying *To Have and Have Not* for the printer in July 1937, he was collaborating with Dutch documentarian Joris Ivens on the film *The Spanish Earth*, a blistering propaganda piece designed to rouse international support for the Republican government (Curnutt xxxv–xliv).

8. *To Have and Have Not* climaxes with Harry holding Vichy officials at gunpoint in his hotel room until they agree to release his mate, Eddie, and allow him and Marie safe passage out of Martinique.

9. The film hit theaters in September 1958, a full four months before Batista fled Cuba.

10. As Gladstein notes, Hawks and his then wife, Nancy Keith, referred to each other as Steve and Slim (181–82).

11. Although Murphy bares his chest only once in the film (in a bedroom scene with Lucy, not a fight scene with a gun), at least two other times in *The Gun Runners* characters doff their shirts for reasons that seem entirely irrelevant to the surrounding scene: they are strictly beefcake moments. In one, Albert tears off his pajama top, asking Murphy, "How do you keep your weight down?" as he starts doing sit-ups, all the while assuring the captain he has no choice but to run the mercenary's guns to Cuba. Promotional stills for the film also feature a topless Albert wielding a machine gun, but that scene is not in the movie. In another moment, Cuban revolutionary Albert's character strikes a deal with in the dressing room of a Havana nightclub changes into his stage costume while barking threats at his American conspirators—also a weirdly distracting bit of blocking.

Works Cited

Across the River and into the Trees. Dir. Paula Ortiz. Tribune/HBO, 2022. Film.

Albrecht-Crane, Christa, and Dennis Ray Cutchins, eds. *Adaptation Studies: New Approaches*. Farleigh Dickinson UP, 2010.

Bambi. From a novel by Felix Slaten. Dir. David Hand. 1942. Sony Pictures Home Entertainment, 2017. DVD.

Beegel, Susan F. "Harry and the Pirates: The Romance and Reality of Piracy in Hemingway's *To Have and Have Not*." *Key West Hemingway: A Reassessment*, edited by Kirk Curnutt and Gail D. Sinclair, UP of Florida, 2009, pp. 107–28.

The Big Sleep. Dir. Howard Hawks. Perf. Humphrey Bogart, Lauren Bacall. 1946. Warner Home Video-Archive Collection, 2016.

The Breaking Point. Dir. Michael Curtiz. Perf. Wallace Ford, John Garfield. 1950. Criterion Collection, 2017. DVD.

Captain Khorshid [ناخدا خورشید]. Dir. *Nasser Taghvai*. Dir. Nasser Taghvai. Perf. Dariush Arjmand. Pakhshiran, 1987. Film.

Casablanca. Dir. Michael Curtiz. Perf. Humphrey Bogart, Lauren Bacall. 1942. Warner Brothers Home Video, 2012. Blu-ray.

Civille, Michael. "'Ain't Got No Chance': The Case of *The Breaking Point.*" *Cinema Journal*, vol. 56, no. 1, 2016, pp. 1–22.

"Cuban Gun-Runners Use U. S. as Armory, Customs Says." *United Press International*, 9 Nov. 1958.

Curnutt, Kirk. *Reading Hemingway's* To Have and Have Not: *Glosses and Commentary*. Kent State UP, 2017.

A Farewell to Arms. Dir. Frank Borzage. Perf. Gary Cooper and Helen Hayes. 1932. Kino Lorber Films, 2011. Blu-ray

A Farewell to Arms. Dir. Charles Vidor. Perf. Rock Hudson and Jennifer Jones. 1957. 20th Century Fox Home Entertainment, 2008. DVD.

Faulkner, William. *Collected Short Stories of William Faulkner.* Random House, 1950.

For Whom the Bell Tolls. Dir. Sam Wood. Perf. Gary Cooper and Ingrid Bergman. 1943. Universal Studios, 2018. Blu-ray.

Hemingway's The Garden of Eden. Dir. John Irvin. 2008. Lionsgate Studios, 2011. DVD.

Gladstein, Mimi Reisel. "Hemingway, Faulkner, and Hawks: The Nexus of Creativity That Generated the Film *To Have and Have Not.*" *Key West Hemingway: A Reassessment*, edited by Kirk Curnutt and Gail D. Sinclair, UP of Florida, 2009, pp. 172–88.

Griggs, Yvonne. *Bloomsbury Guide to Adaptation Studies: Adapting the Canon in Film, TV, Novels and Popular Culture.* Bloomsbury, 2016.

The Gun Runners. Dir. Don Siegel. Perf Audie Murphy and Eddie Albert. 1958. KL Studio Classics, 2019. DVD.

Hemingway, Ernest. *Across the River and into the Trees.* Scribner's, 1950.

———. *Collected Short Stories.* New York: Everyman's Library Classics, 1995.

———. *A Farewell to Arms.* Scribner's, 1929.

———. *For Whom the Bell Tolls.* Scribner's, 1940.

———. *In Our Time.* 1925. Scribner's, 1930.

———. "One Trip Across." *Cosmopolitan*, Apr. 1934, 20–23, 108–22.

———. *The Sun Also Rises.* Scribner's, 1926.

———. *To Have and Have Not.* Scribner's, 1937.

———. "The Tradesman's Return." *Esquire*, Feb. 1936, 27, 193–96.

———. *The Torrents of Spring.* Scribner's, 1926.

His Girl Friday. Dir. Howard Hawks. Columbia Pictures, 1940. Film.

Holmes, Nathan. "Curtiz at Sea: *Captain Blood, The Sea Hawk, The Sea Wolf,* and *The Breaking Point.*" *The Many Cinemas of Michael Curtiz*, edited by R. Barton Palmer and Murray Pomerance, U of Texas P, 2018, pp. 107–20.

Islands in the Stream. Dir. Franklin J. Schaffner. Perf. George C. Scott and David Hemmings. 1977. Paramount Studios, 2005. DVD.

Johnston, Trevor. "*The Breaking Point.*" *Sight and Sound*, vol. 25, no. 2, 2015, p. 112.

Kawin, Bruce F. ed. *To Have and Have Not: Screenplay.* U of Wisconsin P, 1980.

The Killers. Dir. Robert Siodmak. Perf. Burt Lancaster and Ava Gardner. 1946. Criterion Collection, 2015. Blu-ray.

The Killers. Dir. Don Siegel. Perf. Lee Marvin and Ava Gardner. 1964. Criterion Collection, 2015. Blu-ray.
The Killers. Dir. Andrei Tarkovsky, Marika Beiku, and *Aleksandr Gordon. Gerasimov Institute of Cinematography,* 1956. Film.
Leitch, Thomas M. "Twelve Fallacies in Contemporary Adaptation Theory." *Criticism,* vol. 45, no. 2, 2003, pp. 149–71.
———, ed. *Oxford Handbook of Adaptation Studies.* Oxford UP, 2017.
The Resort. Cr. Andy Siara. Peacock, 2022–. TV series.
Reynolds, Michael S. *Hemingway: The 1930s.* W. W. Norton, 1996.
Salten, Felix. *Bambi, a Life in the Woods.* Trans. Whittaker Chambers. Simon & Schuster, 1928.
Schulz, Kathryn. "'Bambi' Is Even Bleaker Than You Thought." *New Yorker,* 24 Jan. 2022, https://www.newyorker.com/magazine/2022/01/24/bambi-is-even-bleaker-than-you-thought.
The Sun Also Rises. Dir. Henry King. Perf. Tyrone Power and Ava Gardner. 1957. 20th Century Fox Home Entertainment, 2007. DVD.
The Sun Also Rises. Dir. James Goldstone. Perf. Hart Bochner and Jane Seymour. NBC, 1984. TV miniseries.
Taken. Dir. Pierre Morel. Perf. Liam Neeson and Maggie Grace. 2008. 20th Century Fox Home Entertainment, 2009. DVD.
To Have and Have Not. Dir. Howard Hawks. Perf. Humphrey Bogart and Lauren Bacall. 1944. Warner Home Video, 2003. DVD,
Today We Live. Dir. Howard Hawks. 1933. Warner Archives, 2009, DVD.
The White Lotus. Cr. Mike White. Perf. Murray Bartlett and Connie Britton. HBO, 2021– . TV series.

To Have and Have Noir
A Tale of Two Hemingway Films

James Plath

Every semester there are more texts I want to assign my 100- or 200-level students than time allows. For that reason, I almost never show a film that is an adaptation of a novel they have already been assigned. I prefer to stretch the syllabus by having the film stand alone as a "text" to broaden students' exposure to an author's oeuvre. Ideally, aside from breaking up the read-and-discuss routine, a film also helps them to see an author differently—through the eyes of screenwriters and directors who aim to distill the strongest visuals and narrative threads from literary texts to create not a facsimile but an effective *new* work of art. When I teach Hemingway, I never assign Hemingway's second (and final) novel set in the United States—*To Have and Have Not* (1937)—simply because I find two film adaptations superior. Watching one of them (or both, if you have the luxury of time) not only offers a change of pace but also shifts the focus from the famous Hemingway style and themes to a discussion of film noir.

Of the various films adapted from Ernest Hemingway's novels and short stories thus far, three common favorites of film critics are Howard Hawks's *To Have and Have Not* (1944), Robert Siodmak's 1946 feature-length version of "The Killers," and Michael Curtiz's *The Breaking Point* (1950), which is also based on *To Have and Have Not*. All three films have been cited as examples of film noir, and the noir aspects have probably contributed to their lasting appeal.[1]

Film noir makes for lively class discussion because, as one film scholar notes, "it has always been easier to recognize a film noir than to define the term" (Naremore 9). That's the approach I take in the classroom, and I follow the students' interests. Rather than wrestle with a debatable definition or dwell too much on origins and history, I cover that material only briefly. If instructors prefer, there are even well-made YouTube videos (e.g., the thirteen-minute "What Is Film Noir") that could be shown instead, followed by a discussion of film noir's recognizable characteristics, which I detail on a handout to simplify matters. Then I give them a cheat sheet to use as they watch the assigned film (see appendix 2). While critical monographs often refer to *The Breaking Point* and *To Have and Have Not* as noir films, seldom do both appear on a single film scholar's radar. This raises the question of just how "noir" either film is. Critics also disagree as to whether film noir is a genre, style, attitude, or all of the above; so if a class speeds through a discussion of noir characteristics, there are always more subtle and complex issues to confront.

As one film scholar summarizes, "Whatever noir 'is,' the standard histories say that it originated in America, emerging out of a synthesis of hard-boiled fiction and German expressionism. The term is also associated with certain visual and narrative traits, including low-key photography [lighting that accentuates contours with shading], images of wet city streets, pop-Freudian characterizations, and romantic fascination with femmes fatale" (Naremore 9). Most scholars agree that while later films can incorporate a noir style, when people refer to noir films, they're usually talking about American crime dramas from 1941 to 1958. The term *film noir*, meaning "black film," was coined by French film critics, first used in 1946 by Nino Frank, who "noticed the trend of how 'dark,' downbeat and black the looks and themes were of many American crime and detective films released in France to theatres during and following World War II" (Dirks 1).

In film noir, it's not difficult to see the marriage of hard-boiled novels and post–World War I German expressionism. The tough-talking, jaded, amoral hero of detective novels and Hemingway's short, clipped way of speaking are a big part of film noir, as are the harsh angles, distorted realities, and chiaroscuro—the deliberate manipulation of uneven light to create striking juxtapositions between darkness and light—that were distinguishing features of German expressionist films. But film noir's contributing influences are many. They include the bleak philosophy of existentialism that became popular during World War II and which emphasized the individual and the idea that nothing exists unless the individual is able to act upon it. Existentialists denied the existence of objective truths and therefore saw life as meaningless, with individuals forced to create their own meaning. Certainly, war and the start of the Cold War were also important factors, given the ever-present threat of a nuclear holocaust. And a large number of returning veterans who had become cynical and disillusioned also were an influence. Early American classic monster movies, which drew heavily from German expressionism, also would have to be considered influences, as would the early Warner Bros. gangster movies that might have been considered "noir" if they hadn't followed the typical rise-and-fall Hollywood arc and hadn't romanticized mobsters. While their lighting and style was often noir-like, the films had a totally different tone from the bleak realism of film noir.

Noir style is especially evident in particular scenes: the upstairs hotel scenes, the basement scenes, and the scene with the resistance members inside a poor village house in *To Have and Have Not;* in *The Breaking Point,* the noir style of filming is less obvious, present mostly in scenes where Harry interacts with Mr. Sing and seedy underworld types and in intimate scenes with Harry and Leona. A fascinating scene is the one where Leona and Harry drink in a little alcove of a club. When temptation is in the air, filmmakers use modified low-key lighting to cast dramatic shadows, but as soon as Harry's wife interrupts them and sits down at the table, the mood—and the style of filming—changes. It becomes less noir-like.

Even without knowing how to describe it, students readily recognize the film noir "look," and begin to see plenty of examples within the assigned films, in addition to Hemingway connections. I have to admit, after talking about literature and symbols and themes most of the semester, watching a film, whether *To Have and Have Not* or *The Breaking Point,* feels like a refreshing break. For one thing, there are additional interesting background stories to share, including the well-known tale of how the first film version of *To Have and Have Not* came about. Hollywood director and Hemingway pal Hawks related, "Once, on a hunting trip, I told [Ernest] that if he would give me the worst story that he had ever written, we would make a good movie out of it. He asked me what I thought was his worst novel and I said *To Have and Have Not,* which I thought was a bunch of junk. He said that he had written it when he needed money and that he didn't want me to make a movie out of it. But finally, he gave in" (Phillips 50).

While "bunch of junk" might seem extreme, as Hemingway scholar Charles M. Oliver notes, Hemingway's third novel is "considered by most critics to be one of his least successful ones," artistically speaking (335). To create it, Hemingway cobbled together two previously published Harry Morgan stories: "One Trip

Across" and "The Tradesman's Return." Then, at *Esquire* editor Arnold Gingrich's urging, Hemingway added a third section to create a full-length work.

In the first section of the novel, Harry is a Key West fishing-charter captain with a "rummy" first mate named Eddy. Harry has a loving home life with his wife, Marie, and three daughters, but the Depression is squeezing them and he's been smuggling liquor from Cuba all summer to make ends meet. So, when a fishing charter loses $650 of tackle and skips out on paying for an eighteen-day rental, Harry feels as if he has no choice but to accept the shady Mr. Sing's job offer of smuggling Chinese undocumented immigrants into the United States. After the Chinese people board his boat under cover of darkness, Harry thinks Sing is going for a gun, and he shoots him, dumps him overboard, and drops the would-be immigrants back in Cuba (while keeping their money). In the second section, Harry and his new first mate, Wesley, are wounded by Cuban authorities while running rum; they dump the liquor and hide from the US Coast guard in the Keys mangroves. Part 3 begins with readers learning that Harry lost his arm and later his boat as a result of the melee. A shady Key West lawyer whom Harry calls "Bee-lips" tells Harry he can get his impounded boat back if he will agree to transport four Cuban revolutionaries, by boat, *back* to Havana. The section's narrator, Albert, who has been working at a low-paying government relief job, agrees to be Harry's first mate for this illicit run. It turns out that the revolutionaries have just robbed a Key West bank, and they shoot Albert when he's slow to cast off. Out to sea, Harry, prepared for trouble, kills all four revolutionaries, but he is mortally wounded in the process. The novel ends with various reactions to his passing. Earlier in the section, to show contrast, Hemingway had inserted conversations among the island's "haves"—well-heeled tourists, among them the flirty and intoxicated wife of a writer who sat next to Harry on a barstool and said, "If it isn't my dream man," after which Harry "took one look at her and stood up." "Don't go," the wife said. "Please don't go." "You're comical," Harry said as he left, underscoring both his hard-boiled toughness and disdain for the "haves."

Those who think the novel a failure point to a patchwork that never quite comes together as a cohesive whole, with inexplicable character shifts and those tourist scenes contributing to a sense of disconnectedness. However, the films are another story. While a third adaptation of *To Have and Have Not—The Gun Runners* (1958), starring World War II hero Audie Murphy—has been so panned that it's not recommended for classroom use, the other two are great options, either singly or together. Regardless of which film(s) I show, I remind students of the differences between film and a written text, and cover the basics of film noir (see appendix 2). When I decide to assign a single film for individual out-of-class viewing, I usually go with *To Have and Have Not*, because it's readily available. I also give students some direction, first by dividing them into three groups, then by asking the members of each group to pay attention, as they watch on their own, to an assigned single noir aspect—the hero, the femme fatale, or the visual style. I find that it's too distracting (and paralyzing) for students to be asked to identify multiple noir features as they watch a film; directing them to focus on a single element ensures that they'll have *something* to say while not losing sight of the forest among the trees.[2]

The following class period, if my students have been good but not great, I take the safe route and ask that everyone who was assigned the noir hero gather in one big group to compare notes, with the femme fatale and visual noir elements people also forming into groups. After they've talked among themselves for a third of the seventy-five-minute period, we reconvene and group members share their observations with the whole class for another third of the period; and for the final third, I walk them through a series of questions that requires them to compare the noir film(s) we just watched to Hemingway fiction with which they're familiar:

- Does the Harry we meet in the noir film(s) seem typical of Hemingway heroes? Why or why not? Is this Harry harder or softer than a typical Hemingway character, more of less likable, more or less cynical, more or less "manly," et cetera? Could you picture Jake Barnes as a noir hero? Why or why not? What about that famous Hemingway style of characters speaking in short clipped sentences? At this point, I read the opening of the novel aloud to them or give them a handout of excerpts from Harry's opening monologue to prompt further comparisons to the noir hero (see appendix 3). I also quote film noir scholar Andrew Dickos, who observed, "The style of its terse, mainly first-person, action prose has its roots in the fiction of both [Dashiell] Hammett and Ernest Hemingway, but the existential context is decidedly modern urban American" (96–97). After that, we discuss any ways aside from dialogue that Hemingway and film noir seem to intersect—ways Dickos hasn't acknowledged. To get there, I walk them through a series of additional questions:
  - Do other Hemingway novels or short stories you know have characters that now seem to embody some of the traits that characterize the noir hero or the femme fatale? What about Margot Macomber, for example?

Or Brett Ashley? Do any characteristics of the Hemingway hero cross over to the noir hero?
- What noir elements can you spot in short stories like "The Killers" or "A Clean, Well-Lighted Place"? Mood? Descriptions? Atmosphere? Underlying philosophy?
- Which Hemingway novels or stories seem well suited for film noir treatment? Which do not? *The Old Man and the Sea* will never be a noir film, for example. Given the key characteristics of film noir, to what extent do Hemingway's fictions generally apply?
- Bottom line: *Is* there a stronger connection between Hemingway's fiction and film noir than the clipped dialogue that Dickos cited?

I take a slightly different approach if the class seems more capable and the numbers work out, assigning what I call "investigative triads," instead of relying on the more familiar three larger groups, to discuss assigned noir topics. For this method, I create groups of three that are composed of one student assigned the noir hero, one assigned the femme fatale, and one assigned the visual noir elements. I ask each triad to first share their observations with one another and then, together, draw some conclusions about Hemingway and film noir—which gets them talking, usually, about the questions I would walk them through before I even get the chance to ask them. To complicate matters (and this is what makes the triad "investigative"), as one person presents their observations, another (they decide who) acts as an advocate, looking for and chiming in with evidence that supports the presenter's interpretation, while the third person acts as a devil's advocate, charged with finding holes in the case. In the triad, each person should have the chance to present, play advocate, and play devil's advocate, and students often find this dialectic method and assigned roles to be a fresh take on more conventional small group discussions. The assigned roles present a more focused challenge and put the burden of discovery on students. In the matter of Hemingway and film noir, they're usually able to work their ways through an interesting discussion in order to come up with both similarities and differences.

For example, students compare the noir hero to what critics have said (or they noticed) about the Hemingway hero and the ways he seems more similar to the noir hero than through just the dialogue alone. They also see on their own that some of Hemingway's female characters function *in part* or *at times* as the femme fatale. And stories such as "A Clean, Well-Lighted Place" and "The

Killers" are drenched with noir atmosphere. If the groups are really getting into it, I let them go two-thirds of the period before we regroup as a full class. Then, when we talk about that femme fatale, for example, it's a short leap to discussing the characters we've encountered in the fiction. How is Brett Ashley a femme fatale? Or Mrs. Macomber? A discussion of film noir really does help students see those characters differently.

If I decide to show both films (usually one assigned outside of class and *The Breaking Point* watched together), I begin the broad classroom discussion with two additional questions:

- Which adaptation has "more noir"? (This is usually a split decision, with students often deciding that *To Have and Have Not* has more moments of classic noir visual style and begins with noir content as well—before veering off into romance and a happy ending. But they usually see that *The Breaking Point* is more faithful to the content, themes, action, and bleak ending of noir films, even if the visual style is limited to certain scenes.)
- Which adaptation feels closer to a Hemingway story and characters?

Students usually are invested in this discussion because these two film adaptations are worlds apart, and the discussion of noir elements versus the fiction gets them talking. Because *The Breaking Point* is closer to the text, they readily gravitate toward that film, but I'll point out that much of *To Have and Have Not* takes place in the hotel bar, and Hemingway and his characters were no strangers to that environment. If they lean toward *To Have and Have Not,* I might remind them that Frederic Henry was technically a deserter who put romance ahead of duty, and we go from there. For me, though, the biggest question comes earlier: Which film do I choose if I can only show one of them?

To Have and Have Not has a number of selling points in addition to Hawks's fun wager anecdote. Not only was it the first film to feature two Nobel laureates in the credits—William Faulkner was hired on as a script doctor—but as a classic film from Hollywood's Golden Age, it also was the first pairing of screen legends Humphrey Bogart and Lauren Bacall, the latter in her very first film. Their age difference aside, they sizzle on camera, with Bacall famous for the seductive line, "You know how to whistle, don't you Steve? You just put your lips together, and ... blow." Then there's character actor Walter Brennan, who amuses students with his intended comic relief as Harry's rummy first mate ("Say, was you ever bit by a dead bee?"), and the novel's fishing scene is recognizable, even if most of what follows is not. Set in summer 1940 shortly after the Nazi occupation of France,

To Have and Have Not turns into more of a romance about helping members of the resistance than a commentary about "haves" and "have-nots." Though now considered a classic, when it was first released, film critics complained that the film's chief weakness was that it was derivative. But even that makes for fascinating classroom discussion. As the *New York Times*' Bosley Crowther quipped in his review, *To Have and Have Not* is *Casablanca* "moved west." He said that despite "surface alterations in some of the characters, you will meet here substantially the same people as in that other geo-political romance" (1).

He's right. After that first fishing scene, it *does* start to feel a bit feel like *Casablanca II*. Initially, Hawks relied on screenwriting veteran Jules Furthman (*Mutiny on the Bounty*, 1935), but because he thought Furthman's first draft stayed too close to the novel, he handed the rewrite job to Faulkner, who had already worked on thirteen films—among them John Ford's Oscar-nominated *Drums along the Mohawk* (1939). There was another issue that makes for a fascinating backstory. As a bonus feature on the DVD release of *To Have and Have Not* reminds us, the Roosevelt administration objected to the original script: "Under the Good Neighbor policy, they tried to force the studio to cancel the film by withholding its export license because it depicted corruption and violence in Cuba" ("Love Story" 1). Hawks's solution was to relocate the film to Vichy-controlled Martinique, which lay just outside the Good Neighbor reach. "In one week's time, Faulkner shifted the story to Martinique, eliminated episodes, created new ones, changed characters, and put them all under the roof of a single hotel" (1). Instead of Rick's Café Américain, the characters spend most of their time in the Hotel Marquis, where the first floor is a nightclub and upstairs there are rooms, one of which is Harry's. Like Rick, Harry makes a point of declaring his neutrality, and like Rick, he helps a Free French leader and his wife. He even has a dry comeback when asked his nationality: "Eskimo" (rather than Rick's "drunkard" retort). And while Rick had the friendship of the piano-playing Sam, Harry is chummy with Cricket (real-life pianist-songwriter Hoagy Carmichael). The *Casablanca* parallels are unmistakable, yet somehow Harry still feels like a Hemingway character—albeit one who, unlike his novelistic counterpart, doesn't die in the end. *To Have and Have Not* is based on the principle that what makes for a good movie is a strong hero who, despite being tough on the outside, is really soft on the inside—a man whom women find attractive, but who's also responsive when a romance develops. The entire third act emerges as a romance between Harry and Marie, though Harry, like the typical Hemingway hero Robert Penn Warren described, lives by a personal code and is skilled at what he does, whether fishing or operating on a member of the resistance despite not being a doctor (79). That's enough of an attraction for Marie, who calls Harry "Steve" after he calls her "Slim"—both in playful reference to Hawks and his wife's nicknames. Their chemistry is palpable, and students are always amazed that the sultry Bacall was only nineteen—the age of an average college sophomore—when she made *To Have and Have Not,* and that she and the forty-four-year-old Bogart fell in love and married. Students are even more surprised to learn that young Bacall was improvising when her character tells "Steve" to whistle if he wants her, and to whistle you just "put your lips together and blow." It became one of the most famous femme fatale lines in film noir history.

The case for choosing *The Breaking Point* is strong but simple: this 1950 film was indeed more faithful to the novel, and Hemingway, notoriously unhappy with most of the Hollywood adaptations, later said that it "suited him" (qtd. in Phillips 62). After it was released, Crowther praised it. "All of the character, color, and cynicism of Mr. Hemingway's lean and hungry tale are wrapped up in this realistic picture, and John Garfield is tops in the principal role," he wrote. "What we surprisingly have here is a good, taut adventure story with some sense of the ironies of life." Coincidentally, it was directed by Michael Curtiz—who also directed *Casablanca.* Though Crowther considered *To Have and Have Not* "one feeble swing and a cut," he opined that *The Breaking Point* was "a four-base hit" (1).

The film opens with Harry in a typical noir voiceover: "You know how it is, early in the morning, on the water? Everything is quiet, except for the seagulls, a long way off. And you feel great. Then you come ashore, and it starts. In no time at all, you're up to your ears in trouble, and you don't even know where it began." This Harry is tough enough, but softened a bit to make him more likeable. An added domestic scene early in the first act establishes him as a loving husband and father who only now has gotten to the point of despair. "I get teed off sometime," he tells his wife. "No sooner, no sooner I get my head above water and somebody pushes me down again." Throughout the film, this Harry is more consistently hard-edged and with more noir "attitude" than his *To Have and Have Not* counterpart.

Though Harry's wife wants him to end their financial woes by working on her father's lettuce ranch in Salinas, he snaps, "I'm a boat jockey, and that's all I know." Screenwriter Ranald MacDougall gave him a returning vet's dilemma: "Ever since I took that uniform off," Harry says, "I'm not exactly great." A decorated PT-boat World War II veteran, he's turned cynical, but he hasn't been smuggling rum the way his book counterpart had been doing all summer. His involvement with Mr. Sing is also more morally defensible. The film is set in Newport Beach, California, with Harry taking that first fishing charter (and his gold-digger "girlfriend") to Mexico for an extended period. This femme fatale (Leona, played by Patricia Neal) has some zingers, too. When she first boards his boat, Harry snaps, "Do you fish?" and Leona responds, "Ooooo. I don't think I like you." Later, as she sunbathes on the bow, she flirts with Harry. "Don't you want to be friendly?" she asks. He responds, "Sure I wanna be friendly, but my wife wouldn't like it." "You're kidding." "No." "Oh, so you're one of those." "Uh-huh."

When the charter skips town on an early flight, stiffing Harry and leaving Leona stranded, she shows up on the dock looking to Harry to get her back to the States. By running out on him, the man also left Harry stranded in Mexico, lacking the money to pay the exit fee to leave the harbor. It's a desperate situation that brings about a desperate act. And in *The Breaking Point* Harry doesn't just think Sing is pulling a gun—he sees it, grabs it, and engages Sing in a life-or-death wrestling match. Here, Sing's death is self-defense, while in the novel it's Harry's paranoia and preemptive attack that kills him. In this film, Leona, a stowaway, witnesses the incident, then tries to use it as leverage to get to Harry, though he stands firm. That, too, makes him more sympathetic—a noir hero who happens to be a nice guy.

The Breaking Point also has an interesting backstory. When Garfield was hired and read the screenplay, he suggested a few changes that would incorporate more elements from the novel—including a brief scene in which Harry "brings trinkets home from his travels for his wife and daughters" (Zacharek 1). But Garfield's association with the picture also was responsible for its quick descent into relative obscurity. After the film was shot but before it was released on September 30, 1950, Garfield's name turned up on an anti-Communist pamphlet—*Red Channels: The Report of Communist Influence in Radio and Television*—"perhaps partly because of his connection to the artistically liberal Group Theatre, but also because his wife, Roberta Seidman, had briefly been a member of the party. Inclusion on that list meant death for an actor's career, and Warner Bros. did little to promote *The Breaking Point,* almost certainly because of Garfield's involvement" (1). Garfield made only one more movie after *The Breaking Point*—*He Ran All the Way,* another film noir—before dying of a heart attack at the age of thirty-nine in May 1952.

For teachers who have to be careful what they show, it's worth mentioning that neither film adaptation would warrant more than a PG rating by today's standards, but *The Breaking Point* does have more onscreen violence, with one of Hollywood's more memorable shootouts. Yet Harry's end line in the novel—"No matter how a man alone ain't got no bloody fucking chance" (220), which encapsulates the book's theme—is tamely rendered without the f-bomb in *The Breaking Point* and completely absent from the more romantic *To Have and Have Not,* despite that film's heavier noir style.

Film is a more visual medium, I remind students, deriving most of its "signs" from what is seen, whereas novels depend on verbal signs. Since the silent era ended, film has also been codependent on sounds as well as silences, while novels consist only of silences, with any suggestions of sounds dependent on readers' ability to interpret those verbal cues and bring sounds to life in their imaginations. In film, characters talk and directors typically add noise (ambient or effects) as well as music. Likewise, while a novel has access to characters' interior lives, unless the director has chosen to employ a narrative voiceover, viewers have only body language, what a character says and does, and what others say about the character, to speculate about a character's inner thoughts. Film is start-to-finish storytelling to a captive audience, so the director has to simplify and compress the narrative by cutting unnecessary characters and side plots. Unlike books, which readers can put down and pick up again, reading at their own pace, a film is a start-to-finish experience. Reading is solitary, and readers can go over passages as many times as they want to grasp meaning or nuance; film is social, with an audience reaction—even more pronounced in the forties and fifties, when both of these Hemingway films debuted—often influencing the way someone responds to a film.

As George Bluestone notes in his often-cited *Novels into Film: The Metamorphosis of Fiction into Cinema,* when the filmmaker "undertakes the adaptation of a novel, given the inevitable mutation, it is that he does not convert the novel at all. What he adapts is a kind of paraphrase of the novel—the novel viewed as raw material. He looks not to the organic novel, whose language is inseparable from its theme, but to characters and incidents which have somehow detached themselves from the language and, like the heroes of folk legends, have achieved a mythic life of their own" (62). That is, the filmmaker is looking to create not a facsimile but rather a completely new art form. Regardless of which of these two excellent film noir adaptations of *To Have and Have Not* I show the class, we often conclude by identifying raw materials the filmmaker gleaned from the novel and discussing how the characters and incidents of the film took on a "mythic life" apart from Hemingway's novel—for better or for worse.

Appendix 1: Plot Summaries

To Have and Have Not (1937 Novel)

- Set in Key West (southernmost Florida). Harry (forty-three) is married to Marie (forty-five), with whom he has three daughters. He's a fishing charter captain who sometimes smuggles contraband from Cuba to Florida to make ends meet, but he's trying to stay legit.
- The novel consists of three parts, with part 1 an expanded version of "One Trip Across," part 2 a considerably altered version of "The Tradesman's Return," and part 3 a long, added section that incorporates characters representing the "haves" and ending with the novel's climax.
- Harry narrates. Part 1 opens with Harry in a Havana café where wealthy Cubans are trying to talk him into taking them to the United States, but Harry turns them down. As the Cubans leave, Cuban revolutionaries gun them down in the street.
- Harry and "rummy" first mate Eddy take a fishing charter out again, and Mr. Johnson loses $650 worth of Harry's fishing gear when he doesn't follow instructions and has the drag set too tight. He skips town without paying, leaving Harry in Cuba with no cash.
- Forced to deal with the shady Mr. Sing, Harry agrees to pick up undocumented Chinese immigrants and drop them anywhere along the US Keys. But later, when he thinks Sing is reaching for a gun, he kills him, dumps the body overboard, drops the immigrants off at the nearest Cuban beach without returning their money, and returns to Key West.
- In part 2, Harry inexplicably has a different first mate, named Wesley, and both of them are shot while fleeing Cuban authorities as they were smuggling liquor to Key West. Hiding in the mangroves and seriously wounded, Harry dumps the liquor to avoid being caught by the US Coast Guard.
- In part 3, Harry has lost his arm because of the wound, and his boat has been impounded. He says to Albert, a relief worker making $7.50 a week, who narrates this section, "I used to make thirty-five dollars a day right through the season. Taking people out fishing. Now I get shot and lose an arm, and my boat, running a lousy load of liquor that's worth hardly as much as my boat. But let me tell you, my kids ain't going to have their bellies hurt and I ain't going to dig sewers for the government for less money than will feed them" (97). He tells Al, "What they're trying to do is starve you Conchs out of here so they can burn down the shacks and put up apartments and make this a tourist town. That's what I hear" (98).

- At Freddie's Place (modeled after Sloppy Joe's), a lawyer nicknamed Beelips acts as middleman for four Cuban undocumented immigrants wanting Harry to take them back to Havana. Harry doesn't ask why. He steals his boat back from the navy yards, but US customs confiscates it again, so he rents Freddie's boat.
- It turns out the Cubans robbed the bank in Key West that's just a block from the docks, and when Harry's new first mate Albert doesn't cast off the line right away, the Cubans shoot and kill him. Out at sea, Harry kills the four Cubans, but is mortally wounded. "No matter how a man alone ain't got no bloody fucking chance," he says, delirious, after being picked up by the Coast Guard.
- On the docks, Albert's wife wonders where he is and, distraught, falls into the water.
- As the novel concludes, Marie thinks about Harry after he dies in the hospital, and Harry's heroics are ironically lost when one Coast Guard captain misinterprets the crime scene: "They must have got to fighting among themselves. . . . They must have had a dispute on how to split the money" (244).

To Have and Have Not (1944 Film)
- Set in Martinique in Summer 1940, shortly after the fall of France. Harry (Humphrey Bogart) is unmarried and unattached, the captain of the charter-fishing boat *Queen Conch* out of Key West. His rummy first mate is Eddie (Walter Brennan). Harry has a room at the Hotel Marquis. We first meet him as he banters with the authority responsible for issuing papers so he can leave the port, and it's revealed that he has been spending the past two weeks taking a client out fishing the Martinique waters.
- That same day, they take Mr. Johnson out fishing, and when he hooks into his second big billfish Johnson loses a rod and reel because of his carelessness. Harry insists on payment, but Johnson tells him he has to get money when the bank opens the next morning. As they return to the hotel, an undercover policeman overhears Johnson comment about Vichy and wants both of their names, which underscores the political tension.
- That evening at the hotel nightclub, the owner, Frenchy (Marcel Dalio), tells Harry that some Free French resistance members are coming to see him to try to hire him to smuggle human cargo into Martinique. Harry is unwilling to get involved in "local politics."

- "Anybody got a match?" the young and sultry Marie (Lauren Bacall) asks, just outside Harry's open hotel room door, where he and Frenchy had been talking. Marie is a globetrotting pickpocket whom Harry later sees take Johnson's wallet at the Hotel nightclub. They look inside the wallet and find $1400 in traveler's checks and a plane ticket for a flight leaving before the bank opens. He was planning on stiffing Harry.
- They confront Johnson together, and Harry insists on him signing over traveler's checks; just then, Vichy police open fire on the Free French underground members as they were leaving—the same men Harry met with earlier in his room—and stray fire kills Johnson before he can sign checks. Harry grabs his wallet and takes $500, less than the $850 he was owed, but all there was.
- Harry and Marie are questioned by the rotund Capitaine Renard (Dan Seymour) of the Gestapo, who confiscates the money Harry took plus his own money and his passport. Harry tells Marie (whom he calls "Slim") that she should leave because things are going to get messy, but she has no money to leave with.
- Viewers are led to believe that Harry changes his mind about picking up a resistance member so he can get Slim the money she needs to leave Martinique. Under cover of darkness, Harry and Eddie pick up Paul de Bursac and his wife, whom Harry is surprised to see accompanying him, but a patrol boat spots them. Harry shoots out the spotlight, but in the burst of gunfire de Bursac is wounded when he tries to surrender rather than hitting the deck, as Harry instructed.
- Back at the hotel, Harry learns that Slim did not leave and is instead waiting for him. Frenchy hired her to sing with the piano-playing Cricket (Hoagy Carmichael). Frenchy also hid the de Bursacs in his hotel basement, and Harry is called upon to remove the bullet from Paul de Bursac, because there are no other options. He does, and earns Mrs. de Bursac's gratitude (and Slim's jealousy).
- Harry learns that the de Bursacs' mission is to go to Devil's Island to help the leader of the Free French resistance escape. Harry is not interested in taking them.
- The Gestapo officers return to the hotel and question Harry again, telling him they know it was his boat that shot at their patrol boat. Harry plays it cool until he learns that they have Eddie in custody and are going to "break" him by denying him alcohol. That infuriates Harry, who moves to

a drawer to "get matches" but grabs a gun instead and shoots one of them, then subdues the other policeman.
- Harry pistol-whips the Gestapo captain until he agrees to phone in Eddie's release and sign their harbor passes. Still angered by how the Gestapo was treating Eddie, Harry decides to take the de Bursacs to Devil's Island and leave Martinique immediately with them and Slim and Eddie. Like *Casablanca*'s Rick, he has evolved from political neutrality to political commitment—or has he? One suspects that the commitment is still based on Harry's individual reasons. The film ends on a peppy, romantic note, with Slim wiggling her hips in Harry's direction and the three of them heading out the hotel door.

The Breaking Point (1950 Film)
- This version is set in Newport Beach, California, where Harry is a fishing-charter captain who has never done anything wrong before. Harry is married to Lucy, and they have two girls.
- The film begins with a domestic scene. Harry (John Garfield) and Lucy (Phyllis Thaxter) are depicted as having a truly happy and loving marriage, more than their analog characters in the novel.
- Wesley (Juano Hernandez), his first mate, also has a family, and they live in cracker-box houses near the water and each other.
- A rich charter hires them to take him to fish Mexican waters for an extended period, and he brings a woman along, much to Harry's consternation; when the rich man skips town, he stiffs Harry and abandons the woman, Leona, who comes to Harry's boat looking for a ride back to the States.
- With no money to pay the exit fee, Harry has no choice but to agree to smuggle Chinese immigrants from Mexico to the United States for Mr. Sing. At sea, as they prepare to load onto his boat, Sing pulls a gun and Harry wrestles with him. After He kills Sing and dumps him overboard, Harry gives the Chinese people back their money and drops them off where they started before heading back to Newport Beach . . . with stowaways Wesley and Leona as witnesses.
- The next morning, the Coast Guard impounds Harry's boat because the Mexican authorities identified it as the craft one of the Chinese immigrants pointed out. They look for the body but can't find it.
- At a lounge, Leona comes on to him again. "Turn it off, turn it off," he says in response to her flirtation. But she reminds him she's being a "good girl" and

not talking about what happened in Mexico, so he should treat her "nice." They continue to drink all night until Lucy shows up and takes Harry home.
- When Harry returns home, he sees that his wife has changed her hair to match Leona's short, blonde cut. Harry tells her he likes it but adds, "You look better than any of them."
- When Phillips, who owns a lien on Harry's boat, comes by and says he's going to take possession if Harry doesn't catch up with his payments in short order, Harry works hard by offering cheaper charters and Lucy takes a job mending sails.
- Still needing money to keep his boat, Harry meets with the shady lawyer and his hoodlum clients at Christian's Hut Bar. When he learns he's to drive the getaway boat for a racetrack robbery, Harry tells himself he's doing it for Lucy and the reward. He thinks his only way out of this mess and his debts is to drive the getaway boat and somehow stop them all. So he stashes guns just inside the engine compartment.
- Wesley shows up to work on the boat at the wrong time, just as the hoodlums drive up to the pier after robbing the racetrack. They shoot Wesley as he starts to ask what's going on, and once out to sea Harry manages to kill all of the men but is mortally wounded.
- The film ends on the dock with a dying Harry being taken to the hospital and Wesley's son standing alone on the pier, wondering where his father is. As in the book, the Coast Guard officers misinterpret what happened on the boat, Harry's actual acts of heroism, and the good intentions behind them.

Appendix 2: Film Noir Characteristics

(These lists are compiled from observations made by Roger Ebert and several critics and scholars, especially Steven M. Sanders, Andrew Dickos, and Ephraim Katz).

Characters
- The main POV character is usually a male loner who feels trapped, disillusioned, cynical, doomed by fate (temperament or circumstances).
- Often amoral, he has a shady past or present and is capable of violence, though he's clearly a "good guy."
- He talks in short, clipped sentences and uses hard-boiled language, and he likes to think of himself as a man who lets his actions do his talking.

- He's old-school, a man heavily influenced by the past.
- He's denied conventional social or domestic happiness because he rejects it or finds it unattainable.
- He and the other men in his world often wear dark fedoras, suits, and ties; the grittier heroes' suits look as though they may have slept in them.
- He becomes involved in some mystery or crime, often because of his involvement with a femme fatale, a beautiful, sultry, mysterious woman who's dressed to kill; she has a problem but is often a problem herself—often deceitful, with a dark past, minor criminal tendencies, or a criminal heart.
- Film critic Roger Ebert described noir characters as being "weaker than they thought they were" and "capable of evil that they didn't think they could commit" (1).

Setting/Atmosphere
- *Film noir* is French for "black film"; French critic Nino Frank coined the term in 1946, for its dark, tense, and brooding atmosphere.
- Noir films were popular from the post-Depression 1930s through the early 1950s, the result of a world weary of war and not yet ready to embrace cheery topics.
- The settings are often urban, isolated, "mean streets," with scenes that take place mostly at night or in darkened, shadowy interiors.
- Dingy realism prevails, with scenes often set in nightclubs and lounges, boxing rings and gyms, hotel rooms, pool halls, and hole-in-the-wall dives.
- Noir exists in a pessimistic world, where fatalism and existentialism coexist.
- To this, Ebert would add locations that "reek" of "the back doors of fancy places, of apartment buildings with a high turnover rate, of taxi drivers and bartenders who have seen it all."

Plot/Narration
- Even when they're not mysteries, noir films feel like a gauntlet the main character has to run, a problem he has to solve, or a maze he has to negotiate.
- They are usually narrated by the main point-of-view character, who often is heard in voiceover, talking grittily about where he is and what he's doing.
- Flashbacks are a popular device, used more to tell us how the character came to this moment rather than to give us great insight into his character; often flashbacks are a window into the main character's thought process as he tries to figure things out

- There is a lack of comic structure in the sense that there is usually no happy ending and very few moments of humor.
- Plot devices like temporary amnesia, nightmares, and daydreams are frequently used to show how a character's psyche is as dark or troubled as the external world.

Themes/Motifs/Symbols
- Frequent motifs/symbols include telephones, guns, newspaper headlines, getaway cars, portraits (art and art collections), neon signage, cigarettes and cigarette lighters, and trench coats.
- Frequent themes are instability, confusion, paranoia, despair, and the ubiquitous prevalence of crime and corruption.
- In the noir world, there are more losers than winners, more survivors than losers, and good and evil sometimes blur.
- Ebert called it the "most American film genre, because no society could have created a world so filled with doom, fate, fear and betrayal, unless it were essentially naïve and optimistic" (1).

Style
- The famous noir style is characterized by low-key lighting that casts heavy shadows.
- Noir films are almost always shot in black and white.
- Chiaroscuro (the manipulation of light and shading or shadow) is used to create additional uneven light that emphasizes a noir world even in settings that normally might not seem noir-like.
- A subjective (point-of-view) camera is used frequently to jarring effect, forcing viewers to see things from the point of view of characters who aren't often likable.
- Foregrounded objects shot at a low angle or canted (tilted) shots reinforce the off-kilter world of noir.
- Mirrors and reflective surfaces are often used to multiply an image in order to suggest a fractured state of mind or circumstances.
- Harsh and extreme camera angles, especially during moments of tension, underscore the gritty nature of the action.

Appendix 3: Harry's Opening Narration

The novel begins with Harry talking:

> You know how it is there early in the morning in Havana with the bums still asleep against the walls of the buildings; before even the ice wagons come by with ice for the bars? Well, we came across the square from the dock to the Pearl of San Francisco Café to get coffee and there was only one beggar awake in the square and he was getting a drink out of the fountain. But when we got inside the café and sat down, there were three of them waiting for us.
>
> We sat down and one of them came over.
> "Well," he said.
> "I can't do it," I told him. "I'd like to do it as a favor. But I told you last night I couldn't."
> "You can name your own price."
> "It isn't that. I can't do it. That's all."
> The two others had come over and they stood there looking sad. They were nice-looking fellows all right and I would have liked to have done them the favor.
> "A thousand apiece," said the one who spoke good English.
> "Don't make me feel bad," I told him. "I tell you true I can't do it."
> "Afterwards, when things are changed, it would mean a good deal to you."
> "I know it. I'm all for you. But I can't do it."
> "Why not?"
> "I make my living with the boat. If I lose her I lose my living."
> "With the money you buy another boat."
> "Not in jail." (3–4)

After this, the discussion escalates. The three men persist. One turns nasty. Tempers flare.

> "Listen," I told him. "Don't be so tough so early in the morning. I'm sure you've cut plenty of people's throats. I haven't even had my coffee yet."
> "So you're sure I've cut people's throats?"
> "No, I said. "And I don't give a damn. Can't you do business without getting angry?
> "I am angry now," he said. "I would like to kill you."
> "Oh, hell," I told him. "Don't talk so much."(11)

Soon the discussion escalates. Tempers flare. One of the men gets nasty.

"Listen," I told him. "Don't be so tough so early in the morning. I'm sure you've cut plenty of people's throats. I haven't even had my coffee yet."

"So you're sure I've cut people's throats?"

"No, I said. "And I don't give a damn. Can't you do business without getting angry?

"I am angry now," he said. "I would like to kill you."

"Oh, hell," I told him. "Don't talk so much."(11)

Notes

1. According to aggregate sites Rotten Tomatoes and the Internet Movie Database, *The Killers* received a 100 percent "fresh" rating at the former and a 7.7 out of 10 at the latter, while *The Breaking Point* earned a 100 percent "fresh" rating and 7.5/10, and *To Have and Have Not* elicited a 94 percent "fresh" rating and 7.8/10, as of May 5, 2024. On noir, see especially Dickos, Dirks, and Naremore.

2. I remain stubbornly old-school when it comes to using Moodle or Google or other online platforms, especially since students were forced to engage each other that way in high school. But of course, instructors who aren't as averse to it can easily build online comments into an out-of-class film assignment or substitute them for out-of-class student groups.

Works Cited

"What Is Film Noir?" *YouTube*, uploaded by Rocco Acee, 29 June 2013, https://www.youtube.com/watch?v=K-2y2k_cKr8.

Bluestone, George. *Novels into Film: The Metamorphosis of Fiction into Cinema*. U of California P, 1973.

Crowther, Bosley. "The Screen in Review; 'Breaking Point,' Adapted From Hemingway Story, Starring John Garfield, at Strand." *New York Times*, 7 Oct. 1950.

———. "'To Have and Have Not,' With Humphrey Bogart, at the Hollywood—Arrival of Other New Films at Theatres Here." *New York Times*, 12 Oct. 1944.

Dickos, Andrew. *Street with No Name: A History of the Classic American Film Noir*. UP of Kentucky, 2002.

Dirks, Tim. "Film Noir, Part 1." *AMC Filmsite*. Accessed 17 Mar. 2019. https://www.filmsite.org/filmnoir.html.

Ebert, Roger. "A Guide to Film Noir Genre," *RogerEbert.com*, Jan. 30, 1995, https://www.rogerebert.com/roger-ebert/a-guide-to-film-noir-genre.

Hemingway, Ernest. One Trip Across," *The Complete Short Stories of Ernest Hemingway: The Finca Vigía Edition*. New York: Scribner, 1991, pp. 381–409.

---. *To Have and Have Not.* New York: Scribner, 1996.

---"The Tradesman's Return," *The Complete Short Stories of Ernest Hemingway: The Finca Vigía Edition.* New York: Scribner, 1991, pp. 381–409.

"A Love Story: The Story of *To Have and Have Not.*" Dir. Jeff Kurtti and Michael Pellerin, Warner Home Video, 2003. DVD

Katz, Ephraim. *The Film Encyclopedia: The Complete Guide to Film and the Film Industry,* 7th ed. Collins Reference, 2012.

Naremore, James. *More Than Night: Film Noir in Its Contexts.* U of California P, 1998.

Oliver, Charles M. *Ernest Hemingway A to Z: The Essential Reference to the Life and Work.* Facts on File, 1999.

Phillips, Gene D. *Hemingway and Film.* Frederick Ungar, 1980.

Sanders, Steven M. "Film Noir and the Meaning of Life," in *The Philosophy of Film Noir,* edited by Mark Coward, UP of Kentucky, 2005, pp. 91–106.

Warren, Robert Penn. "Ernest Hemingway." *Ernest Hemingway: Five Decades of Criticism,* ed. Linda Wagner-Martin. Michigan State UP, 1974, pp. 75–102.

Zacharek, Stephanie. "All at Sea." Liner notes for The Criterion Collection Blu-ray release of *The Breaking Point.* Dir. Michael Curtiz. Criterion Collection, 2017. Blu-ray.

From the Harbor to the Hotel

Visual Equivalents in Howard Hawks's *To Have and Have Not*

Timothy Penner

If director Howard Hawks is to be believed, the impetus behind one of Warner Bros. Studios' most celebrated and storied movies, *To Have and Have Not* (1944), began with a boastful insult directed at Ernest Hemingway while the pair were on a hunting trip. "I can make a movie out of your worst book," Hawks claimed (Kawin 15–16). When Hemingway inquired about which book Hawks considered the author's worst, Hawks replied, "That god damned bunch of junk called *To Have and Have Not*" (16). Whether we can trust the veracity of this story, it has become part of the film's often-repeated lore, even as Hawks's telling tends to change in detail and scope with each iteration. Perhaps it is apt that his version alters so much, since the critical conversation around the movie often revolves around the substantial changes that took *To Have and Have Not* from a disjointed and experimental novel to a canonical example of classic Hollywood filmmaking.[1]

Scholars like Bruce Kawin, Frank Laurence, Gene Phillips, and Mimi Reisel Gladstein have filled many pages with thorough research and convincing arguments about the reasoning behind the substantial shifts in the adaptation process. Their work offers intriguing ways to understand the substantial intermedial changes at play with regard to Hemingway, adaptation studies, and the mid-century studio system.[2] While any investigation of *To Have and Have Not* owes a debt to the considerable scholarship by the aforementioned theorists, my intention here is not to examine the practical changes to the story as it was adapted, nor the reasons behind those changes.

Rather, I propose a reading that posits Hawks's film, with regard to the field of adaptation studies, as a prime example of how a film can express a novel's thematic and social concerns using visual, rather than written, language, despite significant narrative deviation. To show how this phenomenon operates, I first lay out the theoretical framework of what George Linden has termed *visual equivalents,* before offering a reading of the film that reveals the way its mise-en-scène and screen geography visually express the theme of class ignorance (in spite of proximity) central to Hemingway's novel. I also argue against the importance of strict fidelity in intermedial transactions, since, as is the case with biological evolution, cinematic survival is far more contingent on adapting to a new environment than on maintaining fealty to an old one. My approach is built on my own experience of teaching this film as an example of cinematic adaptation in an introductory film course at the undergraduate level; therefore, I will periodically refer to the pedagogical methods I employ in this context.

I like to begin the class by having a conversation with my students about their own experiences of seeing movies based on books, plays, video games, et cetera with which they were familiar before watching the film version. I typically find that my students share the generally held opinion that the original version is often better than the adaptation. Yet, when I ask what they think of *To Have and Have Not,* the general consensus is that the film is much more enjoyable than the novel. I then postpone a conversation about this until after a more thorough discussion of adaptation.

I begin that longer discussion by introducing my class to some important theoretical aspects of adaptation studies by discussing Linden's essay "The Storied World," which proposes that "for a film to be an adequate rendition of a novel, it must not only present the actions and events of the novel but also capture the subjective tones and attitudes toward those events" (169). While this notion is problematic in its insistence on fidelity, Linden's conclusion does lead him to the useful suggestion that a film must employ visual equivalents of the written approaches employed by authors (169). In its simplest form, this can refer to the obvious example of filmmakers using actors to represent characters rather than descriptive sentences; however, it can also scale up to the employment of complex systems of symbolism used to connote thematic concerns.

When a director uses visual equivalents well, that employment often goes far beyond description and into the very heart of what André Bazin calls an author's *form,* which he defines as "a visible manifestation, of style, which is absolutely inseparable from the narrative content" (20). For Bazin, an author's *form* goes deeper than narrative; it is the fundamental shape of the writing. Bazin goes on to say that "faithfulness to a form, literary or otherwise, is illusory: what matters is the equivalence in meaning of the forms" (20). Bazin and Linden both speak to the need for a filmmaker to employ techniques native to the cinematic form rather than try to replicate those used by the author: adaptation should really be understood as an act of translation.[3]

As Linda Hutcheon states, movies (or any works) made from other medial sources are "translations in the form of inter-semiotic transpositions from one sign system . . . to another" (16). Therefore, what is important in the act of this translation is finding visual systems that express a novel's ideas without necessarily replicating the method employed by the author. It should be said that an adaptor *can* employ the same technique as its source material; however, given the differences in the nature of the expressive languages, it need not be a requirement for a successful inter-medial transaction.

At this point in the class, my first-year students have about as much theory as they can take, and so I shift to the film in order to consider how these visual equivalents, and Hutcheon's "inter-semiotic transpositions" operate on a practical level. In preparation, I assign Hemingway's novel as required reading to be done before the in-class screening of the film. I direct my students to pay particular attention to the first chapter, specifically the events Hawks recreates in the film, in order to think about the way the same narrative can be presented in different artistic media. While we discuss some of the choices and reasons behind the differences in characters, locations, and narrative in Hawks's film with regard to the replicated sections, the majority of our discussion revolves around chapter 24, which I also encourage my students to focus on, as it is particularly important in understanding the way visual equivalents operate in the film.

Chapter 24 is a departure from the novel's larger narrative. The previous few chapters have seen Harry Morgan engage in a fatal gunfight at sea before being rescued by the Coast Guard and returned to Key West. Morgan utters some extremely pessimistic final words before drifting into unconsciousness aboard the Coast Guard's boat, and there Hemingway leaves him for the majority of the next chapter.

When chapter 24 begins, the third-person omniscient narrator is describing the situation outside the iron gates that block entry to the former submarine base, now being used as a yacht basin. Henry Carpenter, described as a yachtsman, and his friend Wallace Johnson, a composer who lives off an inheritance, push past the crowd and guard. Once aboard their yacht, the two drink heavily while commiserating about servants, blackmail, and gambling debts. We are told that Carpenter eventually killed himself after his trust fund money evaporated, thinking he could not live on only $200 a month. The narrator then connects these haves to the have-nots by mentioning that Morgan's friend Albert had been providing for a family with $170 less per month before he was killed. We then shift to another yacht, where we enter the mind of a sixty-year-old grain broker who fears that the government has finally caught up with his tax evasion. His thoughts reveal his sham marriage, his lack of sympathy for the other businesspeople he ruined, his history as a novelty salesman, his womanizing, and the fact that he only feels remorse for his rather awful life now because he is about to be caught.

In the next yacht, we find Jon Jacobson and his family, whom the narrator describes as "pleasant, dull and upright" (238). The Jacobsons are wealthy but became so honestly. Jon "is not bigoted and is generous, sympathetic, understanding and almost never irritable" (239). The family's servants are also well paid and think highly of the family, sleeping well aboard their yacht. In the next boat are two Estonians, the Intrepid Voyagers, who travel the world sending stories back to their readers at home. We are told that they are very happy, almost as happy as the Jacobsons.

The narrator then takes us aboard the *Irydia IV*, where we are introduced to Eddy, "a professional son-in-law of the very rich" and his mistress, Dorothy Hollis, the wife of a movie director (241). Eddy is snoring away while Dorothy struggles to sleep. She worries about the state of her marriage, the amount both her husband and her lover drink, and whether or not to take a sleeping aid. The narrator tells us that there are two more yachts, but that their passengers are sleeping. Finally, Harry Morgan and the Coast Guard are reintroduced as the *Queen Conch* is towed back into the yacht basin.

As I go through the events of chapter 24 with my students, I find it useful to create a diagram of the yacht basin. Even the most rudimentary image helps my students to visualize the way Hemingway's narrator is moving through the space, keep track of the characters at play, and gain an understanding of their physical proximity to one another. I also lay out the parameters of Hemingway's iceberg theory, since Hemingway's penchant for cutting away anything that was not vital means that this lengthy passage, with no obvious narrative significance, should nevertheless be carefully considered. For instance, Hemingway's choice to bookend the exploration of the yachts with the "Key West crowd" at the beginning and the entrance of Morgan's nearly dead body at the end emphasizes the physical proximity of the novel's characters. Hemingway's use of what critic Kirk Curnutt has identified as the literary equivalent of a cinematic tracking shot encourages us to recognize that despite leading very different lives, those with money and those without live those lives very close to one another.[4] The yacht basin is a space where the wealthy wallow in self-pity, agonize over self-constructed tribulations, and (occasionally) sleep easy.

Despite the narrator's ability to drift between yachts and interior thoughts, the characters remain completely oblivious to the reality of their neighbors' experiences. More important, none of the yacht occupants, even the generous Jacobsons, extend a single thought to the many characters who occupy this chapter's fringes and, by thematic reasoning, the fringes of their lives. This context is made obvious by Johnson and Carpenter, who insult and then push a security guard out of their way before paying no attention to "a group of men waiting at the Coast Guard pier" (228). Equally important is Morgan's entrance at the end of the chapter, which reminds readers that his descent into a life of crime, which has now brought him close to his inevitable death, was precipitated by the greed of Mr. Johnson, the wealthy businessman who skipped town without paying Morgan for eighteen days of chartered fishing.

Chapter 24 is not the only one in which Hemingway focuses on oblivious characters. Consider the episode in chapter 19 wherein Richard Gordon, the author of novels of social conflict (197), sees Marie Morgan and is disgusted by her physical appearance, calling her a "big ox" and a "battleship" (176). Richard immediately imagines her home life, what her husband thinks about her body, and what she does in bed. He attributes a number of undesirable emotional traits to Marie based solely on her appearance. He even feels confident enough in his insight to base a character in the novel he is writing on her, because "he had seen, in a flash of perception, the whole inner life of that type of woman" (177).

I find it useful at this point to ask my students questions about the nature of the Morgans' relationship as it is depicted in the novel and to consider it in light of Richard Gordon's assessment of Marie. The irony, of course, is that the Morgans' relationship and homelife are nothing like Richard Gordon imagines, something my students are quick to recognize. Thus, we appreciate that the episode is both a chance for Hemingway to mock the idea of self-important authors—so proud of their own powers of perception—and to emphasize human failure to understand one another, even when sharing physical spaces. This theme ties into *To Have and Have Not*'s other major theme, articulated by Morgan as his final words, that "a man alone ain't got no bloody fucking chance" (225). Essentially, Hemingway is doubling the tragedy of Morgan's pronouncement, because the harsh reality is that connectivity is nearly impossible as long as society separates humanity into classes based on *having* and *not having*; it is a reality that no amount of proximity can overcome.

Hawks and his production team do not directly recreate the yacht basin sequence; however, the underlying theme of ignorance in spite of proximity is expressed visually through the film's primary setting: the Marquis Hotel. According to Kawin, it was William Faulkner who centralized the action of the film to the hotel, a choice that also works to ratchet up the tension and tighten the narrative (35). The hotel comprises three levels: a basement cellar with a hidden room where the hotel's owner, Frenchy (Marcel Dalio), hides the resistance fighter Paul (Walter Szurovy) and his wife, Hélène (Delores Moran); a main floor, where much of the film's action takes place in a large barroom; and a third floor, where Harry (Humphrey Bogart) and Marie (Lauren Bacall) have rooms across the hall from each other. The screen geography emphasizes the proximity of the characters and the events that take place in the spaces, as most of the events literally happen on top of one another. Only Morgan and Marie move freely among all three levels, and even they remain mostly restricted to their own spaces on the third floor; the crossing of each other's thresholds inevitably results in complex (albeit fun for the audience) sexual and interpersonal negotiations.

There are many instances of proximal obliviousness to consider; for instance, the sequence near the beginning of the film where Johnson (Walter Sande) sits in the tavern drinking, completely unaware that Harry is upstairs convincing Marie to return his stolen wallet. Or we can think about Cricket (Hoagie Carmichael), the bandleader who never seems to leave the tavern and yet remains blissfully ignorant of both the international intrigue and developing romance taking place below his feet and above his head.

To spur discussion about the way the levels of the hotel work to obfuscate knowledge despite proximity, I revisit two sequences with my students. The first is a lengthy piece that takes place midway through the second act. The scene opens on a two-shot of Hélène and Harry sitting at Paul's bedside in the hidden cellar room where Harry removed the bullet from Paul's shoulder the night before. The pair discuss Hélène's reasons for having come along with Paul, before leaving the hidden room to continue their conversation in the larger area. As they speak, Marie enters at the top of the stairs, unnoticed. She pauses to listen before interrupting their conversation with a series of snide remarks that clearly express her jealousy. After their conversation ends, there is a crossfade to the third floor where Harry and Marie enter Harry's room. Marie's jealousy is clear as she first attempts to be overly obsequious, offering to untie Harry's shoes and run him a bath, before taking on a mocking tone, repeating Hélène's words about never being angry at Harry again. This line reveals Marie's lack of understanding about the actual nature of Harry and Hélène's conversation. Hélène says she cannot be mad at Harry, not because she is in love with him but because he saved her husband's life.

Marie's misreading of this affection causes her to act in ways inconsistent with the fiercely independent persona she has presented thus far. Harry seems to be put off by Marie's jealousy at first, telling her to walk around him, to show that he has no strings attached. Soon, however, the power of their attraction overpowers their resistances, and the pair share a kiss. It is important to note that while Marie is still not fully aware of the nature of Harry's conversation with Hélène, Harry's assurances that she maintains no romantic hold over him allow Marie to let down her guard. Harry, who has the most knowledge, is able to open himself up to a romantic relationship with Marie only after he is able to understand that her outward actions are the result of an underlying attraction. Their kiss represents a connection that transcends the physical and emotional barriers that have kept their relationship mostly superficial, despite being overtly erotic.

This moment of connection is short lived, however, as it is soon interrupted by Frenchy, who comes to warn Harry that the Vichy police officers are in the bar, plying Eddy (Harry's alcoholic first mate, played by Walter Brennan) with drinks in the hopes of getting information about Paul and Hélène. The confusion presented in Frenchy's reactions to Harry and Marie's inside jokes ("Good thing you didn't get me in that tub" and "Look out for those strings") reinforces the idea of secret knowledge. Despite the deeper understanding Harry and Marie now share, the expression of that understanding, despite feeling natural to them, is befuddling to anyone else. Frenchy's intrusion also reminds us that events continue to transpire around them, events that will have significant ramifications on their lives, even as they have a moment of idyllic pleasure. A jump cut brings us to the barroom where Captain Renard (Dan Seymore) is getting impatient with Eddie's fish story. When Harry sits at the table, the conversation shifts to questions about Paul and Hélène's whereabouts. Renard becomes increasingly frustrated with Harry and Eddie's avoidance of his questions and asks about "the two passengers" three times before Harry responds. The irony of the entire sequence is obvious as the two passengers Renard wants so desperately to capture are literally beneath his feet.

We see a similar visual cue at the end of the film. Harry has trapped Renard and his men in his room upstairs, where he is literally beating them into submission. After a cutaway, we see a bruised Renard on the phone ensuring a safe exit for the main characters. Once their safety is secured, Harry, Marie, and Eddie walk down the stairs into the very crowded main level, where the room is full of sailors and soldiers. We can assume that these service people are on the side of the Vichy government, which has control of Martinique, and are therefore aligned with Renard in principle if not in direct purpose. These figures represent the enforcement of the political apparatus that Harry and his cohort are undermining. As we understand from the screen geography, Renard's beating happens directly above the heads of these would-be enforcers, while the two "passengers," the symbolic representation of the Free French movement, hide out below their feet. Yet, the service people continue in their revelry, ignorant of the high-stakes activities occurring all around them. In fact, the three main characters walk (and dance) directly through the crowd, on their way to circumvent the very power the service people represent.

Just as in Hemingway's yacht basin scene, proximity does nothing to decrease the obliviousness or the political and psychological isolation of the characters. Many of the film's events share the same physical footprint, and yet the characters remain ignorant of the reality of each other's lives and the true nature of the situation of which they are each a part.

It is through this mirroring of thematic concerns that we see a manifestation of Linden's visual equivalents via the inter-semiotic transpositions Hutcheon describes. Even though the production team makes no significant efforts at narrative fidelity, the film reveals significant thematic connections between the two works, themes that each work communicates to its audiences via means that are the most efficacious to their respective mediums. The production team's creation of a hotel which does not exist in the source text allows for a purely visual expression of the novel's themes, and thus achieves what Bazin called the "equivalence of meaning" between the two forms at play (20).

Finally, once my students grasp the way visual equivalents operate within Hawks's adaptation of *To Have and Have Not,* we discuss an observable perspective shift that makes the film version of the story more palatable to mass audiences. Phillips and Gladstein have argued that the film's incorporation of the theme of the hopelessness of a *man alone* leaves Hemingway's premise mostly intact; however, I propose that Hawks has removed the bite from the damning indictments found in Hemingway's novel.[5] Rather than a pessimistic warning uttered by a dying man who has learned the lesson about the perils of isolationism far too late for it to do him any good, in Hawks's film, Harry is able to learn a lesson in time for him to find Hawksian comradery.[6] Unlike Hawks's heroes, the followers of the Hemingway code always end up worse off, either dead, close to death, or else losing everything important to them.

It is important to Hemingway's male heroes that they stick to their principles, but ultimately those principles do not lead to a happy ending. The same can be said about the theme of class obliviousness. Hemingway's dramatization of how the physical closeness of characters from different classes does not by itself result in mutual understanding shows us that bridging the divide between the haves and the have-nots is impossible as long as social conventions facilitate demarcations. Hawks's film, by contrast, posits that these divides can foster useful ignorance. After all, it is the ignorance of Renard and the other representatives of the Vichy government that facilitates Paul and Hélène's escape and therefore assures the continued success of the Free France Movement they represent.

The divergence between Hawks and Hemingway on this point is important because it signifies the effort Hawks's production team made to adapt Hemingway's ideas into something more palatable to general audiences—cutting out the pessimistic existentialism that is so integral to the author's treatment of his heroic characters. It is hard to read any pessimism in the image of Hawks's characters literally dancing out of the scene at the end of the movie. Highlighting this particular change allows me to circle back to my students' initial reaction to the film version of To Have and Have Not in relation to the novel. Despite having expressed a near unanimous resolve that, in general, any movie would be better if it were more like its source material, most of the students preferred Hawks over Hemingway. The recognition of their own reactions helps my students understand the argument against all-purpose paradigms for qualitative assessments of adapted works, since commercial cinema and experimental literature (to use our current example) are very different animals with unique sets of conventions. The success of Hawks's film as an example of inter-medial translation comes from its ability to employ techniques that work best in its medium, whether that be a shift to more palatable themes or to the use of visual equivalents to express those themes, rather than its ability to perfectly mimic its source.

Notes

1. By classic, I am referring to both the cinematic style of filmmaking—continuity or invisible editing, reliance on movie stars, focus on narrative—and to the Hollywood studio system, the vertically integrated factory assembly method through which most American feature films were made between 1910 and 1960. Hawks's *To Have and Have Not* was produced and distributed via the Warner Bros. studio infrastructure and conforms to the stylistic conventions meant to hide the artifice of cinema in order to facilitate an immersive experience.

2. The adaptation studies field began taking shape in the mid-1950s with theorists like Andre Bazin, whose essay "Adaptation, or the Cinema as Digest" remains foundational in the field. In recent years, scholars such as Robert Stam, James Naremore, Thomas Leitch, Linda Hutcheon, and Simon Murray (to name just a few), have attempted to move the field beyond notions of fidelity as they continue to explore the dialogic relationship between not just literature and cinema but all forms of inter-medial transactions. While comparative analysis remains an important aspect of adaptation studies, there is a larger emphasis today on the influence of intertextuality and the real-world, practical mechanisations of media production.

3. Bazin uses the example of Jean Delannoy's 1946 film *The Pastoral Symphony* based on a novel by André Gide, in which Delannoy exploits "Michèle Morgan's beautiful eyes," which Bazin claims "are able to communicate the blind Gertrude's innermost thoughts" (20). It is because Delannoy has "enough visual imagination to create the cinematic equivalent of the style of the original" (20) that he is able to visually express the inner thoughts that Gide related through descriptive prose. Linden writes that film "can never express the content of the novel as the novel expresses it. Different materials demand different modes of expression" (160), hence the need to translate between equivalents.

4. Curnutt refers to the tracking shot in his book *Reading Hemingway's* To Have and Have Not. When describing Hemingway's narration technique during a party scene that was eventually excised from the novel, he writes that Hemingway's approach "parallels the cinematic tracking shot in which the camera eye moves from subject to subject for an extended period of time without a jump cut" (xxxiii). Curnutt again uses the tracking shot to describe the omniscient narration employed in the yacht basin sequence in chapter 24 (xxxiv).

5. Phillips proposes reading Bogart's Harry Morgan as a typical Hemingway code hero and Gladstein draws connections between the novel and the film, to argue for Hawks's fidelity to his source material.

6. The heroes in many of Hawks's films find redemption only after accepting their roles as part of a collective rather than as isolated figures. Consider, for example, Geoff Carter in *Only Angels Have Wings,* Thomas Dunson in *Red River,* and the male leads John T. Chance and the Dude of *Rio Bravo.*

Works Cited

Bazin, Andre. "Adaptation, or the Cinema as Digest." *Film Adaptation,* edited by James Naremore, Rutgers UP, 2000, pp. 19–27.

Curnutt, Kirk. *Reading Hemingway's* To Have and Have Not. Kent State UP, 2017.

Gladstein, Mimi Reisel. "Hemingway, Faulkner, and Hawks: The Nexus of Creativity That Generated the Film *To Have and Have Not.*" *Key West Hemingway,* edited by Kirk Curnutt and Gail D. Sinclair, UP of Florida, 2009, pp. 172–86.

Hemingway, Ernest. *To Have and Have Not.* Scribner, 2003.

Hutcheon, Linda. *A Theory of Adaptation.* Routledge, 2006.

Kawin, Bruce F. *To Have and Have Not.* U of Wisconsin P, 1980.

Laurence, Frank. *Hemingway and the Movies.* UP of Mississippi, 1981.

Linden, George W. "The Storied World." *Film and/as Literature,* edited by John Harrington, Prentice-Hall, 1977, pp. 156–70.

Phillips, Gene D. *Hemingway and Film.* Frederick Ungar, 1980.

To Have and Have Not. Dir. Howard Hawks. Perf. Humphrey Bogart, Walter Brennan, and Lauren Bacall. 1944. Warner Home Video, 2003. DVD.

Hemingway's *Fifth Column*, Howard Hawks, and the Movies

Peter L. Hays

Hemingway's works, both novel and play, influenced the movies of Howard Hawks. Hemingway and Hawks were friends. They fished together out of Key West and Sun Valley and hunted together out of Sun Valley; Hawks and his second wife, Slim, even honeymooned at Hemingway's Cuban home, the Finca Vigía (Mast 10). They also shared a philosophy and (at least in early Hemingway) a style of presentation. According to Hawks's biographer Gerald Mast: Hawks and Hemingway,

> both told stories of men in action, and that action was a personal assertion of existential meaning in a universe of potential cosmic meaninglessness. Both had a special fondness for stories of "Men Without Women" and of men who tried to find and make a place for those necessary women. Both preferred characters who did more than they said, felt more than they spoke. Both built their narratives upon moral systems based on personal definitions of honor and integrity. ... Both developed a style—either verbal or visual—which was distinguished by its spare, bare understatement (245–46)

—as we can see in Hawks's films with his use of Gary Cooper and John Wayne.

Moreover, Hawks said, "I like anything that Hemingway wrote." Hawks bought the screen rights to *The Sun Also Rises* but couldn't figure out how to make a film about a man lacking a penis and resold the rights to 20th Century Fox (245). Fishing with Hemingway out of Key West, aboard the *Pilar*, he recounted:

We were sitting in his boat, fishing.... I said, "I can make a picture out of the worst book that you ever wrote." He said, "What's my worst book?" I said, "That piece of junk called *To Have and Have Not*." "Well, you can['t] make a picture out of that," he said. So we sat around for two weeks and evolved the story that we did which was the meeting of the two people in his story and it had very much the same background. (243, based on the 1977 DGA interview with Joseph McBride)

That background for the film adaptation of *To Have and Have Not* (1944) was, as parts of the novel are, Havana, Cuba, years before the novel's action.[1] In Hemingway's novel, Harry Morgan, a Key West fishing guide, is cheated out of payment by a client, Mr. Johnson, and must find other means to support his wife, Marie, and their daughters during the Depression. He turns to smuggling liquor and people, loses an arm in a smuggling attempt, and finally is forced to take three bank robbers on his boat. He kills them but is fatally wounded. Hemingway also juxtaposes the wealthy vacationing in Key West, the "haves," against the poor and struggling "have-nots." But, as Hawks said, his film would begin earlier and tell how Harry met Marie, years before the events of Hemingway's novel. As such, the film contains very little from the novel other than Mr. Johnson, Eddy the drunk as Harry's first mate, dangerous smuggling operations of people in the Caribbean, and a stalwart boat captain in Harry Morgan. Marie in the movie is not like Marie in the novel. One can see the kind of woman Hawks admired—strong-willed, independent, and witty—unlike Hemingway's more passive Marie. And the novel's economic social criticism is changed in the film to be political and anti-Nazi.

The original screenplay, by Hawks's frequent screenwriter Jules Furthman, set the scene in 1930s Havana, where an unmarried Harry Morgan takes out Mr. Johnson, who loses Harry's tackle and then is killed by Cuban revolutionaries before he can pay Harry his debt—which was much more dramatic, hence filmic, than the novel's Johnson, who skips out by taking an early plane. This first film script—Furthman wrote three, and William Faulkner wrote another, with unscripted changes on the days of shooting—was closer to Hemingway's novel than the released film; the *Queen Conch*, Harry's boat, is a thirty-eight-foot cabin cruiser very much like Hemingway's thirty-eight-foot-long *Pilar*. The movie's setting is Havana, and the potential bank robbers are Cubans trying to overthrow Machado's corrupt regime. The hotel where Harry in the script stays is "a typical Hawks-Furthman hotel-restaurant-bar, run by a comical Cuban couple, Decimo and Benicia" (Mast 248). Yet, comical, English-mangling hotelkeepers are rare in American films.

Two film experts I consulted could not think of other examples than those in Hawks's films. But there is one in Hemingway's *The Fifth Column,* a play written in 1937 about a counterespionage agent for the Spanish Loyalists and his entanglement with a beautiful, long-legged blonde during the Spanish Civil War. (The novel *To Have and Have Not* came first [1937], the play *The Fifth Column* was published in 1938 and produced in 1940, and Hawks's film of the novel in 1944.) The unnamed hotel manager in Hemingway's play is described as a "little man who collects stamps and speaks extraordinary English" (5). For example, while constantly seeking food for his hungry family in Madrid, nearly surrounded by fascist forces, he says, "I just come by see you have any little thing of any kind of sort you don't want to eat." Later, he declares, "When against all my voluntaries initiate slight petition for food only wishing superating quantities" (29). That the hotel manager, "a little man," mangles English is only one part of his characterization: he is an individual, collecting stamps; he knows more English than most of his foreign guests know Spanish, and he tries desperately to feed his family during Franco's bombardment of Madrid.

Whether Hawks saw this play, which ran from March until May 1940 is not known.[2] His biographies focus on his films, not his personal life, which was quite varied and eventful, including numerous women, in marriage and outside of it—somewhat like Hemingway—much traveling; varied pursuits, including planes, cars, and motorcycles; and a long career in films, starting with the silents.[3] Both men enjoyed adventuresome lives, including hunting, fishing, and travelling, and incorporated their life experiences into their art; Hemingway was never a pilot, but he flew from Paris to Strasbourg in 1922 long before airline travel was popular (Reynolds 67–68) and with the RAF on missions during World War II. And, as noted above, Hawks liked everything Hemingway wrote, and *The Fifth Column* was printed in 1938 as part of *The Fifth Column and the First Forty-Nine Stories,* Hemingway's collection of short stories to that date, and separately in 1940, three years before the movie was scripted. Whether Furthman's Decimo and Benicia had such linguistic challenges, the public will not know, for his scripts, the first three for the movie, are in the Warner Library of the University of Wisconsin, available only to scholars.

Hawks ran into trouble with Furthman's script and the planned movie. Because it pointed to corruption in Cuba, the "Office of the Coordinator of Inter-American Affairs objected to Warner Brothers' plan to film a novel that 'might embarrass the Batista regime in Cuba,'" even though the film script set the movie earlier, in the Machado regime; things had not changed much (Macura 40). Inter-American Affairs put pressure on the Office of Censorship, which would deny the film an export license, severely curtailing profits, if the film continued to demean Cuba, a nominal ally in World War II. The one island in the Caribbean not an ally was Martinique, in 1944 controlled by the Vichy French, so the film changed the setting to Martinique, the Cuban rebels became Free French fighters opposing the Nazis, and all licenses were issued (Kawin 31–32).

Hawks was a leisurely director, setting up shots and holding conferences in the morning, and shooting in the afternoons. As neophyte Lauren Bacall demonstrated her acting and singing mettle, and as Bogart fell in love with her, her part expanded and that of Dolores Moran—in what Furthman had conceived as a romantic triangle, as there had been in *Casablanca* with Ingrid Bergman, Bogart, and Paul Henreid—diminished; nevertheless, studio publicity for the movie said two blondes were after Bogie. Thus, Hawks and Bogart considerably changed Faulkner's final script, published by Bruce Kawin, during shooting—as Kawin's thirty-eight pages of notes makes clear.

The Fifth Column's unnamed hotel manager is knowledgeable about the goings on in his establishment. Unlike Dorothy Bridges, who thinks Philip is a playboy only minimally engaging in journalism, the manager is aware of Philip's counterespionage role and warns him of potential threats in the hotel. This creates the irony of an unnamed stranger begging for food who is more knowledgeable about Philip than the woman he loves and thinks of marrying.[4] In the movie *To Have and Have Not*, Frenchy, similarly, is quite aware and politically committed, trying to get Harry to help the Free French. To keep open the hotel, which he owns, Frenchy must keep his political sympathies in check, and seemingly welcome the Vichy police; meanwhile, the Free French fugitives are hidden in the wine cellar below his bar.[5]

Furthman's last film for Hawks (Furthman, like Hawks, had begun in silent pictures, Furthman in 1915) was *Rio Bravo*, in 1959, which he cowrote with Leigh Brackett, using an idea from Hawks's daughter Barbara that became the film's dynamite-exploding conclusion. Again, as in the film adaptation of *To Have and Have Not*, we have a bar and gambling establishment, with a hotel above it. And we have characters with flavored English both owning and running the hotel: Carlos and Consuela Robante. Hawks "takes the stock figure of the comic, cowardly, gesticulating, garrulous Mexican and, by eliminating the cowardliness, while playing up the excitability, builds up a character whose dauntlessness and determination win our sympathy and respect even as we laugh at him" (Wood 43). Comic servants go back to the *commedia dell'arte* and to Don Quixote's Sancho Panza, who usually made more sense than Quixote. Pedro Gonzalez Gonzalez played Carlos, and because, at five foot three, he was over a foot shorter than John Wayne, the height difference created a visual joke. Yet, Carlos literally stands up to Wayne's sheriff: "This is my hotel, and you're a guest under my roof. And I will not be told what I shall do and what I shall not do." Thus, Hawks gives the "little man" with an accent his dignity, just as he had done with Frenchy, the owner of the hotel where Harry and Marie stay, and as Hemingway had done with the short, stamp-collecting, family-protecting, knowledgeable hotel manager in *The Fifth Column*.

Music also plays a part in the three vehicles. Background music is a standard part of Hollywood films, and while *To Have and Have Not* and *Rio Bravo* are not musicals, both feature songs, as does the play, as unifying elements. In the first, Hoagy Carmichael plays piano and sings a number of songs, as Dooley Wilson had in *Casablanca,* here with Lauren Bacall joining in on "How Little We Know." Carmichael's first song, "Hong Kong Blues," has the lines "I need someone to love me / need someone to carry me / Home," describing the states of both Harry and Marie. "How Little We Know" comments on Harry's initial misreading of Marie (called Slim by Harry) and on his own lack of willingness to become involved in the antifascist effort. *Rio Bravo,* with its Dimitri Tiomkin score, also features two Tiomkin original songs and two adaptations. Whether Dean Martin and Ricky Nelson had in their contracts that they would sing in the picture is irrelevant; it certainly helped sell the film to a younger audience.[6] Their singing together occurs after young Ricky Nelson, Colorado Ryan in the film, joins the group in the jail holding Joe Burdette (played by Claude Akins) as prisoner as a new deputy, just after Dude (Dean Martin) refuses a drink in response to "El Degüello," reputedly played by Santa Ana before storming the Alamo; it signifies no quarter, the cut-throat song, and Nathan Burdette (John Russell) has paid Mexican musicians to play it constantly to get on the nerves of those holding his brother. Thus, their singing together, with Stumpy (Walter Brennan) joining in on harmonica and with vocals on the chorus, signals harmony indeed, a coming together as a band against opposition, much as the singing of "La Marseillaise," uniting the French citizens, did in *Casablanca*.[7]

While certainly not a musical, *The Fifth Column* also features music. Philip Rawlings plays Chopin on Dorothy Bridges's record player as a peaceful refuge from both the noise of shelling and his own thoughts, also an indication of a cultured background. But in act 2, after Dorothy has upbraided him ("You waste your time and your life is hateful and stupid" [52]), as Philip prepares to go on a night raid to capture a member of the fifth column, soldiers—the play calls them "comrades"—sing the *"Partizan," "Bandera Rosa,"* the "Comintern" song, and the "Internationale" (54–55). These songs, with their patriotic fervor, are anthems, much like "La Marsellaise," and are calls to arms, much as "El Degüello" becomes one for John T. Chance's (John Wayne) deputies in the jail.

The play and both movies also feature moral choices. In *The Fifth Column*, Philip must decide whether to go off with the lovely Dorothy Bridges or dedicate his life to the fight against fascism, a life that is likely to be considerably shortened. Dorothy is a distraction from his duty, as his fellow agent Max tells him. While Philip enjoys the sex, he says, "I can't afford it" and leaves Dorothy (84). The film's Harry Morgan, initially politically neutral, says his loyalty is to "minding my own business." He, too, makes the moral choice to become politically involved, helping the two free French escape the Vichy police and, possibly, helping a prisoner to escape Devil's Island. In *Rio Bravo*, Chance is morally committed throughout; overly so, as he wrongly accuses Feathers (Angie Dickinson) of cheating at cards, when she had not. But Colorado, who like *To Have*'s Harry Morgan, declines to get involved in the other's problems, does make the moral choice when *his* boss is killed and joins the sheriff in his fight against the town boss/bully. And Dude must also make the choice to stop drinking, which he does when Burdett antagonizes him with "El Degüello."

Some might say that these items may just be coincidences. Any two texts, or even three, examined minutely, will have similarities. Accented hotel managers (one in Spain, one in Martinique, and one in Spanish-speaking Texas) would not be unusual; nor would emotion-stirring music in a movie, though rare in a nonmusical drama—nor would stalwart heroes combatting oppression of any sort. But there is one other factor that ties Hemingway's *The Fifth Column* to Hawks's *Rio Bravo*. In the play's opening, Preston, Dorothy Bridges's lover before Philip, describes Philip's behavior at the bar Chicote's: "He had a cuspidor, and he was going around blessing people out of it. You know, sprinkling it on them" (5). In the silent opening of *Rio Bravo*—no dialogue for several minutes—Joe Burdette taunts drink-cadging Dude by throwing a silver dollar into a cuspidor. As Dude overcomes his disgust in his need for a drink and reaches for the dollar, Chance kicks the cuspidor aside. Twenty-one years after *The Fifth Column,* the unsuccessful play was still influencing movies and American popular culture, through Hemingway's inspiration of popular movies, of the need for bravery and collective action against bullies, local or national.

Appendix: A Guide to Student Learning

One can compare both of Hawks's films as classic Westerns: bad man takes over town, hero resists and fights for the townspeople—Nathan Burdett versus Sheriff John T. Chance in *Rio Bravo,* and the Nazis versus the Free French, imposing their rule on Martinique, with Harry Morgan ultimately rebelling in *To Have and Have Not.* What are some other films with this basic plot?

In both films, there is one character committed to resistance throughout—Frenchy in *To Have and Have Not,* the sheriff in *Rio Bravo*—but at least one character needs to be persuaded to join the resistance. In *To Have and Have Not,* it's Harry Morgan; in *Rio Bravo,* it's both the Colorado and Dude (and in both films, actor Walter Brennan provides comic relief). What are some other films where a protagonist must be convinced to do the "right thing"? What is the trigger—whether it is an event or a person—that causes the reluctant hero to switch from "minding his own business" to fighting for others?

Hawks borrowed liberally from himself and others. The film of *To Have and Have Not,* although using Hemingway's title and name for the main character, employed little else—beyond his boat, the Caribbean, a customer named Johnson, and a drunk named Eddy, and some smuggling (though entirely different cargoes in the two works). Hawks took more from Michael Curtiz's *Casablanca,* including its star, Humphrey Bogart, a singing piano player, the rebellion of a French colony against its dominion by French proxies for the Nazis, World War II, and the Nazis, and smuggling of Free French fighters. Is such borrowing theft, homage (imitation being the sincerest form of flattery), or simply commercial filmmaking?

The early scenes in *To Have and Have Not,* showing Johnson catching and losing fish, are process shots of the fish leaping out of the water. Today such scenes might be done with CGI. What is the difference between the two, and why would each be used today?

Notes

1. Hemingway's novel was made twice more into movies, each closer to his novel than Hawks's film: *The Breaking Point* (1950), with John Garfield and Patricia Neal, directed by Michael Curtiz; and *The Gun Runners* (1958), with Audie Murphy and Eddie Albert, directed by Don Siegel.

2. The play produced in 2008 by the Mint Theatre of New York, by Artistic Director Jonathan Bank, scrupulously follows Hemingway's script; the only change I could

detect (other than stage setting) was substituting a full-length silver-fox coat for the cape that Dorothy purchases, no doubt based on what they could borrow for their performances. Hemingway's play, starring Franchot Tone and Lee J. Cobb and directed by Lee Strasberg, was adapted for the stage by Benjamin Glazer. Those changes have not been published, but I doubt that Glazer would have removed some obvious comedy in the form of a malaprop-speaking hotel manager.

3. Hawks had a degree in mechanical engineering from Cornell (1917), flew planes in South America, taught pilots during the First World War, raced cars and motorcycles, built the car that won the 1936 Indianapolis 500, and loved hunting and fishing—these last two hobbies endearing him to Hemingway and Faulkner (Mast 14). He also was extremely promiscuous, jealous of Bogart for seducing Bacall before he could, and having affairs with *To Have and Have Not*'s costar Dolores Moran and an extra named Dorothy Davenport (extra feature on the Warner Brother's disk). He was forty-four when he married Slim Gross, twenty years her senior. Bogart was twenty-five years older than nineteen-year-old Bacall, and John Wayne was twenty-four years older than twenty-seven-year-old Angie Dickinson when the two filmed *Rio Bravo*, a typical Hollywood casting of older men and younger women.

4. Blond and engaging Dorothy Bridges is clearly based on blond and engaging Martha Gellhorn, with whom Hemingway was having an affair at the time. Dorothy doesn't understand the fighting's locale: "I understand a little about University City, but not too much. The Casa del Campo is a complete puzzle to me. And Usera—and Carabanchel." And she says of her own education, "I'm not typical Vassar. I didn't understand *anything* they taught me there" (5). She eats *civet lievre, foie gras,* and *Poulet de Bresse* smuggled in in embassy pouches, while the locals eat "water soup" (8). And she takes advantage of the starving locals by buying cheaply a silver-fox fur cape, as Gellhorn actually did. It's a demeaning portrait, where she, and sex with her, is "a very handsome commodity. The most beautiful I've ever had" (84). Gellhorn could not have been pleased.

5. Robin Woods says that *To Have and Have Not* embodies "one of the most basic anti-fascist statements the cinema has given us" (26). Marcel Dalio, who played Frenchy, also played the croupier in the earlier Bogart film *Casablanca*, also about fighting the Nazis. Dalio was a Romanian Jew, living in France, who had starred earlier in two of Jean Renoir's films. While he was filming *Casablanca*, the Nazis were killing his parents in concentration camps.

6. The movie featured four then current television stars: Walter Brennan, from *The Real McCoys;* Ricky Nelson, from *The Adventures of Ozzie and Harriet;* Ward Bond, from *Wagon Train;* and John Russell, from *Lawman*. John Wayne had discovered Pedro Gonzalez Gonzalez on Groucho Marx's *You Bet Your Life* in 1953 and signed him to a contract to appear as comic relief in Wayne's films.

7. Hawks stole—or *borrowed*—liberally, from others and himself; if it worked once, why not use it again? The rescue of two Free French fighters in *To Have and Have Not* came straight from director Michael Curtiz's *Casablanca*, as did the singing piano player and Bogart. "Steve" and "Slim," the nicknames for the Harry and Marie characters, came from the nicknames Hawks and his wife had for each other. The character name

"Feathers" came from a silent film script Hawks had written for Joseph von Sternberg's *Underworld* (1927), where the protagonist helps a drunken friend, much as Chance helps Dude. "Chance" was the nickname of Hawks's girlfriend in the 1950s, and Walter Brennan, who played drunk Eddie in *To Have and Have Not* with a shambling, loose-jointed walk, played the limping cripple Stumpy in *Rio Bravo*, in both movies helping the protagonist, Bogart or Wayne. Feathers's mocking of Wayne comes from Bacall's insolence toward Bogart. And Bacall's line, on her second kiss of Bogart—"It's better when you help"—is essentially repeated by Feathers's in *Rio Bravo*.

Works Cited

The Fifth Column. Dir. Jonathan Bank. Mint Theatre, 2008. DVD.
Hemingway, Ernest, *The Fifth Column and Four Stories of the Spanish Civil War*. 1938. Scribners, 1969.
———. *To Have and Have Not*. 1937. Scribners, 1962.
Kawin, Bruce, ed. *To Have and Have Not*. U of Wisconsin P, 1980.
Mast, Gerald. *Howard Hawks, Storyteller*. Oxford UP, 1982.
McBride, Joseph. *Hawks on Hawks*. U of California P, 1982.
Macura, Sergej. "Discursive Intersections and Film-Making Constraints: *To Have and Have Not*." Belgrade English Language and Literature Studies: BELLS90 Proceedings, Vol. 2, 2020, pp. 35–49.
Reynolds, Michael. *Hemingway: The Paris Years*. Basil Blackwell, 1989.
Rio Bravo. Dir. Howard Hawks. 1959. Warner Bros. Films, 1986. DVD.
To Have and Have Not. Dir. Howard Hawks. 1944. Warner Bros. Films, 2003. DVD.
Wood, Robin. *Howard Hawks*. 1968. British Film Institute, 1981.

Part III

Later Works and Myths

Teaching *The Garden of Eden*

Suzanne del Gizzo

Confession: I have never taught John Irvin's 2008 adaptation of Ernest Hemingway's *The Garden of Eden*. That may sound like a strange admission, since this collection compiles reflections on teaching Hemingway and film. I accepted the invitation to write this essay because I wanted to think through why I have not taught the film (despite teaching at least three courses in which it would easily fit) and how I might teach it. That process has convinced me that—despite many formidable challenges—teaching Irvin's adaptation of *The Garden of Eden* in conjunction with the novel may help a new generation of readers learn about Hemingway's craft and his all-too-often-missed subtlety as a writer; it may also clarify the reason Hemingway's writing has been so notoriously difficult to adapt to the screen. In brief, the film version of *Garden* objectifies the characters and their sexual encounters, and in this way, it misses the point of the novel, which I read as an exploration of vulnerability and intimacy that results in a touching protest *against* such objectification. Understanding how the film fails to capture this protest not only highlights the respective strengths of the different media—film and writing—but it also may help students learn to read Hemingway by paying attention to "white spaces between the lines," to the imbrication of his language, and to his attention to placement and pacing of scenes, or, as Hemingway might have expressed it, to the seven-eighths of the iceberg that is under water.

Before I could figure out how I would teach Irvin's *Garden*, I had to confront the fact that I have never taught it even though I teach several courses where it might legitimately be included (Literature into Film, Gender and Literature, and a Hemingway seminar). I have identified three sound reasons. First, it's complicated! As a heavily edited posthumous publication, the novel presents challenge enough in the classroom. This history of the book (its connections to the author's life as well as the story of how and when he wrote it), the controversy about its publication, and the still greater controversy around Tom Jenks's editorial decisions are daunting even for seasoned Hemingway scholars. Introducing the novel requires introducing students to manuscript studies (or at least the fact that manuscript study is a "thing") and to thorny questions about authorial intention, since there is a dubiousness about delivering this novel to students simply as just another Hemingway novel. In other words, one cannot teach *The Garden of Eden* responsibly without some context regarding the "story of" and "issues around" it.

Related to this is the second reason I may have avoided teaching adaptation to date: despite all the limitations of the text we do have, *Garden* is a transformative novel in Hemingway studies. Published in 1986, when Hemingway's macho persona was finding a less and less sympathetic audience in academia, the novel resuscitated Hemingway's reputation and relevance with its portrayals of gender fluidity and sexual experimentation. We would never be able to read Hemingway as a hypermasculine, reductively cis-hetero author again. Despite this, the book does not completely exonerate Hemingway from all the old charges. After all, Catherine, though powerful and rich, is presented as possibly crazy; David, though he goes along with her experiments, ultimately winds up in a less challenging, more conventional relationship with the infinitely malleable Marita; and that's all before we get to the question about what to do with the emotionally brutal father-son elephant-hunting story encysted in the main narrative. All to say, Hemingway scholars have a lot of skin in the game of how *Garden* is read and unpacking those complexities for new readers takes time.

Third, and finally, there is the fact that the film isn't very good. Even though Hemingway's works have a reputation for uninspired adaptations—the dialogue can feel stilted and dated, and it is difficult to capture the emotional complexities of his characters who are usually more vulnerable and fragile than their outward behavior and dialogue would suggest—this adaptation feels particularly forced and uncomfortable. In fact, after a long string of misses when Hollywood tried to put Hemingway on the screen, I wondered why Irvin would try it on in the first place. It turns out there is quite a story around the making of the film as well. As Irvin explained in an interview on *One True Podcast,* a program dedicated to Hemingway's work and life, he admired Hemingway as a writer for many years and embraced the opportunity to direct a film based on a novel that he understood as yoking Hemingway's masculinity and sensitivity together. The production, however, was plagued by insufficient funding and artistic differences, and in the final stages, producers took the film from Irvin and gave it to another editor. Irvin speculates that the producers wanted a more overtly erotic film with faster, less lyrical pacing. From his comments, it appears that Irvin and film's producers were in a tug-of-war with two elements of Hemingway's writing—the producers, it seems, wanted to highlight Hemingway's hard, bright, strong surfaces, while Irvin wanted to explore his vulnerable, softer, more complex depths.

If Irvin is right, the producers wanted to make the film because the book is sexy. They wanted a sensational and sensationally erotic film with gorgeous, young, privileged people cavorting against the bright blue Riviera sky buying things and playing with gender and sex roles in polyamorous relationships. To be clear: all this is, of course, a part of the book, but this overcommitment to the surface of the story is where the film fails. It is also where the film becomes a promising tool for helping novice readers understand the richness of Hemingway's famously simple style. By putting the novel side by side with the film and asking some key questions about their similarities and differences, students may come to recognize how Hemingway's novel develops intimacy and interconnection that underpin and supercharge its erotic play, making the work a moving experience, not just a sexual playground.

For all the reasons to do with complexity around the novel and film, I believe *Garden* is probably most rewardingly taught in a Hemingway seminar, where students will have spent some time learning about the author, his reputation, and his life. Although it can stand on its own, *Garden* benefits from context, particularly an awareness of inter- and extratextuality. For example, students should be familiar with how Hemingway understood and presented his writing style (the iceberg method and the theory of omission). They should know that from the start of his career, Hemingway's simple style left him open to misreading and misunderstanding. As Hemingway wrote to Max Perkins in November 1926 responding to a negative review of *The Sun Also Rises,* which found the book trivial, "it's funny to write a book that seems as tragic as that and have them take it for a jazz superficial story. If you went any deeper inside, they couldn't read it because they would be crying all the time" (*Letters* 148). Similarly, it would be useful for students to understand Hemingway's public persona and the exploits that reinforced it. Finally, students should know that

Hemingway was not famous for writing sex scenes. In fact, his sex scenes often have a taint of prudishness or embarrassment. Many are literally elliptical (the scenes between Brett and Jake in Jake's apartment in *The Sun Also Rises* and between Catherine and Frederic Henry in the hospital in *A Farewell to Arms,* for example) or somewhat embarrassingly overblown, as with the earth-moving *la glorias* in *For Whom the Bell Tolls.* David Wyatt argues that part of this awkwardness has to do with the fact that for Hemingway, sex is not just about sex, it is also about the vulnerability that is an integral part of love and intimacy. Carl Eby makes a similar argument, albeit from a different perspective, when he notes that trauma and fear of death catapult Hemingway's characters into eroticism and love. For Hemingway, sex is inextricably linked to vulnerability and loss or fear of loss, and that means his book full of sex, *Garden,* is also the book in which he is most intensely exploring issues of vulnerability.

It is this intimacy and exploration of vulnerability that the film adaptation—as it was ultimately produced—misses. Instead, it seeks to tantalize, and the sex scenes, because they aren't connected to the subterranean themes of vulnerability and loss, come across as gratuitous and borderline pornographic. As a result, the camera does precisely what Hemingway's prose does not: it presents the sex and bodies without sufficiently establishing the stakes of intimacy—without a sense of the vulnerability required to be truly intimate. In this way, the film objectifies the sex scenes and neglects the novel's deeper point that objectification is a form of betrayal and loss.

At the heart of this understanding of the novel is the unsexy father-son elephant-hunting story that David writes intermittently; it is one of several African stories he writes about his father as the sexual experimentation between him, Catherine, and Marita escalates. In this tale, a young David alerts his white hunter father to the presence of a great elephant and then accompanies his father and his father's friend Juma on the hunt. As the hunt proceeds, David's loyalties slowly shift, after he learns that the elephant is on his way to visit the bones of his askari (or friend) killed by Juma years earlier. It is a brutal story about friendship, betrayal, and death. Immediately before the kill shot, David looks into the eye of the wounded elephant and the reader is told, "He had long eyelashes and his eye was the most alive thing David had ever seen" (199). After the elephant is killed, David recalls, "He remembered how the elephant lost all dignity as soon as his eye had ceased to be alive and how when his father and he returned with the packs the elephant had already started to swell even in the cool evening. There was no more true elephant, only the gray wrinkled swelling dead body and the huge great mottled brown and yellow tusks that they had killed him for" (201). In other words, intimacy, life, aliveness, and relationship are dramatized in the hunt; it is David's initiation both into a marketplace logic that encourages individuals to subordinate the dignity of beings to their market value and into the way people and animals, with emotions—the elephant was visiting his friend—die and become merely things. The elephant is objectified, valued for his tusks only. And then David watches as the elephant, killed for those tusks, becomes a thing, "a gray wrinkled swelling dead body," after he is shot. In this way, the novel protests such objectification, or at the very least it is concerned with the losses that result from such objectification. Moreover, there is yet another layer of complexity. Although the young David repudiates his father and Juma, resolving to "never tell anyone anything again," the older David comes to understand his father better through the process of writing the story, which is essentially a way of telling everything to everybody again (181). Writing this story is not simply about recovering identity or masculinity; it is about past and current vulnerability and a willingness to share that enacts vulnerability.

For me, focusing on the elephant hunt is the key to teaching the way the film adaptation of *The Garden of Eden* misses the novel's central point. After all, Irvin insists in his *One True Podcast* interview that he understood the centrality of the elephant hunt to the larger narrative and fought not only to keep it but also to have it filmed, for authenticity's sake, in Africa. In her book about adaptations of Hemingway's and F. Scott Fitzgerald's works, Candace Ursula Grissom praises Irvin's decision to retain the African story writing sequences as a visual representation of "David Bourne's struggle to create a sexual identity for himself through writing," but she observes that the "flashbacks" in the film do not quite work. She isn't alone in this observation (230). *LA Times* film critic Mark Olsen similarly notes that "every time the film switches over to dramatize a story that the writer is working on, a hunting adventure of a boy and his father, the momentum stops dead in its tracks. The true heart of the film is the tempestuous relationship between the writer and his wife, and the way the presence of their mutual lover brings it to a boil, so why Irvin and James Linville [the screenwriter] would be so thoroughly distracted by elephant hunting in the desert is anyone's guess." It is this insufficient integration of the themes and concepts of the elephant-hunt story and its connections to the main narrative that make these scenes ineffective in the film. So why does this happen? What is Hemingway able to do in the novel that the film cannot? And how might this lead us to a better understanding of Hemingway's craft?

To prompt students, I would ask them to reckon with the role of the elephant hunt in the novel and the film by comparing and contrasting them in terms of content, rhythm/pacing, and placement. As they moved through these comparisons, I would also encourage them to define the nature and types of "intimacy" they see in the film versus in the novel.

In the film, the elephant-hunt scene is clearly connected to the main narrative only as a statement of David Bourne's desire to maintain a distinct identity during his uncertain present—a time and situation filled with pleasant but psychologically complex demands for sexual and gender experimentation that make tremendous demands on his sense of self. In the novel, however, the elephant-hunting scenes resonate strongly with Catherine—and David's relationship with Catherine—as well. This connection is most often achieved through language and tropes that are underdeveloped or missing from the film. For example, although the film makes a few references to Catherine's interest in tanning, it does not capture the novel's depiction of her obsessive desire get as dark as she can. Moreover, this darkness is loosely but consistently connected to both Africa and the couple's escalating sexual experimentation—as if getting darker allows Catherine to become less inhibited. Similarly, the film does not pick up on the way David compares Catherine's smoothness to ivory; he observes after they make love, "You're just like ivory. That's how I always think. You're smooth like ivory too" (169). This connection to the elephant is significant for at least two reasons. First, the elephant is hunted for his ivory tusks, and second, by this point in the novel David is sleeping with Marita. Although Catherine encourages David's sexual relationship with Marita, he initially resists; arguably, David, more conventional than Catherine, finds such a relationship a betrayal of his wife. Catherine is thus linked to the elephant through the word *ivory* and through David's feeling of having betrayed her as he betrayed the elephant. In other words, the elephant-hunt story echoes (albeit in complex ways) two central themes in the novel: betrayal (shifting allegiances) and objectification (ivory).

The connection between the elephant hunt and David's relationship with Catherine is further hindered because the film—both in the script and in the performance by Mena Suvari—flattens out Catherine's character. Catherine's internal struggle—her desire for approval, her displays of power, her struggle with dependence and independence—are vital to the novel's meaning. Catherine grapples with intimacy as she invites people, David and Marita, into physical intimacy with her only to grow restless and look for the next thrill. Of all the characters in the novel, Catherine has difficulty accepting complexity, despite her seeming talent for creating it both in her relationships, with the ménage à trois, and on her body, with her desire to simultaneously become as light in her hair and as dark in her skin as she can. Despite these experiments to hold and bring opposites together, Catherine struggles to understand complexity and intimacy. For example, Catherine rejects one of the earlier African stories:, "It's bestial. So that was what your father was like." David responds, "No, . . . But that was *one way* he was" (157; my emphasis). In her rejection of the story and David's father's complexity, Catherine does not appreciate how David's writing makes him open and vulnerable, nor does she appreciate how writing helps him achieve a greater level of intimacy with his father. Marita, however, is able to hold two opposing ideas at the same time. After reading one of the African stories, she asks David, "Was this when you stopped loving him?" David replies, "No I always loved him. This was when I got to know him." She responds, "It's a terrible story and it's wonderful" (154).

While Catherine invites complexity, she finds it difficult to maintain, in part because she wants to be able to control it in ways that prevent her from being truly vulnerable or intimate with others—and it is here readers encounter Catherine's vexed relationship to objectification. At the start of the novel, Catherine appears to detest objectification and commodification. For example, she resents the "clippings" (reviews of his latest novel) as representing David's life as an author in a marketplace. Later, she condemns David's father for his supposed casual liaisons with native women. However, on closer inspection, it is not the objectification she minds; it is that she does not control it. Catherine is extremely wealthy, and she uses that wealth to try to control David—as she disingenuously contends at one point, "I never interfere, I've only tried to make it economically possible for him to do the best work of which he is capable"—and to satisfy her personal whims (156). However, her wealth also arguably undermines her ability to be truly intimate with people, as it allows her to think of them as objects and to become easily frustrated when they don't follow her rules or satisfy her changing desires.

Many critics have sympathetically focused on Catherine as a frustrated artist looking for a creative outlet—they point to her laments that she can't write or paint anything and to her sporadic attempts to study Spanish—but she is arguably better read as an "art dealer," one who admires art but is more suited to buying and selling it than making it. Catherine lacks the empathy required both to be truly intimate and to be an artist. She poignantly reveals when lamenting her lack of artistic ability, "There's nothing except through yourself" (53). Despite her desire to love David, her approach to life and her self-absorption cause her to use him more as an object. She wants him to write their story—the honeymoon narrative—for her, and in bed, she asks him to change to be her girl to satisfy her desire, which is not to say that David isn't game, but merely that she wants to shape him into some*thing* or some experience she desires. She views David's work on the African stories as a betrayal—in part because he is expressing his agency. When Catherine offers to reimburse David with money for the African stories she has burned, readers understand that, although she feels some degree of remorse about it, she sees all her exchanges as reducible to monetary transactions. It is worth noting again the complex connection between the elephant-hunt story and David and Catherine's relationship. Although he has earlier compared her smoothness to "ivory," which seems to align her with the hunted elephant, when she burns David's stories and offers to reimburse him, he is the one that has been killed for his tusks. But Catherine is not a simple character, nor is she simply evil (and again, her complexity evokes David's father). Throughout the novel, she longs for love and acceptance that she seems incapable of offering others, and in this way, Catherine and other characters' interactions with her highlight the different meanings of intimacy in the novel.

Moreover, Catherine's restlessness defines much of the novel's pace. As noted, Olsen observes that every time the elephant hunt is presented on the screen, "the momentum stops dead." In part, this has to do with an intentional change in pacing—David's writing days in the novel and in the film—are meant to feel as though they are "out of time," slow, and methodical, a break from the daily rituals that structure his life with Catherine and Marita—sex, swim, drink, repeat. The stories have a destination, a point he works toward, which distinguishes them from the cyclical but uncertain (depending on Catherine's mood) quality to his daily life. Irvin identifies the tension around the pacing as one of his issues with the film's producers—and the resulting tug-of-war causes the film to feel uneven. Irvin claims that he wanted a slow, lyrical pace, inspired by both the highly ritualized activities of the book and by the title, *The Garden of Eden*. He rightly saw that the pacing—the tension between cyclical ritual and forward momentum—helps to create the tension in the novel. Against the cyclical rituals of their present, readers see two types of movement in the text—the purposeful, methodical movement of David writing the stories (and within that the equally purposeful movements of his father in action in Africa) and the erratic, uncertain movements of Catherine as she changes her physical appearance, requests changes of location, and invites Marita into the couple's relationship. Moreover, Hemingway invites readers to understand pacing explicitly as an element of the novel; there are repeated references to the "speed" of events related to Catherine. Catherine is fearful of speed (which may foreshadow one possible ending Hemingway drafted, in which she, like her father, dies in a car crash). She tells David after one of their early sexual experiments, "It's the only way to slow things," and later when enjoying a drive, she notes, "It never lasts, . . . I always eat that stretch too fast" (48, 87). In a conversation with the perceptive Captain Boyle about the development of his relationship to Catherine, David asks, "How fast will it go?" (65). These associations with Catherine and her fear of, but association with, speed contrasts greatly with David's slow, disciplined pace when writing. Because writing and its pace are presented as an act of recovering intimacy with his father, Catherine's speed can be understood as making intimacy (being present and truly appreciating things) difficult. As with the landscape on her drive, her interactions become a blur.

The filmmakers did not exploit this tension in the novel's pacing; rather, they fell prey to it. Irvin's observation about a lyrical pace is only part of the story. Lyricism and a slow pace, with a camera that lingers, could have established intimacy, but to capture the exploration of intimacies at the heart of the book, that intimacy would have to be contrasted to the livelier tempo Irvin believes the producers wanted. It would be interesting to explore with students how such tension in pacing might be achieved and how pacing could be used to help viewers understand the differing versions of intimacy in the text.

Pacing, of course, results not just from characters discussing openly their attitudes toward speed; it also has to do the placement of the scenes: how and where the elephant hunt is introduced into the principal honeymoon narrative. Placement is where the filmmakers and readers most directly wrestle with the status of *Garden* as a posthumously published, heavily edited text. It is here an instructor could address the value of manuscript study. What might we learn by seeing how and when the elephant-hunt story was composed? Did Hemingway experiment with the placement of the African story fragments in the main narrative? Grissom speculates: "Hemingway was in the process of employing his iceberg technique by interjecting several layers of meaning at various levels of thematic depth. . . . However, because he never completed the novel, Hemingway's placement of the African flashbacks remains somewhat inconsistent" (231). This complicates our ability to argue definitively about the meaning or pacing of the text based on the placement of the African stories, but instructors could invite students to discuss what might have worked in terms of placement and pacing, given thematic exploration of intimacy and vulnerability.

A pedagogical digression: we write essays like this and publish books like this against an apocalyptic backdrop—not just the COVID-19 pandemic, but also the major transformation of higher education and the humanities in particular, which the pandemic has likely accelerated. To employ an overused word, the humanities are in "crisis," and every day I work, write, and teach literature with this in mind. This essay signals two fledgling but significant changes in my pedagogy over the past year. First, I find myself less interested in a Catherine-like high-speed chase through multiple novels and stories in my courses, where inevitably I find that I "eat . . . a stretch too fast." I am finding more meaningful experience teaching slowly, diving deeply, giving the students and me the space and time to appreciate intimately the work in question, from multiple perspectives and using multiple lenses. With his iceberg method, Hemingway richly rewards such an approach. Second, more and more frequently, I recruit the idea and practice of creativity as a valid approach when seeking to meaningfully engage students in my literature courses. I have felt increasingly free to dismantle the sacredness of the text and/or a posture of critical subservience to it, preferring to ask students to empathetically engage texts as cocreators. In other words, rather than a straightforward character study, I ask students to rebuild the characters we read as if they were writing them, challenging the students to unpack their motivations, identify metaphors and why they work (or don't), describe decisions around the style of dialogue, et cetera. In other words, if we believe, and I do, teaching literature helps to teach empathy—so obviously and sorely needed in our society at the moment—it may be worth strategically breaking down our sense of critical distance and allowing ourselves and our students to become more intimate with texts. For me, such approaches are recovering the humanity in literature and the humanities.

Teaching *The Garden of Eden* actively enables those pedagogical approaches. The very complexity around teaching *Garden* as a novel—not to mention pairing it with the film—that I identified at the start of this essay invites an instructor to slow down, dive deep, give themselves and the students time to appreciate complexity. It also invites creative play. The fact that the text as we have it is "unfinished" and "unsanctioned" by the author might be seen as not a liability but an opportunity, a license to play with what might have worked, what might have allowed the themes and tropes Hemingway appeared to be developing work thematically and structurally. Moreover, the themes of intimacy and vulnerability in *Garden* allow an instructor to speak directly about not just those themes in the text but also the role they play in reading and in authentic learning.

We will never know what the film may have looked like if John Irvin had been allowed to finish the edit. However, there is one scene—not in the novel—that suggests he may have had a sense of the issues around objectification in the novel, and I would invite students to consider why that scene is there and what it communicates. At the beginning of the film, Irvin added a wedding scene—and it is bizarre. The beautiful, bucolic setting serves as backdrop to two events: in the foreground we see a filmmaker with a crank camera shooting a recreation of Manet's *Le Déjeuner sur l'herbe* with its naked woman and clothed men picnicking and, in the background, we see David and Catherine's wedding luncheon. The stark contrast between the camera eye capturing an "art" scene (complete with its oddly objectified woman) and the ritual a personal commitment and intimacy powerfully presents in visual form the tension at the heart of the novel. In a film version that seeks to be faithful to the book in so many ways, this addition is notable and intriguing. The other truly interesting decision concerns the soundtrack. During the sex scenes, the otherwise traditional score transitions to music that seems inspired by Erik Satie, with its halting measures and irregular rhythms, which mimics the speeding up and slowing down in the novel.

For many years, scholarship around *Garden* focused on the way it transformed our understanding of Hemingway's hypermasculine persona, but this transformation was understood largely in terms of the novel's depiction of sexual play and gender-role reversals. However, thinking about teaching *The Garden of Eden* as a novel and film pairing against the backdrop of the pandemic and changes in higher education amplifies another aspect of the novel—its focus on differing notions of intimacy and the role of vulnerability in intimacy, a theme that, curiously, Hemingway develops most powerfully in the masculine space of the hunting story. In addition, authentic intimacy in the novel is held up in sharp contrast to objectification and by extension commodification. The elephant's "alive eye" loses all dignity when it is killed and made an object, prized for the market value of its tusks; David is "objectified" by Catherine both as a lover and for his writing. Similarly, we know Hemingway struggled with the commodification of his persona and that he did not finish or publish *Garden*, which kept that work out of the marketplace in his lifetime. *Garden* reveals that Hemingway struggled to balance the vulnerability of being a writer with the commodification of writers and their work.

These elements are more visible when compared with the film, which misses these key themes and gives us—for the most part—the simple, sexy narrative without the book's elements of linguistic and structural complexity. Because Hemingway's simple style was always vulnerable to superficial misreading, comparing the book and the film can help readers deepen their appreciation of Hemingway's craft.

Works Cited

Eby, Carl P. "Reading Hemingway Backwards: Teaching *A Farewell to Arms* in Light of *The Garden of Eden*." *Teaching Hemingway and Gender*, edited by Verna Kale, Kent State UP, 2016, pp. 104–14.

Grissom, Candace Ursula. *Fitzgerald and Hemingway on Film: A Critical Study of the Adaptations, 1924–2013*. McFarland, 2014.

Hemingway, Ernest. *The Garden of Eden*. Collier, 1986.

Hemingway's The Garden of Eden. Dir. John Irvin. Lion's Gate, 2010. Film.

———. *The Letters of Ernest Hemingway:* Vol. 3, *1926–1929*, edited by Rena Sanderson, Sandra Spanier, and Robert W. Trogdon, Cambridge UP, 2015.

———. Interview with Mark Cirino. *One True Podcast*, 12 June 2020, https://www.hemingwaysociety.org/node/875.

Olsen, Mark. "Movie Review: Hemingway's *The Garden of Eden*." LATimes.com, 9 Dec. 2010.

Wyatt, David. *Teaching Hemingway and the Art of Emotion*. Cambridge UP, 2015.

Teaching Hemingway through Fiction Film
Midnight in Paris and *Hemingway & Gellhorn*

Tatiana Konrad

Fiction is frequently associated with the imaginative and the unreal. As such, when fiction texts are used to discuss history, they are complex to deal with. When delving into historical events, preference is often given to nonfiction rather than fiction that attempts to portray and interpret those events. Yet fiction is a valuable resource teachers and learners may explore in their practice; literature and films are powerful texts to work with when discussing important historical issues, including war and genocide.

Prominent historical figures also frequently draw attention of various writers and filmmakers, who often choose to narrate the story not in a documentary but in a *fiction* mode. Films like Woody Allen's *Midnight in Paris* (2011) and Philip Kaufman's *Hemingway & Gellhorn* (2012)—the primary focuses of this chapter—are illustrative examples. While these films, rather straightforwardly, are classified as fiction, they include characters based on real people, such as Ernest Hemingway. This chapter analyzes these cinematic examples and illustrates how they may be used as tools to better understand Hemingway as a man, an American, and a writer. More specifically, I discuss the two films from three distinct perspectives—literary studies, film studies, and pedagogy—and consider ways of teaching Hemingway myths as poststructural truths.

In *Docu-Fictions of War: U. S. Interventionism in Film and Literature* (2019), I examine the potential of fiction films to use in exploring various *truths* about real events. More specifically, I analyze the mode of fiction and argue that all fiction texts are different. Among other types, there is fiction that "adopt[s] elements of documentary and, in its unique way, record[s] reality too" (Prorokova

2). I call such fiction *docu-fiction* (2). Focusing exclusively on war docu-fiction, I investigate its educational component and contend: "War docu-fiction does not *teach* history per se, yet it helps one *understand* history, interpreting it and presenting it in a more dramatic yet perhaps more memorable and approachable way than a straightforward historical account" (9). As such, I view fiction as a fascinating source that scholars and educators may work with to understand and interpret various historical figures and events. Fiction presents us with a different, but no less valid, kind of truth.

Fiction plays a significant role in our understanding of history; it is a powerful mode to deal with real and imaginative worlds. For example, Marc Ferro argues: "The fiction film is despised, because it dispenses only a dream, as if the dream formed no part of reality, as though the imaginary were not one of the driving forces of human activity" (80). For Ferro, fiction film, like, in principle, any other film, "has a value as a document," because every film engages in the complex process of knowledge production and its communication through both visual and verbal components (81).

It is crucial to understand that even history textbooks, which we tend to consider the *truest* material one may use to teach/learn about the historical past, are questionable. For example, Hayden White foregrounds the twofold nature of history, arguing that, on the one hand, "history has never claimed the status of a pure science, ... it depends as much upon intuitive as upon analytical methods, and ... historical judgments should not therefore be evaluated by critical standards properly applied only in the mathematical and experimental disciplines"; yet, on the other hand, "history is after all a *semi*-science, ... historical data do not lend themselves to 'free' artistic manipulation, and ... the form of his [the historian's] narratives is not a matter of choice, but is required by the nature of historical materials themselves" (27). History is a way to interpret events, decisions, and figures; it is a method of classifying certain events, decisions, and figures into relevant and irrelevant; it is a mode of producing knowledge that is selective and is at once both true and untrue.

Using fiction to teach about historical events and figures is a phenomenon common among educators. Even in history lessons, teachers draw on fiction because, according to Donna E. Norton, "through historical fiction, children can begin to visualize the sweep of history" (qtd. in Rodwell 18). Additionally, fiction is frequently viewed as much more fun to work with—and by saying this, I by no means want to compromise or undermine fiction as a mode of expression; instead, I attempt to pinpoint its advantage over mere chronicles or other forms of documentation. To specify, both fiction and nonfiction are legitimate modes of documenting information; yet they function differently and, therefore, in education may be utilized for different purposes, only to enrich the processes of teaching and learning. Consider former educator Sarah K. Herz's reflection on her own vast experience in employing history in the English classroom:

> When students examine the past as outlined in a historical novel, they become immersed in characters moving through time and place and they begin to perceive the continuity of time. The events in a novel become more significant because the student is required to understand them in order to appreciate the novel. By reading about a historical character in a novel, students begin to place that character's life in the past and begin to connect this section of the past to the society they live in and soon realize how studying the past helps them to understand the present. (qtd. in Rodwell 18-19)

One may, therefore, persuasively argue that when using fiction "students are able to recall the historical information more easily because it has been associated within the context of the plot, character, setting and theme of the novel" (19). It does not mean that nonfiction should be substituted for fiction. Both are crucial in teaching various historical events and figures, nonfiction largely dominating this process. Yet, introducing sessions in which an instructor and their students engage in a discussion of history through fiction is important, as this can show students the variety of materials that are out there, as well as explain how to deal with texts that tackle serious issues through fiction.

From the perspective of poststructuralism—which acknowledges the existence of multiple truths—one may argue that every story is a truth. Yet it might be dangerous to baldly say this to students, without providing enough explanation of what poststructuralism is and how the ideas developed by the leading representatives of this intellectual movement (Jacques Derrida, Michel Foucault, and Jean Baudrillard) contribute to our understanding of such notions as truth, myth, authenticity, and reality. Depending on the level of the course being offered, the instructor may use a cultural studies textbook to explain poststructuralism's key ideas and concepts or directly engage with the original writings of poststructuralists (such as the above-mentioned authors) to examine truth, myth, authenticity, and reality, and the ways these phenomena help us understand a fiction text. In the end, one might still wonder: how do we, educators, deal with these truths, and how are the students to interpret them?

Believing that pedagogy's primary focus is on "the process of production and exchange that takes place in the interaction of teacher, learner, and the knowledge jointly produced" (Rodwell 30), I claim that the success of the lessons in which fiction is the core material particularly depends on this mutual work between teacher and student.

It is effective to start the lesson that will discuss fiction texts with these words from historian Inga Clendinnen: "There is no such thing as a real story. Stories are told or written, not found" (qtd. in Rodwell 132). This comment on the tangibility of stories will instantly make students think about such notions as reality, authenticity, and truth. Initiate a discussion among and with the students to uncover the complexity of storytelling as a practice and stories as products and emphasize the fluidity of fiction.

The instructor may continue the lesson with the general discussion of what students think fiction is and how conflicting are the feelings that they experience while watching fiction that deals with real-life events and persons. The expected answer is that they watch fiction often and, indeed, enjoy the films that attempt to recreate certain historical events, but in principle, they never trust them because they explicitly say that what is shown is fiction. A brief discussion of what students make of fiction films that explicitly say they are "based on true events" or, for example, of mockumentaries or pseudo-documentaries, will help them think again of such terms as *fiction* and *documentary*.

As both a historical and literary figure, Hemingway may effectively be taught through his own oeuvre as well as the numerous nonfiction narratives that address his works and life. Yet teaching him through fiction can be a fascinating experience, too. I suggest focusing on two films, *Midnight in Paris* and *Hemingway & Gellhorn,* and teaching Hemingway from three perspectives: the Man, the American, and the Writer. Because of time constraints, students must watch both films in advance, so during the sessions the instructor is free to show only selected clips.

This course can be effectively taught on the undergraduate level, and specifically to students in their first or second year of studies. The semester course can focus broadly on Hemingway and his works (twelve to fourteen sessions of an hour and a half each). The material discussed in this chapter can be offered during two sessions, each focusing on one film. This is the type of course in which student participation and input are of primary importance, so each session is designed to allow sufficient time and space for students to explore questions raised by the instructor as well as formulate and answer their own questions. The number of students can vary from fifteen to thirty.

The two films should be introduced to students in the second half of the course, by which point they are already familiar with some of the key aspects of Hemingway's life and writing style and the main themes of his works. The discussion of *Midnight in Paris* and *Hemingway & Gellhorn* will then be productive and help broaden the students' knowledge.

Midnight in Paris covers an earlier period of Hemingway's life, specifically the 1920s and his stay in Paris (1921–28), where Hemingway worked as a foreign correspondent for the *Toronto Daily Star* and wrote some of his works. The session can focus on Americans in Paris, that is, expatriates.

Instruct the students, as part of their homework, to write down the names of famous people mentioned in the film and ask them to identify Americans among them. In class, ask students to share this information with each other, and then ask how many names they know from the list, and for what these people are famous.

Familiarize students with the life of famous Americans in Paris in the 1920s. Specifically, focus on some of the key figures, including Ernest Hemingway, Gertrude Stein, John Dos Passos, Maxwell Perkins, and F. Scott Fitzgerald. Instructors might invite students to share knowledge about famous expatriates, but they should be prepared to deliver the key facts in a concise, yet sufficient manner. Some of the sources that could be useful for preparation include Donald Pizer's *American Expatriate Writing and the Paris Moment: Modernism and Place* (1997) and Craig Monk's *Writing the Lost Generation: Expatriate Autobiography and American Modernism* (2008). These works focus on autobiographies of American expatriates in Paris and some of their famous writings.

Select a few scenes from *Midnight in Paris* that focus on 1920s Paris, and ask your students to identify the elements that help the viewer imagine the atmosphere of this specific time and place. Focus on scenes that portray Hemingway the man (which are, indeed, very few). Discuss these author portrayals with your students; ask them what the portrayals tell us about Hemingway as both an American and a writer, expecting that each question will elicit a different answer.

At this juncture, it proves helpful to share some details about Hemingway's life in Paris: Michael S. Reynolds's *Hemingway: The Paris Years* (1989), Paul Brody's *Hemingway in Paris: A Biography of Earnest Hemingway's Formative Paris Years* (2014), and Robert Wheeler's *Hemingway's Paris: A Writer's City in Words and Images* (2015) may be particularly useful in preparation. Prepare short slides to highlight some of the key facts from Hemingway's life in Paris. Having presented this information, invite students to compare these facts to the way Hemingway is depicted in the film. Discuss the limits and advantages of the portrayals of Hemingway's life in Paris in *Midnight in Paris,* exploring the way Hemingway the man affects how Hemingway the character is constructed and how Hemingway the character shapes audience perception of Hemingway the man (*and* the brand).

Finally, demonstrate for the class the film's technique of oscillating between the past and the current moment. Discuss the extent to which the interventions in the past stand for our current attempts to learn history, including the history of Hemingway's years in Paris. Focus specifically on the main character, Gil (Owen Wilson), and ask students how time travel helps him learn the history of American expatriates in Paris and its continuous impact on America's (and France's) present.

Next, have the class focus on Gil and examine the parallels between him (he is a writer excited about his interactions with the people from the past, but particularly with Hemingway [Corey Stoll] and Gertrude Stein [Kathy Bates], who become interested in his novel) and Hemingway. Discuss how this intended comparison of Gil to American writers from the 1920s helps us understand Hemingway as a famous and successful American writer. Drawing on the nostalgic depictions of the past, examine with your students how Gil's travels in time are a way to escape the present, and how they help romanticize Hemingway as an expatriate.

Hemingway & Gellhorn focuses on the relationship between the writer and his third wife, Martha Gellhorn. It is set between 1936 and 1945. The film can be particularly useful to analyze the issues of manhood and masculinity of the 1930s and Hemingway as a man of his time. A discussion of the film can follow the session when the instructor and students talk about Hemingway's novel *For Whom the Bell Tolls* (1940). The aim of the lesson is to examine the film's portrayal of the Spanish Civil War (1936–39) and discuss how Hemingway's experience in that conflict inspired him to write the novel.

Instruct students to pay attention to the war scenes depicted in the film while they watch the film outside of class. In class, show the scenes again, and ask your students to take notes of what they see. Have them answer specific questions: Who are the people depicted on screen, and what kind of society? How does the viewer understand that the action takes place in Spain? Ask students to discuss the role of the Spanish Civil War in the film, first in groups and then turn this into a general discussion: What did Hemingway do in Spain? How did the war affect him as a human and as a writer?

After discussing the role of the war, move to the analysis of the role Hemingway plays in the film. Some pertinent questions to have the class consider might include: How does the film portray Hemingway? What kind of a man was he, according to the film? And, according to the film, what was his role in the war? What scene depicting the writer appeals to your students the most? Why and how? What does the film teach us about masculinity in the 1930s? Discuss how the film may be juxtaposed with Hemingway's novel *For Whom the Bell Tolls*. Do you see how the Spanish Civil War could inspire Hemingway to write this novel? Are the images of war similar in the film and the novel? Are they different? Ask students to provide examples from both the film and the novel as they formulate their answers.

Finally, discuss this revealing quotation from Hemingway, regarding fiction versus nonfiction and his war experiences:

> I write fiction and I find that all publishers want biographical material only so they can use it to make your fiction seem a "document." I do not claim even to have been in the war and it is impossible for me to furnish a military history to a publisher. If he wants to he can say that I served on the Italian front which is true enough and ample but I would prefer no military mention at all. I have forbidden Scribners ever to use any personal publicity because I want the stuff to be judged as fiction without any attempt to tie it up with documentation. (qtd. in Gatzemeyer 114)

Significantly, Hemingway spoke these words regarding his earlier novel *A Farewell to Arms* (1929), which deals with World War I; yet they can be aptly used to discuss his experience in the Spanish Civil War and the war as an inspiration for *For Whom the Bell Tolls*. Here I focus the discussion on fiction's role in creating knowledge about war, on how one may study war through Hemingway's oeuvre, as well as the way Hemingway's fiction recreates scenes of war and thus helps us understand the history of which he became a part.

Although *Midnight in Paris* and *Hemingway & Gellhorn* are fictional depictions of Hemingway's life in the 1920s–40s, the two films may be used to teach Hemingway in a meaningful way. It is important to combine these cinematic examples with nonfiction materials and guide students through the history of

Hemingway's life, explaining to them that the two fiction films will never teach them history proper; yet these texts will help them understand certain aspects of the writer's life, sometimes even more effectively and accessibly than nonfiction materials. These depictions interpret Hemingway as a man, writer, and American; they interpret the role of people, places, and events in Hemingway's life and invite the audience to participate in the act of interpreting.

Students should be informed of materials that can help them learn more about Hemingway that are not limited to nonfiction texts. Introducing various narratives in the classroom can, to a great extent, improve both the teaching and learning processes. Given the large number of texts that exist on Hemingway and his life, however, it is important to select the materials carefully, to make sure they indeed help students learn in a new way. Using fiction films in class represents one such option—one that may yield meaningful learning.

Works Cited

Brody, Paul. *Hemingway in Paris: A Biography of Ernest Hemingway's Formative Paris Years*. CreateSpace, 2014.

Ferro, Marc. "The Fiction Film and Historical Analysis." *The Historian and Film*, edited by Paul Smith, Cambridge UP, 1976, pp. 80–94.

Gatzemeyer, Jace. "Review of *Teaching Hemingway and War*, edited by Alex Vernon." *Hemingway Review*, vol. 36, no. 1, 2016, pp. 114–16.

Hemingway & Gellhorn. Dir. Philip Kaufman. Perf. Nicole Kidman, Clive Owen, David Strathairn, and Rodrigo Santoro, HBO Studios, 2013. DVD.

Midnight in Paris. Dir. Woody Allen. Perf. Owen Wilson, Rachel McAdams, Kurt Fuller, and Mimi Kennedy, Sony Pictures Home Entertainment, 2011. DVD

Monk, Craig. *Writing the Lost Generation: Expatriate Autobiography and American Modernism*. U of Iowa P, 2008.

Pizer, Donald. *American Expatriate Writing and the Paris Moment: Modernism and Place*. Louisiana State U Press, 1997.

Prorokova, Tatiana. *Docu-Fictions of War: U. S. Interventionism in Film and Literature*. U of Nebraska P, 2019.

Reynolds, Michael S. *Hemingway: The Paris Years*. Blackwell, 1989.

Rodwell, Grant. *Whose History? Engaging History Students through Historical Fiction*. U of Adelaide P, 2013.

Wheeler, Robert. *Hemingway's Paris: A Writer's City in Words and Images*. Yucca, 2015.

White, Hayden. "The Burden of History." *Tropics of Discourse: Essays in Cultural Criticism*. Johns Hopkins UP, 1978, pp. 27–50.

Films Like White Elephants
Hemingway in Woody Allen's *Manhattan* and *Midnight in Paris*

Stephen Whittaker

Ernest Hemingway and Woody Allen walk into a classroom: melodramatic posturing and glib satire ensue. Or so you might expect from their pop-culture caricatures. If these important American artists have something in common—in a time when each of is saddled with a reputation for adolescent sexism, if not outright misogyny—it might be that since the #MeToo awakening, both are tricky bets pedagogically. Their presumed manners may differ, one ponderous and the other trite, but they both result in a view of women as furnishings for the male ego.

But we experienced something much more engaging and thought-provoking in The Reluctant Muse, a recently completed continuing education course. What we found was that for most of his career, Allen has been struggling to come to terms with Hemingway and that the results of the process shed a good deal of light on Hemingway. And we found in the films and fiction of both artists a self-conscious discourse very much attuned to the uses to which men—men very like themselves—put women.

Just how this course came to be needs some explanation. The eminent Sondra Myers is Senior Fellow for International, Civic and Cultural Projects and Director of the Schemel Forum at the University of Scranton. For the Schemel Forum for Cultural Enrichment and Education in the Community, I have offered courses on Homer; Woody Allen; and various modernist writers, such as Colum McCann, Toni Morrison, and James Joyce. In my day job, I teach modernism and film, as well as classics and rhetoric. But I was hesitant when, in 2018, Sondra asked me to offer a new course on Woody Allen. Ronan Farrow, Allen's son with

Mia Farrow, has played an important role in the #MeToo movement, publishing groundbreaking essays in the *New Yorker* and winning the Pulitzer Prize in the process. Regarding allegations that Allen molested Ronan's sister Dylan when she was a child, Ronan Farrow has said, "I believe my sister."

I realized that if we were even going to try to do a course on Allen's work, the complex themes and dynamics of sexuality and art would have to be addressed directly. As I pondered how to approach this difficulty, I happened to be working on a paper on connections between Hemingway's early story "Hills Like White Elephants" and the novel *The Garden of Eden* (1986), unfinished at his death, thirty-four years after the publication of "Hills," for the summer 2018 Hemingway Conference in Paris. In one of those epiphanies that sometimes inform our work, I saw, or imagined that I saw, how the Hemingway work afforded a way to approach the Allen problem. Allen, of course, had conjured a Hemingway character in *Midnight in Paris* (2011), a character many of whose lines on writing are virtually lifted from *Garden*. I understood that just as Hemingway was reworking ideas from his earlier work in *Garden,* so was Allen in *Midnight.* Both artists' works are relentlessly recursive. One such Woody Allen work from thirty-two years before, *Midnight, Manhattan* (1979), just happened to star Hemingway's granddaughter Mariel—just happened to?

Woody Allen's character, Isaac, in *Manhattan* has an exploitative relationship with Tracy, played by Mariel Hemingway. The man in Hemingway's "Hills Like White Elephants" likewise attempts to reduce the girl to an object for his own use. This intriguing similarity may or may not imply a specific source for Allen in Hemingway-the-writer, but because of the fraught nature of the clear thematic connection, we would need a theoretical foundation and language to approach it. So, we offered the Reluctant Muse course in the fall semester of 2018. Thirty-five people took it, ranging from current university students to alumni to faculty colleagues and spouses to members of the Scranton community.

A Critical Language: Adrienne Rich's "Writing as Re-Vision"

Adrienne Rich's 1971 essay "When We Dead Awaken: Writing as Re-Vision" has four things to recommend it for the study of Hemingway and Allen: it makes clear that feminist criticism has a rich pedigree among male artists; it challenges the idea that there might be a clean division between the artist and her or his work; it links the concepts of artistic influence and self-re-vision; and, most importantly, it lays out in the sharpest terms the dynamic of the male artist's use of the female.

In lecture, one can supply context for Rich's essay. It continues the work of Virginia Woolf's *A Room of One's Own* in critiquing T. S. Eliot's immensely influential "Tradition and the Individual Talent." Woolf, most poignantly in her imagining of a tragic end for Judith Shakespeare when her impulse to become an artist runs up against the cultural limits assigned to her sex, argues that a tradition which has erased the lives of women and the contributions of female artists has limited utility in empowering female life and creativity. Rich extends Woolf's feminist critique by demolishing Eliot's picture of life and art as being of necessity hermetically separate entities. She does this by weaving together the story of her own life and her development as an artist. Both women want to preserve Eliot's central idea of making and responding to art as perhaps *the* defining human activity. But they demonstrate that for the female artist, the tradition is at best an ambivalent construct and that the antiseptic separation of art and life is itself only imaginable as a concomitant patriarchal construction of women as physical and psychological luxuries. The linked assumptions—that the artistic tradition is gender neutral and that the artist's independence from *his* art arises from that perceived neutrality—comprise a complex model that denigrates the dignity of women as human beings and makes inconceivable their lives as artists.

Rich's essay begins by linking its own title to Ibsen's play *When We Dead Awaken* and George Bernard Shaw's *The Quintessence of Ibsenism*. For the pedagogy of a classroom in which some students may mistake feminism for an attack on men or on the male artists being discussed, it is rhetorically and pedagogically canny that Rich begins her piece by finding a foundation in the work of two male artists. It is perhaps no coincidence that the article first appeared in a pedagogical issue of *College English*. Rich describes Ibsen's play as being "about the use that the male artist and thinker—in the process of creating culture as we know it—has made of women, in his life, and in his work; and about a woman's slow struggling awakening to the use to which her life has been put" (34). Rich quotes Shaw's observation that in this dynamic "women can die into luxuries for men."

Rich tells us, "I have hesitated to do what I am going to do now, which is to use myself as an illustration" (38). She recognizes the necessity of this challenge to the boundary between art and life in order to approach the way this artificial partition has served male prerogative.

The essay moves fluently between Rich's life and art. She discusses her influences and shows us how they manifest in her work. She demonstrates how certain ideas recur and evolve in her poems. Her magnificent poem "Planetarium," quoted in full, examines how biography, autobiography, art, and artistic tradition weave together in the making of a work of art, a tradition, and a life (47–48).

Students in the course read Rich's "When We Dead Awaken," and our discussions use her terminology. However, my own thinking is also informed by the critics discussed below, whose work the students are not expected to read, and the thinking of those critics certainly frames our approach in the classroom. As for varieties of feminism, the waves of feminism principally refer to the political agendas of each period. Rich is typically identified as a second-wave feminist because of her attention to class and sexual orientation. However, since she grounds her thinking in that of Virginia Woolf, the prototypical first-wave feminist, Rich's own terminology is sufficient for the purposes of the course.

As can be seen in what follows, in our course, Adrienne Rich's essay helped us articulate the relation between the male author and his female muse, connect the exploited girl in "Hills" and the one in *Manhattan*, see the way Hemingway and Allen each engaged in a re-vision of his own work, and see more clearly the extent to which Allen understood his debt to Hemingway.

The Genetics of Influence: "Hills Like White Elephants" and *Manhattan*

This section might also be headed: "The Hemingways in *Manhattan*" or "Mariel and *Manhattan*: Two of Ernest's Granddaughters."

Students will reliably underread "Hills" and *Manhattan* as simple stories of leisure-class dissipation, the first done as melodrama, the second as farce. The scholarship on "Hills" and a consideration of the use of sources in *Manhattan* can move the discussion into a consideration of how each explores the male use of a female life.

My own scholarly interest in "Hills Like White Elephants" begins with Gary Elliott's 1977 argument that the beaded curtain touched by the girl suggests a rosary and embodies a religious motive for her desire not to go through with the abortion. Elliott thus identified the presence of the Hail Mary in "Hills" and began the reading by subsequent critics of that presence as a marker of Catholic orthodoxy. I am interested in arguing that the story is an example of what I want to call a modernist Annunciation, where the father demands that the girl *not* bear his child. I see this reading as akin to the bitterly irreverent *nada* prayer in "A Clean, Well-Lighted Place," and this way of interpreting the story makes clear that it is a consideration of the most fundamental questions of human dignity, of the nature of fertility and free will.

This theological reading is not central to our work in the Hemingway and Allen course. Elliott's reading does, however, anticipate a crucial insight developed by Stanley Renner. Renner argues in "Moving to the Girl's Side of 'Hills Like White Elephants'" that the conclusion of Hemingway's short story, by leaving in question the girl's decision regarding whether to terminate her pregnancy, clarifies the fact that the subject of the story is the girl's evolving agency (27). Renner stresses that it is in the story's specific setting that "Hemingway works out the story's conflict, which revolves around the development of his female character" (28). Renner continues: "So firmly does the story's sympathy side with the girl and her values, so strong is her repugnance toward the idea of abortion, and so critical is the story of the male's self-serving reluctance to shoulder the responsibility of the child he has begotten that the reading I have proposed seems the most logical resolution to its conflict" (38). He argues that the girl achieves agency by the end of the story and will not get the abortion that the man wishes. Students can readily follow Renner's demonstration that the subject of "Hills" is the tentative emergence of the girl's character from the man's shadow.

Elliott's and Renner's insights allow us to understand that Hemingway is certainly examining critically the gender dynamic of male exploitation anatomized by Rich. The problem with seeing *Manhattan* in a similar light, of course, comes from the fact that the film, even more than the short story, seduces its viewers with the very glamor it is critiquing. Only by carefully analyzing the motives of the central male character, Isaac, do students begin to see that Allen is constructing a suave and charming villain.

As a matter of course, viewers recognize *Manhattan*'s debt to F. Scott Fitzgerald's *Great Gatsby* with the opening black-and-white sequence of romantic shots of the city couples with Gershwin's luscious *Rhapsody in Blue* performed by the New York Philharmonic. Fitzgerald's use of the original 1924 Paul Whiteman recording while writing *Gatsby* is legendary. Fitzgerald's themes of dissipation and self-indulgence are easily recognized in the film. Several of its themes and plot points can be traced to Fitzgerald.

Many critics, feminist and otherwise, have pointed out that the relationship between Scott and Zelda Fitzgerald was fraught. In reaction to early depictions of Zelda as jealous of Scott's gifts and success and more than a little mad, we have come to see Scott as having coopted Zelda's narrative in his fiction in a way that preempts her ability, as an aspiring artist, to metabolize her own story into her art. In a magnificent turnabout, in *Manhattan,* which opens with Isaac trying to find a voice with which to begin his own first-person book, we see Isaac's life coopted by the book his ex-wife, Jill, played by Meryl Streep, is publishing. His ex's having come out as lesbian, Dianne Keaton's Mary opines, explains Isaac's infatuation with "the little girl" Tracy, played by Mariel Hemingway. Mary pigeonholes Isaac psychoanalytically when she mentions Nabokov, the author of *Lolita* (193). Isaac cringes upon hearing excerpts from Jill's book, read aloud by his friend Yale (Michael Murphy): "Making love to this deeper, more masterful female made me . . . made me realize what an empty experience, what a bizarre charade sex with my husband was" (258).

Mary has already mocked Fitzgerald as a member of her and Yale's "Academy of the Overrated" (193). Isaac responds with growing pique that he thinks "all those people are terrific, everyone that you mentioned." The ironies of the scene can be easily picked out, beginning with a charming film character's facile dismissal of an author whose fiction is a source for the filmic world she inhabits. The more complex irony, of course, is that her cavalier takedowns are made to a character played by Ernest Hemingway's granddaughter. That Ernest himself was not consigned to the Academy may be attributed to the fact that such snobs would not have thought anyone rated him highly. In practical terms, the film's fourth wall would surely not have survived criticizing the grandfather to the granddaughter. As it is, the moment surely raised the question for us: is Ernest Hemingway present in the film as more that a supplier of one quarter of Mariel's DNA?

The film's opening sequence, Isaac's tentative predation of various hackneyed styles, contrasts sharply with Allen's own use of previous artists: Fitzgerald and, yes, Nabokov in fiction, as well as Bergman and most especially Federico Fellini's *La Dolce Vita.* If Hemingway is here, we found, it is in the distance between what people say and what they mean or feel. When Tracy argues with Isaac about his desire to break up with her, she notes this distance: "You keep stating it like it's to my advantage when it's you that wants to get out of it" (245). When Isaac tries to persuade Tracy to take him back, he says of her meeting people in London: "You'll be with actors and directors. You know, you're . . . you know, you go to rehearsal and you-you hang out with those people. You have lunch a lot" (271). The surface meaning of the dialogue is not the significance of the interaction. This is Hemingway's technique, not that of Fitzgerald's earnest narrator Nick Carraway. We see it everywhere, in the conversations in the final book of *A Farewell to Arms* between Frederic and Catherine, in the self-deceptions of Jake and Lady Bret in *The Sun Also Rises,* and in the little story published between these two novels, "Hills Like White Elephants," where we see the girl's growing awareness that the man's arguments are all for his benefit and control of her as a body. It is interesting that it is the actress Hemingway who repeatedly pierces the facade of Allen's hypocrisy, his playacting.

This is Hemingway's psychological and stylistic essence: that we construct narratives which reveal our fears and our desires only latently. Allen, like Hemingway, shows us how we suffer from the very delusions we construct. "Hills" and *Manhattan* both show us the girl's struggle to liberate herself from the narrative imposed on her by an older, exploitative male who values the emotional and sexual solace she can provide him over her own personhood. In each of these stories, despite the glamorous posturing of the man, the girl is certainly being encouraged to dive into a luxury for him. One girl wishes to protect her unborn child, the other wishes to nurture her nascent art career. The final shot of him in *Manhattan* shows us Isaac struggling against an awareness of his own self-serving and self-deluding narrative. Hemingway's short story ends, it has been argued, with a hope that the girl has emerged, is in the moment of emerging, as a person in her own right. The girl in *Manhattan* certainly has. Less clear is whether the man Isaac has become fully conscious.

This brings us to a startling aspect of Woody Allen's relationship with Mariel Hemingway. I shared with students this paragraph found under the "Legacy" section of the film's Wikipedia entry:

> In her memoir *Out Came the Sun* (2015), Hemingway detailed Allen's visit to her family home in Ketchum, Idaho, upon completion of filming. After intimating that he wanted to take her to Paris, Hemingway warned her parents "that I didn't know what the arrangement was going to be, that I wasn't sure if I was even going to have my own room. Woody hadn't said that. He hadn't even hinted it. But I wanted them to put their foot down. They didn't. They kept lightly encouraging me." When Hemingway stipulated the procurement of a separate hotel room, Allen "called for his private jet the next morning and left Idaho."[1]

It is hard to imagine our discussion of this complicated and alarming story of the exploitation of the young female character within *Manhattan,* followed by what seems the alleged exploitation of the young actress outside Manhattan, without the critical framework provided by Adrienne Rich's essay. She gave us terms for approaching the forms of exploitation, for understanding the blurring of art and life, and for thinking about the nature of influence. For me, this was probably the most important part of the course, a course that I had feared from the outset would be caught between the horns of rage and denial.

Perhaps we found slight consolation in the fact that at the end of both *Manhattan* and "Hills" we saw clearly that the man in each—both of whom in some regard resemble their authors—whose presence seemed to control the narration, was not, in fact, the subject of the story, let alone its hero. Each narrative effectively ends in a self-indictment and asks a question, the contemplation of which suggests that in each work the story is about *her*, the girl's transformation, in the face of *his* narrative paralysis. In each story, the girl commands agency over her own narrative. And it seemed worth considering that these insights arose from the complicated, and without doubt, flawed psyches of two of our greatest male artists who, like Isaac, were struggling to awaken.

The Ache of Return: *The Garden of Eden* and *Midnight in Paris*

For our second pairing, we dove into Hemingway's unfinished novel, *The Garden of Eden,* and Woody Allen's critically successful *Midnight in Paris.* Hemingway, as a character, makes a substantial appearance in the film. With the publication of *Garden,* Edwin McDowell noted immediately the minor industry devoted to the posthumous tidying up and publication of Hemingway's work. Serious scholarly objection to the posthumous editing and publication of Hemingway's far from linear manuscript began with Susan Seitz. Fortunately for our purposes, the questionable shape and the just-so, even trite, plot resolution of the published version were less important than the manuscript's engaging narrative and frequent direct statements about the writing process and the life of a writer. These we were able to compare with Allen's purported hatchet job on Hemingway.

Thomas Brady's early case for the dismissal of Allen's depiction of Hemingway in *Midnight* has recently been much more compellingly made by Wieland Schwanebeck's thoroughgoing albeit ambivalent dismissal of Allen's use of Hemingway in *Midnight.* Schwanebeck is primarily interested in challenging the distinction in Oscar award categories between original and adapted screenplays. He argues that *Midnight* should have been considered an adaptation rather than an original work. The work adapted was not *Garden*, of course, but a four-decades-earlier use of Hemingway as a cliché in one of Woody Allen's stand-up routines.

Russ Fischer had previously made this connection, writing: "For those who haven't seen *Midnight in Paris*, the scenario Allen is joking about with Hemingway and Gertrude Stein is a central aspect of the film. For those who have seen the movie, you'll know that this is only a part of the film, and that going from stand-up routine to film script is a lot more complicated than just fleshing out a couple of characters." (The routine has been excerpted on YouTube.) In the 1960s piece, Allen reminisces of his having met Hemingway and the Paris circle: "I was in Europe many years ago with Ernest Hemingway." Allen assumes the persona of an urbane aesthete who deigns to give Hemingway occasional guidance. Its running gag is Allen's thoughtful suggestions being punctuated with "And Hemingway punched me in the mouth." Schwanebeck and Fischer both connect the stand-up bit to the similar scene in *Midnight* when Hemingway declines to read Gil's manuscript:

HEMINGWAY. If it's bad I'll hate it because I hate bad writing and if it's good I'll be envious and hate it all the more. You don't want the opinion of another writer.
GIL. But there's no one I really trust to evaluate it—
HEMINGWAY. Writers are competitive.
GIL. I could never compete with you—
HEMINGWAY. You're too self-effacing—it's not manly. If you're a writer, declare yourself the best writer—but you're not the best as long as I'm around. Unless you want to put the gloves on and settle it.

Students readily see, however, the difference between the stand-up Hemingway and the figure in *Midnight*. The earlier is clearly a mere parody used for a gag. That of *Midnight* is something more than a figure of fun, though obviously he still conforms to cultural stereotypes of the real Hemingway. The point here is that Allen is engaging in a re-vision of his earlier take, perhaps even giving the master more of his due.

We asked two questions. Were the ideas spoken by the Hemingway character close to those of the real Hemingway? For this we turned to *The Garden of Eden*, which features a writer remarkably forthcoming on his views of the writing process. But this move depended on a prior question: can we legitimately presume that the opinions of *Garden*'s central character, David Bourne, resemble those of his author?

In her brilliant treatment of the long genesis, psychological complexity, and spectacular incompleteness of Hemingway's unfinished novel, "Hemingway's *Garden of Eden*: Resistance of Things Past and Protecting the Masculine Text," Rose Marie Burwell demonstrates how the artificial published edition of the work "almost obscured the pervasively self-reflexive mode of this work which Hemingway could not complete though he had worked on it for thirteen years (1946–1959)" (198). Her essay affords a compelling demonstration "of evidence of Hemingway's presence in the narrational structure beyond the unity of Hemingway and David Bourne that reviewers assumed" (200). For the purpose of considering Woody Allen's apparent reliance in *Midnight* on the declarations regarding writing that occur in *Garden,* Burwell allows us to see in a comparison to the two works whether Allen's Hemingway character is something like the real Hemingway. Hemingway's own reviewers underread the Hemingway-like character in *Garden,* just as Allen's critics underread his treatment of Hemingway in *Midnight.* Both sets of critics saw in their respective auteur's work little more than parody, whether the product of failing artistic capacity or of habitual glibness.

Guided by Burwell's argument that it is not unfair to see a lot of Hemingway in David Bourne, our reading of *Garden* allowed us to compare that view of Hemingway with Woody Allen's. On this score, we were able to see the daily pattern of life common to both depictions, even though Bourne's social and artistic isolation make him distinct from Hemingway. The Hemingway characters (Bourne and Hemingway) are serious and committed artists whose daily routine includes, after the dedication to their art, drinking, eating, and socializing with other artists and aesthetes; honest estimation of the gifts and frailties of others; and erotic adventures. On this last score, we found common ground between Allen's Hemingway's and Hemingway's Bourne's simultaneous presentation and critique of the hypermasculine persona often attributed to Hemingway. This manly man is critiqued seriously and psychologically by Bourne's gradual exploration of androgyny.

Woody Allen and Ernest Hemingway share an appreciation of the complicated relationship between exterior performance and interior experience. This appreciation may, in fact, be one of Allen's deepest debts to Hemingway. Arguably the most celebrated example of the distance between what is said and what is felt in Hemingway's work is the long scene between Frederic Henry and Catherine Barkley toward the end of *A Farewell to Arms*. Both Allen and Hemingway are fascinated by this distance and return to it repeatedly. Hemingway probably came to this technique via Joyce's depiction of the way the flow of consciousness is both concealed and revealed by behavior. For all three artists, the phenomenon is a profound psychological truth, essential to the realistic portrayal of human character and characters. Allen certainly draws on both earlier writers, as well as on psychoanalytic practice. Allen's work also explores this distance via the two corresponding approaches to acting: physical technique and the Method.

But for the anachronism, we might be tempted to say that the *Garden* Hemingway is a product of what in acting is called the Method: developed out of a careful consideration of a character's interior life and experience. The critique in *Midnight* seems, at least at first, to arrive as a product of old-fashioned physical acting or superficial mimesis. Thus, the Hemingway of *Midnight* feels at first like satire. We asked whether Allen's Hemingway has been deprived of interiority as a suggestion that the real Hemingway's view of manhood is in fact cartoonish. Most critics read Allen's portrayal this way. But this reading omits two features of Allen's oeuvre: that though Allen's characters are clearly psychological, he generally rejects the Method because it requires the actor, if not the character, to really understand himself; and, as we saw with *Manhattan*, Allen's engagement with, and veneration of, the Jazz Age, has persisted throughout his career.

That psychological subtlety and rejection of the Method can coexist is one of the most remarkable features of Allen's oeuvre. In *Alice,* for example, the title character, played by Mia Farrow, entertains an ambition to become a writer. She imagines that her successful publisher friend Nancy Brill, played by Cybill Shepherd, might help her, since Alice had previously aided Nancy in her career. It takes Alice's Muse, played by Bernadette Peters, to set her straight. While Alice is naive and idealistic, her Muse is psychologically trenchant and analytic. At one point, her Muse points out that Nancy is refusing to help Alice precisely *because* the successful woman sees the less successful both as competition and as a reminder of her own humble beginnings. The Muse then asks how anyone like Alice, who is "not psychological at all," can possibly become a writer.

Tellingly, this scene is mirrored in *Midnight* in the scene quoted above, just before Hemingway offers to settle the matter of writers' competitiveness by putting on the gloves. The scene combines the psychological insight about the anxiety of influence from *Alice* with the punchline, pardon the pun, from Allen's Hemingway stand-up routine. Allen has certainly subjected the stand-up material to a revision, one that stresses the artist's authentic psychology. Gil, Allen's alter ego, stammers in praise of Hemingway: "Liked? I loved—everything you wrote." And the film attributes the insight to the Hemingway character, who cautions Scott Fitzgerald, regarding Zelda: "This month it's writing, last month it was something else. You're a writer—you need time to write—not all this playing around—she's wasting you—because she's really a competitor—don't you agree?" Allen depicts his own alter-ego taking a psychology lesson from the Hemingway character.

Likewise, consider how Gil's question to Hemingway about fearing death in battle prompts the veteran into a peroration on the profound power and meaning of sex, the gist of which is succinctly echoed by Isaac's ex-wife's book, as read by Yale. The conversation in *Midnight* goes like this:

GIL. Weren't you scared?
HEMINGWAY. Of what?
GIL. Getting killed.
HEMINGWAY. You'll never write well if you fear dying. Do you?
GIL. It's my biggest fear.
HEMINGWAY. But it's something all men before you have done and all men will do.
GIL. Yes but—
HEMINGWAY. Have you ever made love to a truly great woman?
GIL. My fiancée is very sexy.
HEMINGWAY. And when you make love to her, you feel true and beautiful passion and you at least for that moment lose your fear of death.
GIL. I don't know about that—
HEMINGWAY. I believe that love that's true and real creates a respite from death.

Note again Hemingway's seriousness about sex versus Gil's triteness. This opposition was one of the most serious indictments leveled against Isaac in *Manhattan:* the inability to distinguish between "very sexy" and "true and beautiful passion." The Hemingway character, not the Allen surrogate, comes off as a fully human being.

As for the character Hemingway's ideas on writing in *Midnight*, I found it a good exercise to draw students' attentions to a few quotes from *Garden* for comparison. Here are just four of dozens:

> Be careful, he said to himself, it is all very well for you to write simply and the simpler the better. But do not start to think so damned simply. Know how complicated it is and then state it simply. (37)

> He put the note and the key in his pocket and went back into the work room and sat down and wrote the first paragraph of the new story that he had always put off writing since he had known what a story was. He wrote it in simple declarative sentences with all of the problems ahead to be lived through and made to come alive. The very beginning was written and all he had to do was go on. That's all, he said. You see how simple what you can not do is? (108)

> He was completely detached from everything except the story he was writing and he was living in it as he built it. The difficult parts he had dreaded he now faced one after another and as he did the people, the country, the days and the nights, and the weather were all there as he wrote. (128)

> When it's right you can't remember. Every time you read it again it comes as a great and unbelievable surprise. You can't believe you did it. When it's once right you never can do it again. You only do it once for each thing. And you're only allowed so many in your life. (230)

Setting aside the sensationalism surrounding the bicurious subject matter and the travesties of the published version, there are few more satisfying moments to be had than in reading Hemingway's elaborate account of the writing of the safari story. The narrative alternates between present and past, between frame narrative and the story being conjured. David Bourne's re-vision is as sophisticated a playing with frames of reference as any to be found in Woody Allen's films, and if you are familiar with *Another Woman* (1988) or *Purple Rose of Cairo* (1985), you realize that that is saying a lot. Hemingway's treatment of the fluidity of form is never better. And it anticipates nicely the temporal and narrative displacements of *Midnight*.

We realized that truth when Allen returned to Hemingway in *Midnight* from his work of three and four decades before there was a good humored—I have to use Gil's word—*love* for the elder artist's work. Likewise, we found in Hemingway's own re-vision of the difficult negotiations of agency, sex, fertility, and the attempt to root glamor in grammar mooted in "Hills" a comparable mastery.

Conclusions: *Midnight* in *The Garden of Eden;* or, the Dionysian and the Apollonian

In our course, The Reluctant Muse, exploring the presence of Ernest Hemingway's work, persona, and DNA in Woody Allen's work and life gave us a very fruitful way of coming to understand both artists.

The problem of disentangling the life and the work is sometimes an aesthetic problem, as with Joyce's Stephen Dedalus or with Fellini's Guido Anselmi. With artists as various as Paul Gauguin and Louis C.K., as Shen-yi Liao has recently noted, "the relationship between the art and the artist" is obviously a moral issue (198). To some extent with Hemingway, and more emphatically with Allen, the disentanglement is both an aesthetic and a moral problem. In Hemingway, the problem of art and life can be argued to arise directly from the injunction: write what you know. But what Hemingway knew was, much of the time, the moral problems of his own experience. The moral questions that attend Allen's work are, it must be noted, self-consciously part of Allen's aesthetic. Because of Allen's habitual blurring of the boundary between autobiography and art, this moral problem is constitutive of the aesthetic experience of *Manhattan*, in a way it is not, say, even in an extreme case such as Nabokov's *Lolita*, the referencing of which novel in *Manhattan* in the presence of Hemingway's underage granddaughter is a complex moment whose effect has become only more incendiary with time.

Only within the rubric of Adrienne Rich's ideas on gender and art were we able to explore the autobiographical dimension of Hemingway's and Allen's work, to understand the ways both artists revised themes in their subsequent work and how Allen benefitted from Hemingway's process, and how—despite their liability to charges of misogyny or exploitation themselves—each artist clearly participated in a tradition of male artists struggling to come to terms with a culture in which male artistic work both participated in, and struggled to free itself from, the use of women. That is, we were able to contextualize the terrible ambivalence with which the exploited female submitted to, engaged with, or rebelled against the shared project. At the same time, we were able to apprehend the artists' own consciousness of the problem.

Allen, we concluded, recognizes, refers to, and mines this entanglement in Hemingway and so uses Hemingway as a foundation for his own exploration of the nexus of the predation of the muse and the reality of her ambivalence.

More gently, we were able to see how for many, it is hard to tell Woody Allen and Ernest Hemingway apart. They are icons of American culture whose work seems often to submerge in self-parody. Hemingway's style is a feast, truculently immovable, of declarative macho unintentional self-parody, and Woody Allen's take on Hemingway in *Midnight in Paris* is a facile gag played on this shallow take on Hemingway and consistent with the postmodern superficiality of Allen's take on almost everything. We found that *Midnight in Paris* is to *Manhattan* much as *The Garden of Eden* is to "Hills": in each case the later work directly approaches material and concepts approached more circumspectly and tentatively in the earlier. And we very much found that Allen, like Hemingway, was coming to terms with the meaning of Hemingway's worldview.

Parodies of Hemingway's style have been a cottage industry at least since E. B. White's "Across the Street and Into the Grill" in the 14 October 1950 *New Yorker*, which ends with "I commute good, thought Pirnie, looking at his watch. And he felt the old pain of going back to Scarsdale again" (28). We were able to see through the idea that Hemingway's declarative style reflects a superficial, even trite, worldview or that his prose flounders in unintended self-parody, both of which ideas can be seen in a colleague of mine's recent derision, "'He stepped into the stream. It was a shock.' Really?"

Though the presentation of Hemingway in *Midnight in Paris* has occasioned accusations of Woody Allen's characterization as superficial and lazy, most of the lines delivered in the film mirror things said or thought by the autobiographical character in Hemingway's *The Garden of Eden*. And they are anything but trite. Furthermore, Allen's own autobiographical surrogate, Gil, performed by Owen Wilson, clearly idolizes Allen's Hemingway. Indeed, Allen's treatment can justifiably be read as hagiography. Allen's idealizations of the American tradition and of Paris constitute a mainstay of his filmic language. Gil, who shares more than a name with the existentially complex character of the same name in *Purple Rose of Cairo* (1985), is at once naive and perspicacious, an authentic sensibility and an artistic fabrication.

That Woody Allen is doing something more interesting than mocking Hemingway emerges with a reconsideration of his earlier film *Manhattan*,

Allen's most explicit celebration of the American literary and artistic traditions from which he sprang. The use of Fitzgerald and the Gershwin soundtrack clarify that this is the city glamorized by *The Great Gatsby*. But the dialogue owes more to Hemingway than to Fitzgerald. Characters speak, but the meaning is never in the words they utter. Allen's self-obsessed Isaac knows himself hardly at all. The genius of the film is that it seduces us with the glamor of character and setting, leaving us to work out the hollowness of this glamor much as the end of "Hills" leaves us to discover a similar vanity. We are in the epistemology of *The Sun Also Rises* here:

> "Oh, Jake," Brett said, "we could have had such a damned good time together."
> Ahead was a mounted policeman in khaki directing traffic. He raised his baton. The car slowed suddenly pressing Brett against me.
> "Yes," I said. "Isn't it pretty to think so? (198)

Manhattan ends with Tracy saying: "What's six months if we still love each other? You have to have a little faith in people." Tracy is performed by Mariel Hemingway, born Mariel Hadley Hemingway in 1961, daughter of Jack Hemingway, granddaughter of Ernest Hemingway and Elizabeth Hadley Richardson. Typically of Allen, the casting becomes crucial. In her apparent simplicity, Tracy sees through Isaac's sophistic polish. Her authenticity belies her apparent naivete. Her final lines foil Isaac's emptiness and dissimulation, just as Jake's do Brett's. *Manhattan*'s manifestation of Hemingway is literally genetic.

Isaac's attempted appropriation of Tracy's life for his own use in *Manhattan* closely mirrors the man's attempted manipulation of the girl's life in "Hills." Each sophisticated older man tries to bend the girl to his own pleasure. Each interaction conjures an exotic, hedonistic ethos. Laying the film and the story side by side allows the student to see that Allen and Hemingway both conceal a savage critique of that ethos. A patient classroom comparison of the text or subtext working of "Hills" and *Manhattan* makes clear Hemingway's stylistic influence on Allen and enables the students' more subtle readings of both authors.

In *Manhattan* and *Midnight in Paris,* we find two occasions where Allen explicitly relies on Hemingway in the exploration of the conflict between glamor and authenticity. Allen's films thus provide a means by which the student can learn to move between the language of cinema and that of fiction and come to appreciate the complex relationship between Hemingway's apparently simple style and its complex content. Correspondingly, a story such as "Hills" can help the student limb the moral hideousness anatomized in *Manhattan* and illuminate the complicated, even affectionate, playfulness of the depiction of Hemingway in *Midnight in Paris*.

Note

1. As of March 2019, this had disappeared from the film's Wikipedia page, where I found it in October 2018.

Works Cited

Allen, Woody. "Lost Generation. From 'Standup Comic: 1964–1968,'" uploaded by nxa12, 15 May 2009, https://www.youtube.com/watch?v=z85zt_EUySg
———. *Manhattan. Four Films of Woody Allen.* Random House, 1982.
Brady, Thomas. "Woody Allen Has a Laugh at Hemingway in His Latest Film, *Scarriet* (blog), 5 June 2011, https://scarriet.wordpress.com/2011/06/05/woody-allen-has-a-laugh-at-hemingway-in-his-latest-film/.
Burwell, Rose Marie. "Hemingway's *Garden of Eden:* Resistance of Things Past and Protecting the Masculine Text." Texas Studies in Literature and Language, vol. 35, no 2, Summer 1993, pp. 198–225.
Eliot, T. S. "Tradition and the Individual Talent." The Sacred Wood: Essays in Poetry and Criticism. Methuen, 1920, pp. 42–53.
Elliott, Gary D. "Hemingway's Hills like White Elephants," *Explicator,* 35, Summer 1977, pp. 22–23.
Farrow, Ronan. "My Father, Woody Allen, and the Danger of Questions Unasked (Guest Column)." *Hollywood Reporter,* 11 May 2016, https://www.hollywoodreporter.com/news/general-news/my-father-woody-allen-danger-892572/.
Fischer, Russ. Listen to the Stand-Up Routine That Is the Origin of Woody Allen's Oscar-Winning "Midnight in Paris" Script," /*Film,* 1 Mar. 2012, https://www.slashfilm.com/520244/listen-50year-standup-routine-origin-woody-allens-oscarwinning-midnight-paris-script/.
Hemingway, Ernest. *The Garden of Eden,* edited by Tom Jenks, Scribner, 1986.
———. *The Sun Also Rises. The Hemingway Library Edition.* New York: Scribner, 2014.
Liao, Shen-yi. "The Art of Immoral Artists." *Routledge Handbook of Philosophy and Media Ethics,* edited by Carl Fox and Joe Saunders, Routledge, 2023, pp. 193–204.
McDowell, Edwin. "New Hemingway Novel to Be Published in May." *New York Times,* 17 Dec. 1985.
Midnight in Paris. Dir. Woody Allen. Sony Pictures Home Entertainment, 2011. DVD.
Renner, Stanley. "Moving to the Girl's Side of 'Hills Like White Elephants.'" *Hemingway Review,* vol 15, no. 1, Fall 1995, pp. 27–41.
Rich, Adrienne. "When We Dead Awaken: Writing as Re-Vision." *On Lies, Secrets, and Silence: Selected Prose 1966–1978.* W. W. Norton, 1995, pp. 33–49.

Schwanebeck, Wieland. "Oscar's Unrecognized Adaptations: Woody Allen and the Myth of the Original Screenplay." *Literature/Film Quarterly*, vol. 42, no. 1, 2014, pp. 359–72.
Seitz, Susan M. "The Posthumous Editing of Ernest Hemingway's Fiction," Diss. U of Massachusetts Amherst, 1993.
White, E. B. "Across the Street and Into the Grill." *New Yorker*, 14 Oct. 1950, p. 28.
Woolf, Virginia. *A Room of One's Own*. 1929. Penguin, 2000.

Appropriations of Hemingway in *The Long Goodbye* and *A History of Violence*

Scott D. Yarbrough

As an icon of American masculinity in all its faults and virtues, Hemingway has perhaps never shone more brightly in the ether of the popular press than he has this last decade. At a rough estimate, there have been at least seventeen biographical studies published since 2010, from complete biographies to studies on Hemingway in various wartime roles, to books on his relationships with women, along with books about his relationship with writers like Ezra Pound and John Dos Passos, his work with the Red Cross, his youth in Oak Park, and his life in Cuba, his boat, and his brain.[1] There have been at least five novels written about his relationship with his various wives in the last decade as well (most significant among them *The Paris Wife* by Paula McClain).

This outpouring of interest of this signifying and iconographic writer is matched by representations of him in the film media. He has been lampooned in Woody Allen's *Midnight in Paris* (2011) and mauled in the HBO film *Hemingway & Gellhorn* (2012). The 2015 movie *Papa Hemingway in Cuba* came and went with less of a splash than a fishing lure cast into the gulf. Despite these more overt depictions, however, Hollywood has used the Hemingway brand, model, and mystique in more subtle and complex ways.

Over the years, teaching Hemingway's texts has become more difficult and challenging because very often the students cannot see the text itself beneath the obscuring patina of the author's variously described personas. Terms like *toxic masculinity* have entered our popular lexicons, and the kind of manhood seemingly espoused by the Hemingway persona is out of fashion, seeming to many students an atavistic relic of a less enlightened time. As an exercise in upper-level and graduate courses, I find a brief detour through the ways Hemingway is appropriated as an image to be useful; then as a counterbalance we look at the appropriations of his texts as well. Film proves a particularly valuable medium for showing this to students.

Unlike such contemporaries as F. Scott Fitzgerald and William Faulkner, Hemingway never had to go to Hollywood; instead, Hollywood came to him. Even when adaptations of his novels bore very little similarity to the texts they were based on (most notoriously, 1958's *The Gun Runners,* a loose adaptation of *To Have and Have Not,* starring Audie Murphy), the films boasted their relationships, however tenuous, to Hemingway. He was the most prominently and effectively *branded* author of his time, and in many ways, he continues to be the most significant representative of the author-as-brand phenomenon. Although a quick Internet search reveals furniture created in the so-called Hemingway safari style, ink pens meant to somehow reflect Hemingway, a variety of fishing flies, restaurants, bars, and hunting paraphernalia that all strive to associate themselves with the name, one can hardly imagine other literary writers treated similarly by the mercantile world: a John Updike real estate company, a Philip Roth line of sleepwear, a Doris Lessing set of gardening tools, and so on. Similarly, although genre characters such as James Bond, Harry Potter, and Katniss Everdeen (from the *Hunger Games* trilogy) may have great, and in some cases even lasting, cache, these characters' creators are far less known or recognizable.

Scholars and devotees have long decried the schism that has developed between Hemingway's runaway image and his texts. In some ways, Hemingway, with his varied experiences and autobiographical writing, was tailormade to suffer this condition. As Nina Ray explains in her study on Hemingway's imminent marketability, the wish of various companies to participate in—and benefit from—the branding of Ernest Hemingway is perfectly understandable.

Nevertheless, the ultimate result is exactly the one scholars and the author himself have feared. As the American public has become increasingly more preoccupied with mass culture and less inclined to pick up novels and collections of short stories, the dusty popular culture signifier of the Hemingway persona has all but subsumed his work. Rather than the death of the author, we have witnessed the death of the text. With the dissolution of Hemingway's work into the flotsam and jetsam of mass cultural currents, however, film, the dominant medium of current popular culture, has appropriated Hemingway in two widely divergent ways: through use of his name and culturally iconic image as tropes and signifiers, and through subtler and perhaps even unconscious incorporations of his texts into films.

The Image in Spite of Itself

In the short story "On Writing," a grown Nick Adams tellingly confesses (to himself) that "Everything good he'd ever written he'd made up. None of it ever happened" (237) Here, Nick's voice is Hemingway's own.

As detailed by Leonard J. Leff in *Hemingway and his Conspirators* (1997) and Bruccoli and Baughman in *Hemingway and the Mechanism of Fame* (2006), Hemingway initially was glad just to be paid for his work. As Leff has pointed out, it didn't take long for the editors and marketing personnel at Scribner's to realize that identifying the characters with their author would be a useful strategy in selling Hemingway's novels. Reluctant to be seen as a hack writing for money, Hemingway was at first disinclined to participate too much in publicizing his own works; before long, however, he had joined in with characteristic interest and zeal. Quite possibly no one at Scribner's, nor the author himself, ever thought that they would succeed in developing the Hemingway public persona to the extent they did. At any rate, by the early 1930s Hemingway found himself in the midst of celebrity's central paradox: once you've worked so hard to make yourself a public image, upon succeeding you lose control of that carefully developed image. The number of current examples that help prove this point are rather staggering. I can point to famous flameouts such as Justin Bieber and Lindsey Lohan, but students are almost always better at developing this list than I am.

We consider how, as a literary brand, Hemingway has been ever ubiquitous. We engage in a bit of a scavenger hunt, dragging up brief references to Hemingway quotations in movies like *Se7en* (1995) and *Prozac Nation* (2001); we consider how he has been portrayed as a drunken buffoon in *The Moderns* (1988); a young wounded Red Cross driver whose alcoholism and depression have little to do with genetics, brain chemistry, trauma, or upbringing and everything to do with being spurned by Agnes Von Kurowsky, as played by Sandra Bullock in *Love and War* (1996); an adrenalin-junkie adventurer who only occasionally takes time out to write in an eponymous miniseries (1988); he serves as the inspiration for a comic travelogue in *Michael Palin's Hemingway*

Adventure (2000), and as an extant (if not actually present) symbol of machismo in *Wrestling Ernest Hemingway* (1993). We enjoy the postmodern oddness of *Hemingway: The Hunter of Death* (2001), which has Hemingway leading an expedition to shoot a sacred mammoth in Kenya, accompanied by his Spanish lover, Renata; a frustrated bullfighter godson; and secret agents working for the Mau Mau rebels. And, of course, we consider his representation in Woody Allen's *Midnight in Paris* (2011) and the HBO film *Hemingway & Gellhorn* (2012).

Indeed, his public persona so overwhelms his texts that film adaptations are often skewed to make any autobiographical elements even more overt. Gregory Peck's Harry Street in *The Snows of Kilimanjaro* (1952) is clearly meant to serve as a Hemingway amalgam; George C. Scott's Thomas Hudson (*Islands in the Stream,* 1977) overtly reflects Hemingway's persona as much as Hudson's. Given the very public and by any standards exciting nature of Hemingway's life, the tendency to make all texts autobiographical is tempting. Nevertheless, the focus on the author's persona further obscures the texts.

Arguably, Hemingway's persona has become so recognizable that film directors can reference him, however obliquely, and in doing so perform a kind of cultural shorthand. When Robert Altman made *The Long Goodbye* (based on Raymond Chandler's penultimate Philip Marlowe novel) in 1973, Hemingway had been dead for twelve years. At that point, his celebrity profile was in some regards more complex than it is now. Although he was still a signifier of machismo and an avatar of the Lost Generation as the wounded ambulance driver, big game hunter, war correspondent, and also as a serious writer, nevertheless, his alcoholism, marital issues, and suicide were more highly visible and remembered. These aspects of his public life served as recognizably dark counterweights to his hypermasculine, adventurous public persona.

In Raymond Chandler's *The Long Goodbye* (1953), detective Philip Marlowe's friend Terry Lennox comes to him in the middle of the night and asks for a ride to the Tijuana airport. Marlowe gives it to him and learns later that Lennox is accused of killing his wife. Marlowe can't believe his friend would do such a thing, yet before long Lennox has presumably committed suicide in a small town in Mexico and has written a confession. Due—he thinks—to his brief notoriety for aiding Lennox's escape, Marlowe is hired to find the missing writer Roger Wade, who has gone off somewhere on a bender. In Chandler's novel, Wade is a popular writer of sword-and-romance historical novels. He decries himself for never having taken his work seriously, and his work as a novelist, as described, better evokes a Frank Yerby or Rafael Sabatini than Hemingway.[2] Altman's adaptation of Wade to the big screen sweeps away Chandler's characterization and instead uses a clearly identifiable Hemingway simulacrum. Wade is in his early forties in the novel. He is in more or less good shape despite his alcoholism and is suspected of having cheated on his wife (Marlowe's client Eileen Wade). I give my students a summary of the novel and show very brief clips of other more faithful Chandler adaptations, including Bogart from Howard Hawks's *The Big Sleep* (1946) and Robert Mitchum in Dick Richard's 1974 version of *Farewell, My Lovely*. In Altman's film, fifty-seven-year-old Sterling Haden's Wade is bearded and in beach shirts and khakis and looks similar to the Hemingway of the 1950s and the *Dangerous Summer* photos. Altman's version of Wade walks with a cane and a limp, as if he'd been wounded in war like Hemingway was (but not Wade). Altman's Wade has troubles with impotence (reminiscent of Jake Barnes from *The Sun Also Rises* as well as some readings of Colonel Cantwell). I also show students pictures and brief magazine clippings from that same late fifties era so they'll see the resemblance for themselves.

Chandler aficionados routinely excoriate *The Long Goodbye*'s adaptation for its many liberties and its general disregard for Chandler's characterization. As biographer Patrick McGilligan has noted, Altman has stated in interviews that "the role was patterned more after Chandler himself—or after a certain empty-shelled type of writer like... Ernest Hemingway, at a time in their careers when the parade had passed them by. 'These people were all frustrated... because they wondered what happened to themselves'" (361–62). Perhaps Altman's interest in Hemingway had been stoked by his beginning work in adapting a film version of *Across the River and into the Trees*, which he later abandoned (545).

Altman's main subtext in the film is similar to his subtext in other films: he wishes to subvert the tropes of what he may have seen as a worn-out genre. The Korean War story of *M*A*S*H* is more a statement about the American sixties; the Agatha Christie–style murder mystery of *Gosford Park* becomes an overt commentary on manners and class. In his rendering of *The Long Goodbye*, the smart-mouthed detective is suddenly a mumbler; instead of fast-talking femme fatales we have nude, hash-brownie eating female yoga instructors who cavort on a balcony across from Marlowe's hillside flat; the threatening gambler mob boss is played for laughs. Similarly, Altman's substitution of a Hemingway pastiche for a writer who in the literary source feels he has denied his gifts and settled for being a hack is perhaps a post-Vietnam poke in the eye at what Altman believes Hemingway signifies: an earlier generation's exemplar of masculine honor, codes, and courage.

In Chandler's novel, the writer is murdered by his wife, who shoots him in the head and then tries to make the scene appear a suicide. In Altman's film, Wade commits suicide by wading drunkenly out into the ocean. This is a particularly bad pun, if nothing else, since *Wade* goes *wading*. Furthermore, Marlowe's friend Terry Lennox is innocent of murder in the novel. In the film, he is guilty and Marlowe executes him in revenge.

More to the point, of course, is that the Leigh Brackett script furthers the Wade comparison to Hemingway by having him commit suicide. Typically, the wandering and digressive plots of Chandler's novels are tightened by the screenplay writers. In the adaptation of the 1946 *The Big Sleep*, which Brackett cowrote with William Faulkner, for example, the role of the gangster and gambler Eddie Mars is strengthened throughout. Additionally, Mars meets his end on screen, whereas in Chandler's novel the reader never learns what becomes of Eddie Mars. In Brackett's adaptation of *The Long Goodbye* for Altman, however, the tightest elements of Chandler's plot are loosened. In the novel, Eileen Wade is the murderer of not only Wade but also society heiress Sylvia Lennox; Marlowe's realization that Terry is innocent of the crime—despite having confessed to it, more or less—places all his suspicions in a new light. With Wade's suicide, Eileen is no longer a suspect. Altman and Brackett's decision to not have Eileen Wade be the killer is less a kneejerk attempt to reverse the femme fatale stereotype than it is an opportunity to again reinforce the Wade-as-Hemingway illusion and allusion. In the film, Eileen is complicit with Terry, but the audience is unsure of the extent of her culpability.

Altman's choice to use a Hemingway avatar in *The Long Goodbye* gives rise to a number of points. First, had Hemingway's public image been less identifiable to a somewhat literate movie audience, then Altman's hijacking of Chandler's Roger Wade would have been an empty exercise that served only to put Altman's always visible thumbprint on the text and nothing more. Students recognize that Altman is purposefully making the same mistake many writers had since Scribner's started its campaign to confuse the author with his characters during its promotion of *A Farewell to Arms* (Leff 118–22). Had Altman instead paid more attention to *A Farewell to Arms* and stories like "In Another Country," "Big Two-Hearted River," and "Soldier's Home" with their declaration of the "obscenity" of "abstract words such as glory, honor, courage," or to Jake Barnes crying over Brett Ashley in *The Sun Also Rises,* saying to himself, "It is awfully easy to be hardboiled about everything in the daytime, but at night it is another thing," he would have realized that Hemingway had made the same subversive moves against outworn codes of masculinity thirty years earlier, even if both he and his reading public had a hard time remembering this (34).

Return of the Repressed

Once more, Hemingway's "On Writing" provides pearls of wisdom for readers reading Hemingway. In it, Nick observes, "The movies ruined everything. Like talking about something good" (237). We find the obverse of this valuation of Hemingway's iconic persona above, beyond, and largely segregated from his actual works when the text is used in a way that offers no reference to its origins or originator. One of the more obvious lifts is John Huston's ending to the 1948 *Key Largo*. Huston tossed away the ending from Maxwell Anderson's play and borrowed from the unused final fight of Hemingway's novel *To Have and Have Not* for Frank McCloud's (Humphrey Bogart) climatic shootout on a boat with Johnny Rocco (Edward G. Robinson). Huston had a long and illustrious history of collaboration on Hemingway films. He was an early writer and director for the 1932 *A Farewell to Arms,* and the uncredited (due to contract issues with Warner Bros.) primary screenplay writer for the 1946 version of *The Killers* (Siodmak directing). As Altman would do later, Huston also tried to develop an adaptation of *Across the River and into the Trees* (Phillips 27–28, 72, 160).

While we watch clips of the other movies, I usually show students the entirety of *The Killers* (1946). *The Killers* is considered a classic film noir, and Siodmak and Huston are given more credit than Hemingway, for good reasons. The film's opening minutes follow Hemingway's 1926 short story closely. However, the majority of the movie constitutes flashbacks painting in the backstory in an attempt to explain two conundrums presented in the film: first, why are the killers after the Swede (Ole Andersen in the story)? Second, where does the Swede's fatalism come from? The film catapulted both Ava Gardner and Burt Lancaster to fame (it was Lancaster's first movie). Although the film departs from Hemingway's short story altogether after its initial rendering, the movie nevertheless trumpets its connection to Hemingway in its opening credits; the title is even listed as *Ernest Hemingway's the Killers*.

David Cronenberg's 2005 *A History of Violence,* however, expressly refers to, or quotes, in a sense, the opening to *The Killers,* yet no credit is given to Hemingway. Josh Olsen's Oscar-nominated screenplay was adapted from a graphic novel by John Wagner and Vince Locke; in some ways the graphic novel's rendering of the scene (in terms of the isolation of owner Tom Stall, the time of day, the framing) is even more similar to Siodmak's *The Killers* than the film *A History of Violence* is.

The Killers opens with the two hired gangland enforcers, Max and Al (William Conrad and Charles McGraw), crossing the street to a small diner. It's dark but not too late, since the diner's dinner specials will not be ready until six o'clock. A young man in his late teens or early twenties (Nick Adams, the protagonist, played by Phil Brown) sits in the foreground; the two gangsters sit at the end of the counter, overcoats and hats still on.

In Siodmak's film, the tension is immediate. The two men try to order something they can't have and are disgruntled when George (Harry Hayden), the diner's owner, separated from the men behind the counter, continues to explain to the two that the dinner dishes are not yet ready. Then Al asks, "You got anything to drink?" As the danger and tension build, the two men assert their power, their ability to carry out great violence in the town of Brentwood, simply by their refusal to be polite and by their casual disregard of the small town. At the same time, the two men's restraint is notable; they threaten through implication and demeanor, rather than by waving their guns and growing heated.

GEORGE. (*in response to Al's question*) I can give you soda, beer, ginger ale—
AL. (*harshly*) I said have you got anything to *drink.*
GEORGE. (*abruptly*) No.
MAX. This is a hot town. What do you call it?
GEORGE. Brentwood.
AL. (*to Max*) Did you ever hear of Brentwood?
(*Max shakes head.*)
AL. What do you do here at nights?
MAX. They eat the dinner. They all come here and eat the big dinner.
GEORGE. That's right.
AL. You're a pretty bright boy, aren't you.
GEORGE. Sure.
MAX. Well, you're not. Is he, Al?
AL. He's dumb.

AL. (*calls down the counter, Nick in the foreground, reading the paper*) Hey you, what's your name?
NICK. Adams. Nick Adams.
AL. Another bright boy.
MAX. Town's full of bright boys.

A History of Violence both completely mimics the scene and operates in an entirely different way. I show my students a series of lengthy clips immediately following our viewing of Siodmak's *The Killers*. *A History of Violence* begins with a series of meaningless murders by the two gangland thugs, Leland (Stephen McHattie) and Billy (Greg Bryk) after the two have knocked over some lonely convenience store. Stephen and Billy enter Tom Stall's diner just as Tom (Viggo Mortensen) is readying to close; the setting is again early evening or twilight, and the camera again focuses on the diner's counter and barstools. The two killers ignore Tom, sitting down at the counter.

LELAND. Coffee, black.
(*Tom looks at them.*)
BILLY. The same. I'll have some of that pie—some of that lemon meringue pie.
TOM. Guys, I'm sorry. I'm—we're closed.
LELAND. (*harshly, shouting last word*) I said . . . *coffee!*
TOM. (*placating*) Ok.
(*Leland smirks.*)

In this exchange, we see a replication of the scene from *The Killers*. Just as the mobsters in *The Killers* insist on being served food not available in the diner, so the killers in *A History of Violence* insist upon being served. There are differences, though. In *History*, a couple is still sitting in the diner; in addition to a cook, the diner has a waitress, Charlotte. Tom realizes Billy and Leland constitute some form of danger and tells her she can go home; Billy grabs her before she can leave and forces her into a booth. Even as Billy's malevolence manifests itself, Leland smiles.

TOM. Sir, we don't—we don't carry much cash here. You gentlemen are certainly welcome to all of it.
LELAND. (*pulling gun*) Oh, I know that, asshole, believe me. *[Standing, shouting]* I do know that.

When the young woman dining with her husband or boyfriend in the booth cries out, Leland shouts at her and turns the gun back on Tom, telling Billy, "Let's show this asshole we mean business."

BILLY. (*turns to look at Charlotte*) What? Her?
LELAND. Yes, her.
LELAND. (*shouting*) Do her!

Unlike in *The Killers,* the scene here builds to a climax of violence: as Billy pulls his gun, Tom breaks the glass carafe of coffee against Leland's head. Leland falls, his gun sliding across the floor. Billy turns and shoots at Tom, missing. Taking up the pistol, Tom fires twice, shooting Billy in the chest. Leland pulls a knife from an ankle sheathe and stabs Tom in the foot. Tom turns and fires a bullet through Leland's head.

As my students readily grasp when we compare the clips in class, the similarities between the scenes are manifest: the two hitmen, the small diner, the ominous mood building like a gathering cloud, the compliant owner behind the counter. The differences are arresting as well, of course. The meth-stoked aggressiveness of the killers in *History* is explosive rather than implicit, and the addition of more potential victims in the diner heightens the stakes of the scene as well. The differences are further reflected in the mise-en-scène of the sequences. It seems to be fully dark in *The Killers,* although it's not yet six o'clock; outside the brightly lit diner, the night appears foreboding and full of shadows. In *A History of Violence,* the setting seems almost the same time— the clock behind Tom's shoulder reads seven, and the diner is closing; but the small-town street outside is cheerily lit, with pedestrians walking to and fro. Inside, the diner's lighting is muted and friendlier than the harsh brightness in *The Killers.* Although the diner in *The Killers* is almost deserted, the diner in *History* has a number of customers, including young parents. When this relaxed, intimate world is invaded, it is as if the sociopaths have stepped into the characters' living rooms.

Tom Stall, like Ole Andersen, has a past in organized crime and as a result is in hiding, having recreated himself as a small-town proprietor of a diner. However, despite the parallel diner scene and a number of other similarities, the two films are thematically at odds. The fundamental difference between them is one of agency. Nick, George, and Sam are powerless before the threatened violence of the professional killers in Hemingway's short story. They have capitulated to the killers' requests before they even are certain that the two gangsters are armed. In *A History of Violence,* Tom Stall is one of those familiar, redoubtable figures out of old western and gangland films: he is an outlaw who has rejected his evil past but is now forced by circumstances to return to his bloody ways. His ability to act throughout the film is circumscribed only by his lack of willingness.

Before the end of the movie, Tom Stall will kill (with his family's help) a team of assailants sent to bring him from his house. Realizing that his cover is blown and his family is at risk, he will return to his former city to confront his mob-boss brother. He will then successfully attack his brother and his brother's bodyguards in their very stronghold. Upon completing a viewing of the entirety of *The Killers* and extensive clips from *A History of Violence,* I ask students which approach they find more satisfying as viewers. Overwhelmingly, most initially enjoy the "fighting back" response in *A History of Violence.* I then assign a writing prompt: What are the thematic implications of *A History of Violence?* What should be their (using more familiar jargon) takeaway from the movie? I then ask them to write a lengthy paragraph asking the same question regarding the story "The Killers" and the 1946 film version, *The Killers.* Their responses are different in each instance, and student appreciation for how much Hemingway achieves in such a tight and constrained story grows as they write their responses.

Cronenberg's film is in many ways an intelligent and well-wrought pulp thriller that asks questions about the evil within our hearts, about our human capacity for violence, and about the nature of forgiveness. Nevertheless, his film offers a fairly simplistic response that is at complete odds with Hemingway's short story. Although the film purports to be a narrative about the aftereffects of horror and the ripples and repercussions of violence, it actually is the opposite. Violence, argues *A History of Violence,* may be sufficiently countered by violence.

Students, then, may consider these movies side by side and in relation to "The Killers." In contrast with *A History of Violence,* we work together to grasp how "The Killers" is of a thematic unity with many of Hemingway's Nick Adams stories as well as a variety of other earlier works. Repeatedly, Nick learns the lesson that life is not only unfair but often a cold, cruel, brutal affair. Bad things not only can happen to good people but almost certainly will. From the time he's a small boy (in "Indian Camp"), through his travels ("The Battler," "The Killers"), through his service in the Great War ("In Another Country," "A Way You'll Never Be"), he comes face to face with the realization that life contains many dark corners and one can never avoid them all. From the beginning, Nick is faced with a choice: either do the best you can to somehow bear up and carve moments out of each day that can make life worth living, or submit to the inevitable decline and fall of the human animal. Like all of us, Nick wishes not to believe in such a stark binary opposition. Throughout his stories, he tries repeatedly to deny the primacy of struggle, despair, and death. Leaving the Indian camp with his father as a small boy and ruminating on the suicide of the laboring woman's husband, he feels "quite sure that he would never die" (70). When Ole Andersen says, "There ain't anything to do" and submits to his fate, Nick is horrified by both the inevitability of Ole's fate and his acceptance of it (221). "It's an awful thing," Nick says to George, and then, "I can't stand to think about him waiting in the room and knowing he's going to get it. It's too damned awful." George replies, "Well, you better not think about it" (222). Just like Ole, George is sure there's nothing to do about his circumstances other than accept them.

Many of Hemingway's works are about people trying to find balance. Even as characters like Nick struggle mightily to hold onto innocence, characters like George, Ole, Catherine Barkley from *A Farewell to Arms;* Brett Ashley and Jake Barnes from *The Sun Also Rises;* the older waiter from "A Clean, Well-Lighted Place"; and Santiago, the titular character in *The Old Man and the Sea* have eaten from the Tree of Knowledge and understand that life can be fundamentally unfair. Hemingway's characters are posed a central question: what are you to do in light of such knowledge? You can either lie in your bed like Ole and await your fate, or you can do the best you can with your life, like Count Mippipopolous, and enjoy the small, good things that go into making each day part of a worthwhile progression into the future. While typical action films or even an intelligent action film like *A History of Violence* seem to be about the Teflon-coated indestructibility of human lives, stories like "The Killers" are about the frailty of lives and souls. This contrast further demonstrates why the happy ending of the film of *The Snows of Kilimanjaro* contradicts the point of the short story; even as Harry learns his lesson about the fleeting vulnerability of life too late, the reader is able to learn from Harry's failings.

In his best work, Hemingway is not so concerned with the act of violence—or passion, or sex, or heartlessness—but instead with what comes next. Even as his varying public personas—wounded survivor, big game hunter, boxer, thrill-seeker, churlish boor, philanderer, war correspondent, and so on—fight for ascendancy, Hemingway's most essential texts demonstrate their continuing relevance and worth. Hollywood may fiddle while Rome burns, but Hemingway sifts through the ashes.

Notes

1. Leading biographers include Dearborn, Hutchisson, Kale, and Bradford. Additionally, see Burns and Novick. On Hemingway's wartime roles, see Mort, *Hemingway Patrols,* and Mort, *Hemingway at War,* and Reynolds. Works on his relationships with women include Donaldson, Hotchner, and di Robilant.

2. Yerby lived from 1916 to 1991 and largely focused on historical romances about the American South, a fact made interesting by Yerby's ethnicity; he was African American. Sabatini (1875–1950) authored swashbuckling pirate novels such as *The Sea Wolf* (1915), *Scaramouch* (1921), and *Captain Blood* (1922).

Works Cited

Bradford, Richard. *The Man Who Wasn't There: A Life of Ernest Hemingway.* I. B. Tauris, 2020.
Bruccoli, Matthew, with Judith S. Baughman. *Hemingway and the Mechanism of Fame: Statements, Public Letters, Introductions, Forewords, Prefaces, Blurbs, Reviews, and Endorsements.* U. South Carolina P, 2006.
Dearborn, Mary V. *Ernest Hemingway: A Biography.* Knopf, 2017
di Robilant, Andrea. *Autumn in Venice: Ernest Hemingway and His Last Muse.* Knopf, 2018.
Donaldson, Scott. *The Paris Husband: How It Really Was between Ernest and Hadley Hemingway.* Simply Charly, 2018.
Hemingway. Dir. Ken Burns and Lin Novick. PBS Direct, 2021. DVD.
Hemingway, Ernest. "The Killers." *The Complete Short Stories of Ernest Hemingway: The Finca Vigía Edition.* Scribner & Sons, 1987, pp. 172–78.
———. "On Writing." *The Nick Adams Stories,* edited by Philip Young. Scribner's, 1972, pp. 233–41.
Hotchner, A. E. *Hemingway in Love: His Own Story.* St. Martin's 2015.
Hutchisson, James M. *Ernest Hemingway: A New Life.* Penn State UP, 2016.
Kale, Verna. *Ernest Hemingway.* Reaktion, 2016.
Leff, Leonard J. *Hemingway and His Conspirators: Hollywood, Scribner's, and the Making of American Celebrity Culture.* Rowman & Littlefield, 1997.
McClain, Paula. *The Paris Wife.* Ballantine, 2011.
McGilligan, Patrick. *Robert Altman: Jumping Off a Cliff.* St. Martin's P, 1989.
Mort, Terry. *Hemingway at War: Ernest Hemingway's Adventures as a World War II Correspondent.* Pegasus, 2016.

———. *The Hemingway Patrols: Ernest Hemingway and His Hunt for U-Boats*. Scribner, 2009.

Phillips, Gene. *Hemingway and Film*. Frederick Ungar, 1980.

Ray, Nina M. "The Endorsement Potential Also Rises: The Merchandising of Ernest Hemingway." *Hemingway Review*, vol. 13, no. 2, 1994, pp. 74–86.

Reynolds, Nicholas. *Writer, Sailor, Soldier, Spy: Ernest Hemingway's Secret Adventures, 1935–1961*. Mariner, 2018.

Contributors

Jean Jespersen Bartholomew received the H. R. Stoneback Award (2020/2022) for her work as an independent scholar in Hemingway studies. A writer/editor as well as educator, Bartholomew has written dozens of columns, articles, film reviews, monographs, and books within fields as diverse as literature, real estate, and healthcare. As a literature instructor, she has designed and taught over ten separate Hemingway courses, often utilizing film, and was recognized for teaching excellence as Outstanding Teacher of the Year (Humanities Division) at College of DuPage, Chicago and Southern Virginia Teaching Peer in Virginia.

Cam Cobb is associate professor with the Faculty of Education at the University of Windsor. His qualitative field research has appeared in such journals as the *International Journal of Inclusive Education*. His literary and film scholarship has appeared in *Cinema: Philosophy and the Moving Image* and other publications. As a rock journalist, Cobb has written for several magazines, including *Shindig!* and *Record Collector*. His most recent book is *Weighted Down: The Complicated Life of Skip Spence* (2024).

Alice Mikal Craven is professor emeritus in comparative literature and an active professor of film studies at the American University of Paris. She has taught at Queens CUNY, the New School, and Science Po, but she has spent most of her career at the American University of Paris. She has coedited books and codirected conferences on Richard Wright and James Baldwin. Her book, *Visible and Invisible Whiteness: American White Supremacy though the Cinematic Lens,* was published in 2018.

Kirk Curnutt is professor and chair of English at Troy University. A member of the board of the Ernest Hemingway Society, he is the author of Kent State University Press's *Reading Ernest Hemingway's* To Have and Have Not: *Glossary and Commentary.* He has written several additional essays on Hemingway's Key West/Cuba potboiler. He also serves as executive director of the F. Scott Fitzgerald Society and is managing editor of its annual *F. Scott Fitzgerald Review.*

Donald A. Daiker is professor emeritus of English at Miami University in Oxford, Ohio, where he taught courses in American literature, the short story, sports literature, composition, and the teaching of composition for 43 years. Don has published eleven books, most recently *Hemingway's Earliest Heroes: Nick Adams and Jake Barnes* (2024). With John Beall, he is coauthor of *Hemingway's Combat Zones: War, Family, Self* (2019). He is a member of the editorial board of the *Hemingway Review*.

Suzanne del Gizzo is professor of English and chair of the Center for Integrated Humanities at Chestnut Hill College. She is also the editor of the *Hemingway Review* and the media committee chair for the Ernest Hemingway Foundation and Society. Suzanne teaches a variety of courses in American literature, gender studies, film, and writing. She has published more than twenty articles in scholarly journals and has coedited three books: *Ernest Hemingway in Context* (2013), *Ernest Hemingway's The Garden of Eden: 25 Years of Criticism* (2012), *The New Hemingway Studies* with Kirk Curnutt (2020).

Marc K. Dudley is professor of American literature and Africana studies at North Carolina State University. He is a contributor to *The Bloomsbury Handbook to Toni Morrison, The New Hemingway Studies,* and *Teaching Hemingway and Race*. He is the author of *Hemingway, Race, and Art: Bloodlines and the Color Line* and *Understanding James Baldwin*. Additionally, he is the editor of the Norton Critical Edition of Sherwood Anderson's *Winesburg, Ohio* and the forthcoming Norton Critical Edition of Ernest Hemingway's *A Farewell to Arms*.

Sean C. Hadley has been published in outlets such as *The Imaginative Conservative, Touchstone* magazine, and the *Hemingway Review*. For the last fifteen years, he has taught in the classical classroom. Sean currently serves as a postdoctoral research fellow with the Classical Education Research Lab at the University of Arkansas.

Until his passing in 2022, **Peter L. Hays** was professor emeritus of English at the University of California, Davis. A noted Hemingway scholar, he served as the editor of *Teaching Hemingway's The Sun Also Rises* (2003) and author of *A Concordance to Hemingway's In Our Time* (1990) and *The Critical Reception of Hemingway's The Sun Also Rises* (2011). He is dearly missed by family, friends, and a great many in the Hemingway scholarly community.

Tatiana Konrad is a postdoctoral researcher in the Department of English and American Studies, University of Vienna, Austria; the principal investigator of "Air and Environmental Health in the (Post-)COVID-19 World"; and the editor of the Environment, Health, and Well-Being book series at Michigan State University Press. She is the author of *Docu-Fictions of War: U.S. Interventionism in Film and Literature* (2019), the editor of *Imagining Air: Cultural Axiology and the Politics of Invisibility* (2023) and *Cold War II: Hollywood's Renewed Obsession with Russia* (2020), and a coeditor of *Cultures of War in Graphic Novels: Violence, Trauma, and Memory* (2018).

Christina Parker-Flynn is associate professor of film and literature in the English Department at Florida State University, where she teaches courses that primarily concentrate in film theory and adaptation studies. She is the author of *Artificial Generation: Photogenic French Literature and the Prehistory of Cinematic Modernity* (2021).

Timothy Penner is an adjunct instructor in the Department of English, Theatre, Film and Media and a research fellow at St. Paul's College at the University of Manitoba. He regularly teaches courses on film history and theory, trauma literature, Catholic cinema and literature, and escapist art. His work has appeared in *Celebrity Studies, International Studies in Catholic Education,* and *The New Review of Film and Television Studies.*

James Plath is the R. Forrest Colwell Endowed Chair and professor of English at Illinois Wesleyan University, where he has taught American literature, film, creative writing, and journalism since 1988. He is a former teaching Fulbright Scholar at the University of the West Indies in Barbados and a recipient of his university's highest teacher-scholar award. His publications include ten books, among them *The 100 Greatest Literary Characters* (2019), *Historic Photos of Ernest Hemingway* (2009), and *Remembering Ernest Hemingway* (1999). In a previous lifetime he directed the Hemingway Days Writers Workshop and Conference in Key West for ten years.

Stephen Whittaker is professor of literature at the University of Scranton, where he teaches modern literature, film, women's studies, and specialty writing courses in the business and science honors programs. His publications on American and British authors have appeared in such journals as *Studies in the Novel,* the *Legal Studies Forum,* the *James Joyce Quarterly,* and *European Joyce Studies.*

Scott D. Yarbrough is coauthor of *A Practical Introduction to Literary Study* and coeditor of the two volumes on *The Road* in the Cormac McCarthy Casebook series. He has published articles and chapters on McCarthy, Hemingway, and Faulkner, among others. He was the 2008 South Carolina Arts Commission Prose Fellow and is a former president of the South Atlantic Modern Language Association. He is on the executive board to the Cormac McCarthy Society. He serves as vice president of compliance and professor of English at Charleston Southern University. He hosts the *Reading McCarthy* podcast and cohosts the *Great American Novel* podcast.

Index

Academy Award. *See* Oscar (Academy Award)
Across the River and into the Trees (2024 film), 107
Across the River and into the Trees (Hemingway novel), 72, 85, 107, 195, 197
Adams, Nick (character), 4, 6, 10, 11, 13n4, 18, 19, 21, 71n7, 193, 198, 199, 201
Africa, 95, 157, 158, 160
The Age of Innocence (1920 novel), 68
Albert, Eddie (actor), 60, 61, 82, 87, 104, 106n5, 108, 148n1
All About Eve (1950 film), 60
Allen, Woody, 165, 172–74, 179–82, 185–87, 189, 190
Altman, Robert, 194–97, 203
Anderson, Ole "the Swede" (character), 4, 5, 8, 11, 13n4, 13n5, 18, 26, 27, 30, 197, 200, 202
Anderson, Sherwood, 40, 56
Anselmo (character), 38
Antifascism. *See* Fascism
Aristotle, 74, 75, 77, 79, 80, 81n1, 81n2, 82
Ashley, Brett (character), 35, 37, 50, 60–71, 76, 77, 80, 115, 116, 156, 188, 197, 202

Bacall, Lauren, 86, 95, 96, 98, 102, 107, 108, 109, 116, 118, 123, 136, 141, 145, 146, 149, 150
Baker, Josephine, 54
Barnes, Jake (character), 35, 37, 42, 50, 53, 60–71, 73, 76, 77, 80, 114, 156, 179, 188, 195, 197, 202
Batista, Fulgencio, 90, 94, 101, 104, 105, 107n9, 145
"The Battler" (Hemingway short story), 201
Baudrillard, Jean (philosopher), 167
Bazin, André (French critic), 20, 33, 132, 133, 138, 140n2, 140n3, 141
Beach, Sylvia, bookstore owned by, 55
Bergman, Ingrid, 49, 50, 57, 108, 145, 178
The Big Sleep (1946 film), 86, 107, 195, 196
"Big Two-Hearted River" (Hemingway short story), 196
Bogart, Humphrey, 86, 95, 96, 102, 105, 107–9, 116, 118, 122, 129, 136, 140, 141, 145, 148–50, 195, 197

Bordwell, David (American film theorist), 7, 14n6, 15, 19, 21, 33
Bourne, Catherine (character), 154, 156, 158–63
Bourne, David (character), 154, 156–61, 163, 182, 185
The Breaking Point (1950 film), 86, 89, 90, 93, 97–99, 102, 103, 107, 108, 110–12, 116, 118–20, 124, 129, 130, 148
Breen, Joseph, 70
Breen Office, 70
Bridges, Dorothy (journalist), 36, 145–47, 149
Buchan, John (writer), 51
Bullitt (1968 film), 87
"The Butterfly and the Tank" (Hemingway short story), 39
By-Line (Hemingway book), 46, 57

The Cabinet of Dr. Caligari (1920 film), 7
Café les Deux Magots, 56
Cain, James M. (writer), 37
Camera Eye Aesthetic, 20, 87, 163
Campbell, Mike (character), 61, 64, 65, 80
Captain Blood (1935 film), 59, 108, 203
Captain Khorshid (1987 film), 105, 107
Carmichael, Hoagy, 117, 123, 136, 146
Casablanca (1943 film), 79, 86, 93, 101, 102, 106n4, 108, 117, 118, 124, 145, 146, 148, 149n5, 149n7
Castro, Fidel, 94, 104, 105
Censorship, 49, 145
Cerveceria Alemana, 56
Chandler, Raymond, 21, 194–96
Chez Bricktop, 55
Chinese, as undocumented immigrants, 89, 90, 93, 100, 113, 121, 124
Chopin, 36, 52, 146
Christian's Hut, 91, 97, 125,
Citizen Kane (1941 film), 3, 20
"A Clean, Well-Lighted Place" (Hemingway short story), 115, 177, 202
Close-Up, use of, 4, 18, 20,

208

Cohn, Robert (character), 37, 60–62, 63, 65, 67, 68, 71n5, 80n1
Collins, Kitty (character), 8–11, 20, 26, 32n3
The Complete Short Stories of Ernest Hemingway (Hemingway book), 15, 33, 39, 51, 73, 98, 129, 130, 203
Cooper, Gary, 17, 50, 57, 108, 142
Cosmopolitan, 89, 108
Count Mippipopolous (character), 63, 76, 77, 202
Cronenberg, David, 198, 201
"Cross Country Snow" (Hemingway short story), 71
Cuba, 55, 85, 89, 92–94, 101, 104, 106n7, 107n9, 107n11, 142–45, 191
Cuban Revolution, 89, 90, 94, 101, 104
Curtiz, Michael, 86, 102–4, 107, 108, 110, 118, 130, 148, 149

Dali, Salvador, 43, 44, 55
Death in the Afternoon (Hemingway book), 6, 15, 71n8, 72, 74, 82
"The Denunciation" (Hemingway short story), 39, 51
Dickens, Charles, 18–20, 33n1, 34
Dos Passos, John, 56, 106, 169, 191
Double Indemnity (1944 film), 5, 21, 33n3
DuPuis, Kelly (essayist), 42, 58

Ebert, Roger, 125, 126, 127, 129
Eisenstein, Sergei, 3, 15, 19, 24, 33
Eliot, T. S., 175, 189
Ellington, Duke, 54
Elliptical, as style, 4, 6, 12, 13n3, 35, 52, 54, 156
"The End of Something" (Hemingway short story), 71
Esquire, 89, 108, 113
Evans, Robert (actor), 42

A Farewell to Arms (1932 film), 17, 85, 108, 197
A Farewell to Arms (1957 film), 85, 108
A Farewell to Arms (Hemingway novel), 17, 85, 89, 97, 106n1, 108, 156, 164, 179, 183, 196, 202, 206
Farrow, Mia, 174, 183
Farrow, Ronan, 173, 174, 189
Fascism, 44–46, 48, 51, 53, 57, 107, 144, 146, 147, 149
Fatalism, 19, 126, 197
Faulkner, William, 17, 86, 90, 101–3, 106n3, 108, 116, 117, 136, 141, 143, 145, 149, 192, 196
Femme Fatale, 6, 8, 11, 15, 20, 26, 97, 106n7, 111, 114–16, 118, 119, 126, 195, 196
Ferrer, Mel, 60, 61, 82
The Fifth Column (Hemingway play), 35–37, 39, 40, 43, 51–54, 57, 142, 144–47, 150

Film Noir, 3–9, 11–12, 13n4, 14n5, 14n6, 15, 17–24, 26, 28, 30, 31, 33n2, 33n3, 34, 88, 96, 97, 103, 110–12, 114–16, 118–20, 123, 125–27, 129n1
Fitzgerald, F. Scott, 39–41, 56, 157, 169, 177–79, 184, 188, 192
Fitzgerald, Zelda, 184
Fitzgerald and Hemingway on Film, 157, 161, 164
Flashback, use of, 3, 5–13, 14n1, 14n2, 14n6, 20, 24, 25, 28, 29, 31, 77, 157, 161, 197
Flynn, Errol, 42, 50, 59–61, 80, 82
For Whom the Bell Tolls (1943 film), 37, 48–51, 57, 85, 108
For Whom the Bell Tolls (Hemingway novel), 35, 37, 38–40, 43, 45, 47, 53, 57, 97, 108, 156, 170, 171
Franco, Francisco, 38, 43–46, 48, 51, 55, 56, 106n7, 144
Frank, Nino (film critic), 21, 33, 111, 126
Franklin, Blinky (character), 9, 10
Freddy's Bar. *See* Christian's Hut
Freud, Sigmund, 12, 13, 15, 31–33, 111

The Garden of Eden (2008 film), 85, 108, 153, 154, 157, 164
The Garden of Eden (Hemingway novel), 153, 157, 160, 162–64, 174, 180–82, 186, 187, 189
Gardner, Ava, 11, 15, 20, 26, 42, 50, 60, 61, 63, 82, 108, 109, 197
Garfield, John (actor), 86, 97, 102, 105, 107, 118, 119, 124, 129, 148
Gellhorn, Martha, 36, 38, 40, 44, 46, 52, 53, 149n4, 170
George the Cook (character), 4, 6, 10–12, 18, 19, 28, 198, 200, 202
Georgette (character), 35, 63, 64, 80
German Expressionism, 111, 112
Gershwin, George, 177, 188
Gilda (1946 film), 5, 9
Gingrich, Arnold, 113
Gladstein, Mimi Reisel (scholar), 95, 107n10, 108, 131, 138, 140n5, 141
Gordon, Richard (character), 97, 99, 100, 106n7, 135
The Great War. *See* World War I
Green Cat Nightclub, 29
Griffith, D. W., 19
Grissom, Candace Ursula, 157, 161, 164
The Gun Runners (1958 film), 86, 87, 89, 93, 94, 97–99, 103, 104, 106n4, 106n5, 107n11, 108, 113, 148n1, 192

Hammett, Dashiell, 114
Hard-Boiled, 19, 21, 85, 92, 96, 97, 197
Havana, 89, 92, 93, 107, 113, 121, 122, 128, 143

Hawks, Howard, 17, 86, 89, 90–98, 101–3, 106n3, 107–10, 112, 116–18, 131–33, 136, 138, 139, 140n1, 141–47, 148n1, 149n3, 149n7, 150, 195
Hays Code, 7, 69, 70, 72
Hemingway, Mariel, 174, 176, 178, 179, 188
Hemingway, Mary, 178
Hemingway and Film, 72, 82, 130, 141, 204
Hemingway and Gellhorn (2012 film), 165, 168–72
Hemingway: The Hunter of Death (2001 film), 194
Hemingway and the Movies, 22, 33, 141
Hemingway's Second War, 39, 57
Hemingway's Theaters of Masculinity, 27, 34
Hemingway on War, 14n4, 15
Henry's Lunchroom, 18, 28
Hepburn, Audrey, 60
"Hills Like White Elephants" (Hemingway short story), 174, 176, 177, 179, 189
Hitler, Adolph, 38, 43, 44, 46, 55
Horace, 18
Hotchner, A. E., 203n1
Hotel Angleterre, 55
Hotel Florida, 36, 52, 56
House Un-American Activities Committee, 102
Hunting, 99, 112, 131, 144, 149n3, 154, 156–58, 163, 192
Huston, John, 21, 197
Huxley, Aldous, 23

Ibsen, Henrik, 175
Iceberg Theory, 6, 18, 20, 21, 31, 73, 74, 98, 134, 153, 155, 161, 162
"In Another Country" (Hemingway short story), 196, 201
"Indian Camp" (Hemingway short story), 90, 201
In Our Time, 88, 108
Into the Fire (2002 film), 39, 44, 45, 57
Irati River, 64
Irvin, John (director), 108, 153–55, 157, 160, 161, 163, 164
Islands in the Stream (1977 film), 85, 108, 194

James, Henry, 6, 15, 19
Jenks, Tom, 154, 190
Jordan, Robert (character), 35–38, 46, 47, 49, 50, 53, 97
Joyce, James, 33, 56, 173, 183, 186

Key Largo (1948 film), 197
Key West, 85, 89, 92, 94, 99, 105, 107n7, 113, 121, 122, 133, 134, 142, 143

The Killers (1946 film), 3, 4, 5, 7, 9, 14n6, 17, 20, 24, 26, 27, 30, 32–34, 86, 106n2, 108, 110, 129n1, 197–201
The Killers (1956 short film), 106n2, 108
"The Killers" (Hemingway short story), 6, 7, 17, 18, 20, 21, 85, 110, 115, 116, 201, 203
King, Henry (director), 37, 39, 58, 59, 71n4, 82, 109
Korda, Zoltan (director), 78, 79, 82

La Closerie des Lilas, 56
Lancaster, Burt, 19, 108, 197
Lang, Fritz, 7, 14n7, 15
Las Ventas, 56
Laura (1944 film), 33n3
Laurence, Frank (film scholar), 22, 33, 131, 141
Le Carré, John, 51
Le Grand Duc, 55
Leitmotif, 24
Letort, Delphine (French critic), 22, 27, 30, 31, 34
Library of Congress, 45
Lolita (1955 novel), 178, 186
The Long Goodbye (1953 novel), 194, 195, 196
The Long Goodbye (1973 film), 194, 195, 196
Los Angeles Times, 72, 157, 164

MacDougall, Ranald (screenwriter), 90, 97, 102, 118
Machado, Gerado (dictator), 90, 93, 94, 101, 143, 145
Macomber, Francis (character), 77, 78, 80–82, 90
Macomber, Margot (character), 78–81, 114, 116
The Macomber Affair (1947 film), 73, 77–79
The Maltese Falcon (1941 film), 21, 33
Manhattan (1979 film), 173, 174, 176, 177–80, 183, 186–89
Martin, Dean, 146
Masculinity, as theme, 17, 23, 26, 27, 100, 102, 155, 157, 170, 171, 191, 197
McCarthy, Joseph R., 95
McQueen, Steve, 87
#MeToo Movement, 173, 174
Midnight in Paris (2011 film), 165, 168–72
Mimesis, 75, 183
Mint Theater, 53, 148n2, 150
Montoya (character), 65, 66, 68, 71, 76, 80
Morgan, Harry (character), 85, 89, 91, 92, 94, 96, 98–102, 112, 133, 134, 135, 136, 140n5, 143, 147, 148
Morgan, Marie (character), 91, 96, 98, 101, 135, 136
Morrison, Toni, 173

Moulin Rouge, 55
Murder, My Sweet (1944 film), 33n3
Mussolini, Benito, 38, 43, 44, 46

NAACP, 102
Nabokov, Vladimir, 178
Naremore, James (film scholar), 4, 14n6, 15, 110, 111, 129n1, 130, 140n2, 141
Narration in the Fictional Film, 14n6, 15
Nelson, Ricky, 146, 149n6
New Madrid, 46, 57
New Yorker, 109, 174, 187,190
New York Herald, 64, 71n6
New York Times, 57, 117, 129, 189
"Night before Battle" (Hemingway short story), 39
Nihilism, 17, 19, 48
Noir. See Film Noir
Novels into Film, 120, 129

Objectif, 20
Objectification, 26, 153, 156–59, 162, 163
Oedipus Rex, 79, 81
The Old Man and the Sea (1958 film), 60, 73, 115
The Old Man and the Sea (Hemingway novella), 60, 202
"On Disillusionment" (Hemingway short story), 13
"One Trip Across" (Hemingway short story), 89, 90, 92, 99
One True Podcast, 154, 157, 164
"On Writing" (Hemingway story fragment), 197
Orwell, George, 44, 56, 56n2
Oscar (Academy Award), 59, 60, 74, 106n5, 117, 180, 189, 190, 198
Out Came the Sun, 179
"Out of Season" (Hemingway short story), 6

Pablo (character), 35, 38, 43, 47, 48, 50, 53
Palace Hotel, 69
Papa Hemingway in Cuba (2015 film), 191
Paris, 21, 32, 37, 55, 61, 62–66, 68, 70, 71n6, 80, 144, 169, 170, 172, 174, 179, 180, 187
Paris Review, 18, 34
The Paris Wife, 191, 203
Parker, Dorothy, 44
Peck, Gregory, 60, 78, 81, 82, 194
Perkins, Maxwell, 70, 90, 155
Pfeiffer, Pauline, 55
Phillips, Gene D. (film scholar), 64, 72, 82, 130, 131, 141, 204
Pilar (character), 38, 43, 48, 50
Plimpton, George, 18, 34, 71
Poststructuralism, 165, 167

Post-Traumatic Stress Disorder (PTSD), 12
Postwar Crisis, 17
Pound, Ezra, 56, 191
POV, use of, 125
Power, Tyrone (actor), 42, 50, 60, 61, 82, 109
Prentiss Hat Robbery, 9, 10

Radical Externalism, 17
Red River (1948 film), 141
Red Scare, 95
Rembrandt, 22
The Republic (Spain), 38, 39, 44, 45, 46, 48, 52, 56, 107
Revolution, 57, 88, 90
Reynolds, Michael S. (scholar), 109, 150, 172
Reynolds, Nicholas, 57, 204
Rich, Adrienne, 174
Rio Bravo (1959 film), 140n6, 145, 146, 147, 148, 149n3, 150n7
Riviére, Joan, 27, 34
Rockefeller, Nelson D., 101
Roman Holiday (1953 film), 60, 106n5
Romero (character), 65–67, 70
Roosevelt, Eleanor, 38, 39, 44, 46
Rotten Tomatoes, 71n1, 129n1,

Sartre, Jean-Paul, 30, 31, 34, 55
Schrader, Paul, 15
Scorsese, Martin, 68, 90
Scott, George C., 108, 194
Shaw, George Bernard, 175
"The Short, Happy Life of Francis Macomber" (Hemingway short story), 77, 80, 82
Sing, Mr. (character), 92, 93, 97, 99–101, 112, 113, 119, 121, 124
Siodmak, Robert (director), 3–9, 11–15, 17, 19–21, 24, 27–29, 33, 108, 110, 197, 198, 199
Sloppy Joe's, 122
Smuggling, 92, 93, 100, 101, 104, 113, 118, 121, 143, 148
The Snows of Kilimanjaro (1952 film), 60, 194, 202
"The Snows of Kilimanjaro" (Hemingway short story), 59, 99
"Soldier's Home" (Hemingway short story), 99, 196
Soviet Montage, 18, 19, 24, 106n4
Spain, 37–40, 42–44, 46, 48, 50, 51, 53–55, 56n1, 56n2, 57, 58, 66, 80, 95, 106n7, 147, 170, 171
Spanish Civil War, 37–39, 43, 44–46, 51, 53, 55–58, 106n7, 144, 150, 170, 171
The Spanish Earth (1937 film), 39, 58, 107n7
The Spy Who Came in from the Cold (1965 film), 51

Stalin, Joseph, 46, 56, 56n2
"Statement on Sound" (Eisenstein manifesto), 3, 15
Stein, Gertrude, 40, 55, 80, 169, 170, 181
Stravinsky, 55
The Sun Also Rises (1957 film), 37, 39, 41, 42, 48–51, 58–73, 75–77, 80, 82, 85, 87, 109
The Sun Also Rises (Hemingway novel), 35, 37, 38, 40, 41, 49, 53, 57, 59–72, 76, 77, 78, 80, 82, 85, 87, 90, 97, 106, 108, 142, 155, 156, 179, 188, 189, 195, 197, 202
Sun Valley, 142

Taghvai, Nasser (Iranian filmmaker), 105, 107
The Thirty-Nine Steps (1915 novel), 51
"The Three-Day Blow" (Hemingway short story), 71n7
Today We Live (1933 film), 86, 106n3, 109
Todorov, Tzvetan (theorist), 7, 13, 16
To Have and Have Not (1944 film), 51, 108, 109, 112–14, 120, 122, 129n1, 131–34, 138–42, 142–92, 150
To Have and Have Not (Hemingway novel), 85, 87–92, 95, 99, 106n1, 107n7, 107n9, 108–13, 120–22, 140n4, 141, 143, 144, 192, 197, 205
Touch of Evil (1958 film), 29
Tracy, Spencer, 73
"The Tradesman's Return" (Hemingway short story), 89, 101, 106n6, 108, 113, 121, 130
Trauma, 5, 6, 8, 9, 11–13, 15, 156, 193
Trotsky, 46, 56
Trotskyites. *See* Trotsky

Truman, Harry S., 102
20th Century Fox, 50, 58, 60, 82, 108, 109, 142

"Under the Ridge" (Hemingway short story), 39

Vichy Government, 93, 101, 107, 117, 122, 123, 137–39, 145, 147
Victorian, 18, 33n1
Vidor, Charles, 5, 108
Voiceover, use of, 3, 6, 7, 10, 13, 14, 118, 120, 126

Warner Bros., 86, 87, 107–9, 112, 119, 131, 140n1, 144, 149, 150, 197
Wayne, John, 142, 146, 147, 149n3, 149n6, 150n7
Welles, Orson, 3, 7, 12, 20, 29
Wharton, Edith, 68
What Is Cinema?, 20, 33
"When We Dead Awaken," 174, 176, 189
Wide Shot, use of, 20
Wiene, Robert (director), 7
Wilder, Billy, 5, 21
Wilson, Robert (character), 78, 80, 81
"Womanliness as a Masquerade," 27, 34
Wood, Robin (film critic), 21, 149n5
Wood, Sam (director), 37, 57, 108
Woolf, Virginia, 175, 176, 190
World War I, 6, 12, 13, 51, 59, 61, 80, 106n3, 111, 171, 201
World War II, 8, 9, 21
Wrestling Ernest Hemingway (1993 film), 194
Writer, Sailor, Soldier, Spy, 57, 204

Zanuck, Darryl F., 50, 60, 69, 72